THE BRIDGE IN TH[barcode]

The Five Eyes and Cold War Counter-Intelligence

Edited by Dennis G. Molinaro

Established in the 1940s, the Five Eyes intelligence network consists of Australia, Britain, Canada, New Zealand, and the United States. The alliance was integral to shaping domestic and international security decisions during the Cold War, yet much of the intelligence history of these countries remains unknown. In *The Bridge in the Parks*, intelligence scholars from across the Five Eyes come together to present case studies detailing the varied successes and struggles their countries experienced in the world of Cold War counter-intelligence.

The case studies draw on newly declassified documents on a variety of topics, including civil liberties, agent handling, wiretapping, and international relations. Collectively, these studies highlight how Cold War intelligence history is more nuanced than it has often been portrayed – and much like in the world of intelligence, nothing is ever entirely as it seems.

DENNIS G. MOLINARO is an author and researcher with a PhD in history from the University of Toronto.

The Bridge in the Parks

The Five Eyes and Cold War Counter-Intelligence

EDITED BY DENNIS G. MOLINARO

UNIVERSITY OF TORONTO PRESS
Toronto Buffalo London

© University of Toronto Press 2021
Toronto Buffalo London
utorontopress.com
Printed in the U.S.A.

ISBN 978-1-4875-0512-7 (cloth)   ISBN 978-1-4875-3163-8 (EPUB)
ISBN 978-1-4875-2371-8 (paper)   ISBN 978-1-4875-3162-1 (PDF)

Library and Archives Canada Cataloguing in Publication

Title: The bridge in the parks : the Five Eyes and Cold War counter-intelligence /
    edited by Dennis G. Molinaro.
Names: Molinaro, Dennis G., editor.
Description: Includes bibliographical references.
Identifiers: Canadiana (print) 20210191147 | Canadiana (ebook) 20210191155 |
    ISBN 9781487505127 (hardcover) | ISBN 9781487523718 (softcover) |
    ISBN 9781487531621 (PDF) | ISBN 9781487531638 (EPUB)
Subjects: LCSH: Five Eyes (Alliance) | LCSH: Intelligence service – History –
    20th century. | LCSH: Cold War.
Classification: LCC JF1525.I6 B75 2021 | DDC 327.12 – dc23

This book has been published with the help of a grant from the Federation
for the Humanities and Social Sciences, through the Awards to Scholarly
Publications Program, using funds provided by the Social Sciences and
Humanities Research Council of Canada

University of Toronto Press acknowledges the financial assistance to its
publishing program of the Canada Council for the Arts and the Ontario Arts
Council, an agency of the Government of Ontario.

 Canada Council Conseil des Arts
for the Arts du Canada

ONTARIO ARTS COUNCIL
CONSEIL DES ARTS DE L'ONTARIO
an Ontario government agency
un organisme du gouvernement de l'Ontario

Funded by the Financé par le
Government gouvernement
of Canada du Canada

Canada

For Nichole, Leonardo, and Andre

A certain friendly rivalry has developed. They are trying to ruin our universe; we are trying to ruin theirs. Of course, we could probably tamper with its atomic structure, we might even try that in a couple of hundred years or so. However, at the moment we are concentrating on the destruction of that small part of its spiritual structure which has so far become apparent to the mind of man. The attack is more subtle, more satisfying. Certainly more civilized.

– Peter Dwyer, *Hoodman Blind*

Eyes without feeling, feeling without sight,
Ears without hand or eyes, smelling sans all,
Or but a sickly part of one true sense
Could not so mope.

– William Shakespeare, *Hamlet*

There is perhaps no more pleasant pastime than that of listening to the conversations of other people. There are, of course, those lucky few who can place their ear at the keyhole without any moral qualms; but these superhuman creatures are few and far between …There are places where one has excellent opportunities for this fascinating method of listening in; cocktail parties, for instance – but this is most half-hearted eavesdropping, for your real eavesdropper gives his complete and undivided attention to the matter … And your honestly disinterested listener could do no better than to take up his station on the top of the bridge in the parks. Here he can overhear the most delightful snatches of talk … Here he can meditate on humanity.

– Peter Dwyer, "The Bridge in the Parks"

Contents

Foreword

The Cold War came to a stuttering close in 1989 and the early 1990s. A brief, formless "post-Cold War" era was then succeeded in 2001 by the "global war on terror" in which the long-term national antagonism – Soviet Russia and China on one side and the US-led Western alliance on the other – gave way to a conflict zone between states and violent non-state actors. By the end of the second decade of the twenty-first century it had become apparent that tensions and antagonisms between post-Soviet Russia and China and Western nations had hardly disappeared, indeed were resurgent, but they no longer followed the fundamentalist ideological divisions of the 1945–1989 era when totalitarian communism faced off against liberal democratic capitalism.

Scholars can now look back at the Cold War era as one with a historical starting point and an end date, even if the precise timing of beginning and closing is still open to debate. Scholars are now able to examine much more closely than before one crucial area of the Cold War: the role of security and intelligence. The threat of mutual nuclear annihilation closed off options for direct military confrontation between the communist world and the West, the closest brush with Armageddon coming with the Cuban missile crisis of 1962, a deeply sobering experience for both blocs. Bloody proxy wars were waged in Asia and Africa, but direct conflict was avoided, leaving much of the Cold War to be fought by security and intelligence agencies operating in the shadows. As long as the Cold War continued, these shadows were rigorously maintained to evade the scrutiny of inquiring scholars. Protection of national security trumped the search for historical truth. Often what did emerge in journalistic and scholarly inquiries into Cold War espionage and counter-espionage were narratives highly critical of the official line, distrust of authorities being inflamed by the conflictual process of extracting documentary evidence, and suspicions, often quite warranted, of official cover-ups and dissembling.

Now that a generation has passed since the fall of the Berlin Wall, scholarly inquiry into the security and intelligence history of the Cold War has entered into a new and more fruitful time of much greater access to previously secret records (although access is far from complete even now). Scholars today can assume a greater critical distance from the events and personalities they investigate, and benefit from the greater appreciation of the overall context of the Cold War than was available when the Cold War was a current event rather than history. This permits greater objectivity in assessing the behaviour of the security and intelligence agencies and the impact that their operations had upon their own societies and political systems, as well as their performance in the global competition with their adversaries, than was often possible in an earlier era of more politically engaged research.

The present volume offers a taste of what contemporary Cold War scholarship has to offer, especially from a Canadian perspective. The articles assembled here by editor Dennis Molinaro provide a series of revealing snapshots into the "Anglosphere" of the Cold War intelligence community, what today has come to be known as the "Five Eyes," that has survived the end of the Cold War era as a durable intelligence alliance in the twenty-first century. By the mid-1950s the United States had assumed such a hegemonic position in the Western bloc that lesser powers like Canada tended to be seen as mere adjuncts of US power. Forgotten is the influential role that Britain still played among its former imperial possessions – Canada, Australia, and New Zealand – particularly in the realm of intelligence where Britain had come out of the war with high prestige for its successes in counter-intelligence and codebreaking against Nazi Germany, while the United States was still struggling with the transition from the wartime OSS to the CIA. The first great Cold War intelligence battle was fought in Canada, with the defection of Soviet cipher clerk Igor Gouzenko in 1945 and the revelation of extensive spying operations by the Soviets against their wartime allies. We now know that the most influential external voice in shaping the Canadian response to the Gouzenko defection was that of British intelligence.

Readers can find in this volume a good sampling of contemporary Cold War historical scholarship on the Anglosphere intelligence community. Much remains to be done, but this collection points the way to future research priorities.

Reg Whitaker

Acknowledgments

This book began as a discussion on counter-intelligence at the Social Science History Association (SSHA) in Montreal in 2018. It's my hope that the book continues that discussion and furthers the study of intelligence history by not only encouraging the opening of the historical archives of the Five Eyes nations but also by adding nuance to what has often been a subject that pulls people into polarizing positions. The book does not focus on one theme but explores many case studies across all the Five Eyes. In Canada this field is still in its infancy. There are few scholars in the country working in the field of intelligence studies and history; though this number has grown, it certainly hasn't grown far enough. Why is this the case? A major factor has been the lack of primary source material. The fault for this lies squarely at the feet of the Canadian government and its antiquated and archaic Access to Information legislation in addition to its near abandonment of archival funding. The addition of more primary source documents would lead to more of what this volume has attempted to do – that is, to illustrate the complexities and nuances of the field of intelligence history. Too often people portray the intelligence community in black or white terms. The intelligence community is not some monolithic hive mind that seeks to survey everyone and stamp out civil liberties, nor is it innocent of past histories of abuse. The stories of this volume attempt to illustrate those points through the varied experiences of cases from the Five Eyes' Cold War history.

In regard to the historical release of information, Canada is certainly not alone in the battle for primary-source documentation, as all the Five Eyes governments have lagged in this area. However, the field is not as undeveloped in those countries as it is in Canada where it still lacks any kind of relationship with Canada's intelligence community. The fault lies with Canada's intelligence community after it has seemingly hidden itself from society for reasons we can only guess. While secrecy is necessary to do their job, hiding from the public is not. Thankfully this has begun to change over the last several years as the community has become more engaged in public outreach and has tried to humanize itself as it reminds the Canadian public that it is a community that serves them and is a part of the government bureaucracy just like other departments. This is a positive development, and I hope it continues. As the book's introduction will demonstrate, now more than ever, intelligence communities of all the Five Eyes countries need to come together, engage with their respective publics and with each other, and turn their attention to where the modern-day threats lie.

The book owes its existence to a number of individuals and organizations, a list that is by no means exhaustive. My thanks to the Symons Trust Fund for Canadian Studies at Trent University and the Osgoode Society of Canadian Legal History for their generous financial support. My thanks to the ATIP staff and archivists at Library and Archives Canada, Global Affairs Canada, the Royal Canadian Mounted Police, the Privy Council Office, and the Canadian Security and Intelligence Service, who all did the best they could to assist me given the limitations they faced. I would also like to thank the National Archives and Record Administration of the United States, Archives New Zealand, the National Archives of the United Kingdom, and the National Archives of Australia. Much of my work would also not have been possible without the assistance of the Office of the Information Commissioner of Canada and its staff, who often face uphill battles to overcome in pursuit of their duties. Some of my sources also came from the Canadian Foreign Intelligence History Project (CFIHP). My thanks to them for continuing to pursue information release. I would also like to acknowledge the anonymous readers whose review made this a better book, as well as Len Husband, the manuscript committee, and the staff at UTP for their support for this book. This is ultimately a collaborative project. My sincerest thanks to all the contributors to this volume who made the book possible and were ever patient in seeing the project through to completion.

There are also individuals who I would like to thank who helped make this book possible. They include: Rebecca Russell, Rachel Horner, and the staff at Lion's Fence. My thanks to friends and family who have supported my efforts over the years, including Robert Wright; Phil and Theresa Downer; Adam, Miranda, Ella, and Audrey Preston-Lord; Paige and Payson Marrett; Travis Downer; Michele, Lisa, Julian, Sebastian, and Anthony Molinaro; Christina and Gino Molinaro; Hailey and Penny. My sincerest thanks to Andre, Leonardo, and my partner in life Nichole. Their support, patience, and love always kept me driving forward.

THE BRIDGE IN THE PARKS

Introduction

DENNIS G. MOLINARO

There has never been a time since the Cold War that counter-intelligence and espionage have garnered more attention than they have today. Since 9/11 the Five Eyes (FVEY) intelligence community, consisting of the United States, United Kingdom, Australia, Canada. and New Zealand, has been rightly focused on the threat of terrorism, but that often-myopic focus has since allowed their traditional adversary, namely Russia and a new one in the People's Republic of China (PRC), to strategize and conduct espionage operations against the West. Both have engaged in human intelligence (HUMINT) operations as well as cyber-attacks and disinformation campaigns. Examples of these activities appear increasingly in news media. In June 2010 the FBI arrested eleven Russian spies operating for Russia's foreign intelligence service, the SVR. They were part of the Russian "illegals" program, which had sent spies to live as Americans in the United States for decades with the hope of eventually penetrating US policymaking circles.[1] Also in 2010, Britain's domestic intelligence service reported that the number of Russian spies in the UK was now at a level not seen since the Cold War.[2] In March 2018, Russian intelligence defector Sergei Skripal and his daughter Yulia were found in a Salisbury park after having been poisoned by the nerve agent Novichok. UK authorities have since identified Ruslan Boshirov and Alexander Petrov as the Russian military intelligence (GRU) officers who were the likely perpetrators of the attack, which also killed a woman from Wiltshire, Dawn Sturgess, who had unfortunately found and handled the disposed bottle that contained the nerve agent.[3] This attack is in addition to the 2006 poisoning of former Federal Security Service officer Alexander Litvinenko, who lived in the UK and was a fierce critic of Russian president Vladimir Putin, who is believed to be responsible for ordering Litvinenko's assassination.[4] These events are in addition to the FBI initiating a counter-intelligence investigation into a sitting president, that is, former president Donald Trump. The investigation, opened after Trump fired FBI director James Comey, focused on whether Trump was acting on behalf of Russia either wittingly or unwittingly. This investigation was combined with special prosecutor Robert Mueller's examination of Russia's interference in the 2016 presidential election, whether the Trump campaign conspired with them, and whether Trump had attempted to obstruct justice after firing Comey. Mueller's report could not prove obstruction, nor did it vindicate him.[5] However, Mueller did charge thirteen Russian nationals and three Russian entities with interfering in the election by means of an online disinformation campaign via social media sites like Facebook. Mueller also secured many guilty pleas, including Trump's once closest and most trusted associate, his former lawyer Michael Cohen. Trump's subsequent impeachment proceedings did little to assuage people's concerns about Trump's ties to Russia.[6]

But while the FVEY faces espionage operations from its oldest adversary, its greatest new challenge comes not from Russia but from the PRC. While the West was preoccupied with counterterrorism, the PRC was busy strategizing and carrying out its long-term policy of supplanting the United States as a global leader by building its economy and technology sector. A sizeable portion of this activity was done through cyber theft and acquiring intellectual property by buying up Western companies. The PRC sought to steal everything from technology on solar panels to Dupont's formula for the colour white. In 2012 National Security Agency director Keith Alexander referred to this theft campaign as the "greatest transfer of wealth in history." The frequent cyber intrusions resulted in the arrest of Su Bin, an executive living in British Columbia, who was charged with assisting Chinese intelligence, specifically the PRC Ministry of State Security (MSS). Canadian authorities arrested Su Bin at the request of the FBI, and in retaliation, the PRC government arrested two Canadians living in China: Kevin and Julia Garratt. Su Bin did not contest his extradition and pleaded guilty, which ultimately led to the Garratts being freed; in addition, the United States struck a deal with Beijing, an arms treaty of sorts on cyberattacks. The agreement, however, was short-lived as the PRC has continued its cyber intrusions, with the latest occurring in December 2018, leading to the arrest and extradition from Belgium of another individual accused of spying for the Chinese. What's more, China's cyber offensive has led to the deaths of intelligence sources when it worked with Iran to penetrate a CIA messaging system that exposed sources and led to the execution of these sources in China.[7]

But as much as the PRC has used cyberattacks in its espionage offensive, some of its greatest successes have come by way of HUMINT and penetrating the policy circles of FVEY countries, as the Russians had also attempted to do. For instance, as Clive Hamilton has outlined in *Silent Invasion: China's Influence in Australia*, the PRC has engaged in a slow, long-term, and methodical strategy of seeking to gain influence in Australia's power circles through a variety of means: from Chinese state-owned enterprises (SOE) heavily investing in Australia; to leveraging the overseas Chinese diaspora to act in Beijing's interest, including students and professors attending Australian universities; creating community groups to push PRC policy; and attempts to buy influence by wining and dining politicians with trips to the PRC. The PRC's tactics differ from Russia's in important ways. While the most the Soviets could muster in the Cold War was a dozen spies in Australia, the PRC leans heavily on and pressures its overseas diaspora, and uses its embassies and consulates to pressure and control the community, constantly reminding them that their first duty or obligation is to the "motherland." The result, according to Australian intelligence and Chinese defectors, is that at least one thousand Chinese spies are presently at work in Australia. Former counter-intelligence experts in the United States estimate at least 25,000 Chinese intelligence officers and 15,000 informants are at work in the United States. Experts have disclosed that the apparatus does not often break laws, is not overly invasive, but operates on an industrial scale. According to James To, "overseas Chinese are recruited to gather low-grade intelligence by interfering or monitoring, among others, trade unions, women's groups, student associations and, for technology and business strategies, corporations." Intelligence agencies are often equipped to deal with and focus on only traditional forms of spying from intelligence officers, not this kind of "decentralized micro-espionage." In addition, the PRC may use traditional techniques like honeypot traps that seek to ensnare politicians or business leaders in sexual scandals and blackmail them. The result is that overseas Chinese communities are being exploited by the PRC government to do its espionage work. When exposed by Western authorities, the PRC government often tries to deflect the criticism by arguing that Western states are being racist.[8]

Nearly all of this activity is conducted by way of China's United Front Work Department (UFWD), its long-term goal being to divide FVEY nations and steer them and their politicians into supporting the PRC's foreign policy goals, such as its One Belt One Road initiative, its claims to the South China Sea, and its "One China" policy with respect to Taiwan, to name a few.[9] New Zealand has also faced a steady barrage of covert and clandestine influence tactics by the PRC, which have been so successful there that New Zealand's status as a FVEY nation is now seriously being questioned. Academics exposing the PRC's tactics in New Zealand, such as professor Anne-Marie Brady, have been subjected to constant harassment and break-ins.[10]

PRC influence campaigns also appear to be occurring in North America, including in Canada. Reporters in Canada from media outlets such as the *Globe and Mail*, *Global News*, and *National Post* have reported on individuals in Canada with suspected links to the PRC government who are mingling with Canadian politicians and who appear to seek to gain influence, possibly in similar ways to what has occurred in Australia and New Zealand. Advantages of UFWD work for the PRC in Canada could include accessing Canadian resources and technology, driving a wedge between Canada and the United States, and having Canadian politicians adopt PRC-friendly policies. Community groups operating in Canada such as the Confederation of Toronto Chinese Canadian Organizations (CTCCO) have also been reported as having close ties to Beijing and receiving praise from China's Overseas Chinese Affairs Office (OCAO), which now falls under the control of the UFWD.[11]

Canada was also recently thrust into the middle of growing Chinese and American tensions on 1 December 2018, when Canada arrested Meng Wenzhou, the daughter of Chinese mobile corporate giant Huawei, which FVEY countries have accused of being an intelligence-gathering arm of the PRC. The United States accused her of bank fraud by assisting Iran in avoiding US sanctions. Canada arrested Meng, and China retaliated by arresting two Canadians living in China and ordering the death of a third who had been previously sentenced to a fifteen-year jail term on drug charges. As the drama continues to play out, some leading former members of Jean Chrétien's government came out with head-scratching comments, including that the Canadian government should have tipped off Meng about the arrest so that she could flee.[12] A former Cabinet minister in Chrétien's government and Canada's ambassador to China, John McCallum, held a press conference for Chinese media about the arrest, telling them that the PRC had a good case to block Meng's extradition. The move stunned those in political circles and major media outlets, who were not invited to the event. Perhaps coincidentally, McCallum had been identified by reporters as leading the pack in terms of Canadian MPs' free trips to China, to the tune of $73,300. McCallum's continuing comments about what the Canadian government and the United States should do in the case, even after having issued a retraction for his earlier comments, led the Canadian prime minister, Justin Trudeau, to ask for his resignation. Some current and former Canadian politicians, such as former Ontario trade minister Michael Chan, current Ontario MPP Vincent Ke and current Senator Victor Oh, have also been the subject of media scrutiny about what connections they may have to PRC government officials or acceptance of free travel to the PRC. This is not to say that the activities of these individuals were illegal, but rather that they could be interpreted as problematic, at the very least, especially given the PRC's attempts to influence politicians in other FVEYs nations. As Canadian Senator Frum put it, "the part that just slays me is that it's perfectly legal. And the government knows it's legal, and the government doesn't care."[13]

There are signs that the Canadian government is devoting more attention to the subject. In its 2019 Annual Report, Canada's National Security and Intelligence Committee of Parliamentarians (NSICOP) identified the PRC as a national security threat engaged in foreign interference in Canada and stated that "the PRC utilizes its growing economic wealth to mobilize interference operations: with deep coffers and the help of Western enablers, the Chinese Communist Party uses money, rather than Communist ideology, as a powerful source of influence, creating parasitic relationships of long-term dependence."[14]

The same report highlighted that the PRC has been engaged in Canada in much of the same interference activities that it has conducted in places like New Zealand and Australia by targeting Canada's democratic institutions at all levels including politicians and their staff. Perhaps even more troubling, arrests of individuals in Ontario and BC that are alleged to be involved in illegal gambling, also appear to have links to individuals and groups suspected of having ties to the PRC government, and have had access to Canadian politicians including Canada's prime minister.[15]

The rapid spread of the Covid-19 virus throughout the world and the PRC government's attempt to hide and downplay the initial seriousness of the virus have caused international condemnation of the regime and inflamed tensions within China. Within Canada, media have exposed how groups with ties to the UFWD sought to hoard personal protective equipment and ship them to China while the PRC hid the severity of the virus from the world. US intelligence also exposed how China had minimized the virus' severity. The international condemnation has also finally moved the Canadian government ever so slowly to take some kind of stand on China's actions, which has been glaringly reluctant to do. With nations such as Australia and the United States calling for an international investigation into the virus's origins (and the PRC lashing out in response) the emergence of a new Cold War has certainly begun.[16]

With the world's renewed focus on espionage and counter-intelligence, what role can the history of counter-intelligence play? A collective look back at segments and case studies in FVEY counter-intelligence history can help us understand this complicated, and deceptive, world. While writing on one specific theme would be ideal, the realities of this historical field make that exceptionally difficult, as it requires that all Five Eyes countries have the same access to declassified material, which has not been the case. This is a historical field that has limited sources and must fight constant battles to free primary sources from the grips of governments.

This book focuses on stories from each of the Five Eyes partners, revealing how the partners worked together at times, what pitfalls they encountered when it came to targeting and looking for subversives, as well as how situations varied in each country. This volume attempts to add nuance to what has often been a polarizing historical field in which scholars are forced to choose between focusing on abuses and the overreach of intelligence agencies in the Cold War or discussing successfully prosecuted individual cases of counter-intelligence. The volume thus seeks to add complexity to this history, more in line with the "grey" world in which counter-intelligence has often existed. In doing so, it is hoped that policymakers and academics alike can appreciate the difficult and complex world of counter-intelligence and avoid past pitfalls. In addition, the book highlights what has worked well and examines historical cases in which members of the FVEY worked together for a common purpose. It is an important reminder, as current-day adversaries seek to divide this important historical alliance. This history is also continually changing as more sources are beginning to reveal and challenge what scholars thought they knew of this period. The authors in this volume make use of new declassified sources to further complicate an already complex and rich subject.

Into the Wilderness of Mirrors

The end of the Second World War ushered in an era of uncertainty, with Germany defeated and a Soviet army that outnumbered the other Allied forces and occupied half of Europe. The war marked the acceleration of international cooperation when it came to US, UK, and Canadian intelligence sharing. The Gouzenko affair and the discovery of a Soviet spy ring in the UK, Canada, and the United States marked a greater push for intelligence sharing among not only these countries but other democracies as well.[17] But even with the discovery of this ring, each nation had its own security concerns and its own desire to approach and address those concerns as it saw fit. Nations may often disagree on how much of a threat one nation's adversary poses to the others. Any alliance or partnership must establish and agree on who the enemy is. It was in this context that the UK made its attempts to wrangle together and cooperate on intelligence sharing with new and more established members of the Commonwealth and bring them together into a series of Commonwealth Security Conferences. Their purpose was to recognize the seriousness of the new and emerging Soviet enemy in the postwar era. The conferences were an effort by the UK to underscore the danger that this wartime ally now posed and the threat of its espionage activities. They also sought to establish how nations should cooperate and work together to counter the new threat the UK believed had covertly penetrated the West. The Australian Security Intelligence Organization (ASIO) and New Zealand's Security Intelligence Service were born in the era of defections and the Red Scare. Gregory Kealey and Kerry Taylor admit in their chapter that given the UK's role in the creation of those services, they had expected to find an overbearing and paternalistic UK. They thought they would find that the UK sought to steer its allies into toeing the "party line." They instead found UK representatives doing their best to take an educative approach with their Australian, New Zealand, and Canadian allies in an effort to counter and highlight the deception and infiltration efforts of the Soviets.

In histories of intelligence and the Cold War, much has been made of how the boundaries between espionage and subversion have been blurred, and for good reason. Following Gouzenko, the West fell into the period of the Red Scare, led by people like US Senator Joseph McCarthy. The political left became equated with Soviet-style communism. Stalin's death and the revelations of his secret trials and purges only added to the scrutiny of the political left and pushed it into a moment of crisis. In the United States, the hunt for Soviet spies was a very public affair with naming and shaming occurring in sometimes dramatic fashion and largely due to the loyalty hearings led by McCarthy. McCarthy engaged in the witch-hunt with FBI director J. Edgar Hoover as an ally, matching him in his anti-communist fervour, though Hoover had a larger goal: control of the postwar intelligence world. In addition to the Gouzenko spy trial in Canada, the period of the late 1940s and 1950s was marked by numerous high-profile defections, spy trials, and dramas, such as the Julius and Ethel Rosenberg case, the Klaus Fuchs arrest, the Elizabeth Bentley defection, and the

Alger Hiss trial.[18] Countless studies have examined the period of the Red Scare, the hunt for Soviet spies, and the repression of the left and of civil liberties. But although a person's political ideology caused them to be targeted by intelligence agencies, Marcella Bencivenni in her chapter details how sometimes the real political battles played out behind the scenes in the courtroom. At the root of some of these public trials were power struggles between competing personalities and agencies. In other words, even in cases that involved Soviet spies or the policing of politics and the repression of civil liberties, other factors were at play behind these cases. One case that has received far too little study is the case of Carl Marzani, an Italian American radical who during the Second Word War was employed in the Office of Strategic Services (OSS; the precursor of the CIA) and sent to jail in 1947 for having concealed his past communist affiliations. The Marzani case was a prelude to the massive investigation of federal US workers suspected of subversive affiliations that was ordered by President Truman under Executive Order 9835 on 21 March 1947. Unlike other suspected communists, however, Marzani was not accused of treason, sabotage, or disloyalty. Instead, he was indicted simply on charges of having "defrauded" the American government under section 80 of Title 18 of the US criminal code, a statute commonly known as the "False Claim Act." To complicate the case even further, Marzani had resigned from his government job in November 1946, well before his indictment.

The high stakes of the Marzani case were evident from the extensive public attention and press coverage it received at the time. In an atmosphere of growing hysteria, the case became highly symbolic of the ideological battle of the Cold War. Part of the reason this case unfolded in the manner it did, as Bencivenni reveals, was Hoover's hatred of Bill Donovan and all things OSS and his attempt to hold on to the FBI's gains in the intelligence world. If Donovan's OSS was rife with Soviet spies, it would be up to the FBI to protect the nation rather than some "central" intelligence agency Donovan was pushing for. The Marzani case provided a template for further loyalty prosecutions and also revealed the power politics of that period.

Not only did attempts to rout out Soviet spies have a chilling effect on civil liberties, but the period is also known for its horrendous legacy with respect to the LGBTQ community. Across the Western world, in countries where people expected to find a safe haven, homosexuality was considered a crime and suspected individuals were purged from the public service. In places like the United States, Canada, and the UK, LGBTQ members of the public service were viewed by authorities as possessing "character" defects that left them susceptible to Soviet blackmail. In Canada, not only were homosexuals dismissed from these jobs, but authorities attempted to find members of the community throughout the country to ensure none could apply for federal work.[19] In the UK, the purges of gay men from the public service were linked to the defections of Guy Burgess and Donald Maclean in 1951. Pressures also mounted in the United States during the McCarthy era. The purges of gay men in the UK public service were often interpreted in the historical literature as a necessary condition for securing US cooperation and support in the Cold War, but as Lomas and Murphy's chapter demonstrates, historians are extracting more nuance and complexity in these events. While security was a central concern in these purges, fear of scandal was an equal if not greater factor. Indeed, while Whitehall believed there were security risks in employing gay men in the public service, more pressing to the Foreign Office was protecting the reputation of the office from scandal. Lomas and Murphy's chapter reveals that there is still much to be revealed in this shameful saga of the Cold War.

Much like its Five Eyes allies, Australia was gripped not only by its own Red Scare but also with the real threat of Soviet espionage. Because so little is known about intelligence services, it can be relatively easy to conclude that these are organizations that are devoid of humanity and simply bureaucratic machines that grind up those working for them over time. In contrast to other members of the Five Eyes, little is known about officers and sources that worked for ASIO, especially ones with overseas postings. ASIO was concerned as much as the other partners were with counter-intelligence, and Philip Deery's chapter provides readers with an in-depth look into that grey world through the activities of Anne Neill, who was one of ASIO's first recruits. Neill was a trailblazer in a new security service that had few sources reporting on its adversary. She penetrated the Australian Communist Party and even found herself reporting on the party from deep within the Soviet Union. While Deery had intended to find an ASIO that was not overly concerned with Neill and her well-being, that was not the case. His work reminds us that intelligence services are made up of people, and his work provides one of the few glimpses into the lives of officers and sources and their work in the Cold War. Far from being a bureaucracy that cared little about the welfare of its people, ASIO was greatly concerned about Neill, and three different case officers did everything they could to ensure Neill had support. They were especially concerned with the toll her cover operation was having on her personally and on her ability to live the double life she believed she needed to live for her country.

Canada went through a Red Scare that occurred alongside the real threat of Soviet espionage, similar to its Five Eyes allies. Much like in

Britain, it operated largely out of public view as the security services in Canada quietly collected information on students and on gays and lesbians in the public service, and influenced the dismissal of staff from the National Film Board.[20] But the world of counter-intelligence has rarely been clear-cut; distinguishing the spies from the ideologues, and subversion from espionage, wasn't a science, and much of it was (wrongly) placed in the hands of law enforcement, namely the RCMP, which was filled with its own biases, assumptions, and cultural world view about the political left, and communism in particular.

Nowhere was this world view revealed more explicitly than in war planning. Ultimately, the Cold War was about the prospects of war with an enemy that was armed with the same kind of nuclear weaponry as the West, the kind that could end life on earth. But how does someone plan for a type of war that no one has ever fought – a full-out nuclear conflict – and what can that planning for a future disaster reveal about one's cultural world view? The Canadian government tasked the RCMP (along with the military) with identifying and interning individuals who would be a threat to Canada in the event that a future nuclear dystopia came to pass. The result was the creation of Operation Profunc, which ran from 1943 to 1983. Frances Reilly's chapter explores how this operation, aimed at rounding up communists, sympathizers, and their families, exposes the ways in which Canada remained in a perpetual state of emergency, and how the government imagined the threat to the country as coming not just from nuclear weapons but from ideology, as support for leftist politics was equated with support for the Soviet Union.

Threats change, and the security environment is not static. How does an intelligence service change its focus? How does it reorient itself to deal with the emergence of a new threat or an old one that was overlooked? As Canada entered the 1960s and 1970s, new threats emerged, but they came in a different form than nuclear war with another state. Terrorism was a growing concern, be it terrorists entering Canada from abroad or terrorists emerging from within Canada. The best-known terrorist group in Canada at the time was the Front du Libération du Québec (FLQ). They carried out bombings in Quebec and the infamous kidnapping of British commissioner John Cross and the murder of Quebec minister Pierre Laporte. Steve Hewitt argues in his chapter that the 1970s did not mark any fundamental shift from the Cold War world of counter-intelligence to counterterrorism. Instead we witnessed the start of a fusion of the Cold War security milieu with the counterterrorism world of the 9/11 era. The Cold War was very much a part of the twenty-first-century "war on terror," as threats were still being categorized as arriving from abroad rather than as emerging from within.

It was James Jesus Angleton of the CIA who referred to the world of counter-intelligence as a "wilderness of mirrors." It is a world that makes finding enemies like looking for needles in haystacks, that reflects your own ideological biases back at you, and paradoxically, employs deception and disinformation to protect an open democratic society. These themes emerge in discussions of those who have come to be known as the "illegals" and the best way to counter them. During the Cold War, and even in modern times, these were undeclared intelligence officers. Russian illegals were a major concern for Five Eyes countries in the Cold War because these officers sought not only to build their own network of sources but to penetrate the highest echelons of their host country by getting jobs within government or even employing children to aid in the cause, all while blending in as members of society. Methods of trying to monitor these individuals included the use of surveillance teams as well as wiretapping. Recently declassified documents from the 1950s expose how Canada created Operation Picnic, a wiretapping program aimed at Russian illegals and monitoring foreign embassies. As this program wound down in 1954, the government faced a challenge in terms of how to legally permit wiretapping in a democracy.[21] How does a democracy legally permit violations of privacy to counter an enemy that is living as one of its own citizens? It is a dilemma that existed in the past but that still persists today in an era of big data and internet disinformation. As Dennis Molinaro's chapter reveals, much can be learned from the past. In the 1960s, the government opted for secrecy and to shirk its responsibilities by creating a legal framework for the RCMP to monitor threats to the country. The result was that the RCMP was left to try to navigate through this legal grey zone on its own. While the perception of the RCMP in this period was that it was engaged in mass surveillance and was a force unto itself (the McDonald Commission came to a similar conclusion), in terms of wiretapping, the reality was quite the opposite. Targets of wiretaps were selectively chosen, and the RCMP was very firm in ensuring that officers were in compliance with existing legislation. The service's use of wiretapping in the 1960s and 1970s suggests that the RCMP did not abuse its powers during the Cold War, but, rather, successive Canadian governments utilized secrecy to hide behind their intelligence services at a time when Canada needed a transparent and concise legal framework to counter Soviet espionage.

The 1970s was a period in which the RCMP, CIA, and FBI faced scrutiny for the free hand they were given by the government, even if, as Molinaro suggests, the complete story is yet to be told, at least in terms of the Canadian government's role in RCMP actions during the 1970s.

There is little doubt, however, that all intelligence services took their powers to the limit and in some cases beyond what was acceptable in a democratic society. From the FBI's COINTELPRO to the CIA "Family Jewels" and the RCMP's barn burnings and break-ins, transparency and government oversight were best for all involved.[22] John Breen reveals how there is still more of a story to tell in the investigations of US intelligence agencies in the Cold War and how governments in the era colluded with foreign powers and contemplated using disinformation tactics against their own citizens. In addition to shedding a light on government oversight and scandal involving intelligence agencies, Breen's chapter takes readers back to the Richard Nixon era, revealing how, in addition to the Watergate scandal, which ended his presidency, Nixon colluded with Russia and the South Vietnamese, in contravention of US law, to avoid peace before the election, knowing that a peace deal might help his Democratic opponent. Throughout both Nixon's and his successor Gerald Ford's presidencies, both men were obsessed with leaks to the press. Breen reveals how after Nixon's fall, Ford, Director of Central Intelligence William Colby, and the deputy attorney general proposed utilizing leaks of information to disrupt and attempt to mitigate the damage being done by the Church Committee investigations. They proposed using counter-intelligence disinformation tactics against the US Congress and American media. There is no evidence that they carried this out, but it does explain why in 1975 Ford himself leaked that the CIA had plotted assassinations in the past. It was, as some have speculated, a "flashback" tactic. By illuminating what past presidents had been involved in, Ford's tactic, as Breen states in his chapter, was one in which "if everyone is to blame, no one is to blame."

Writing intelligence history, unlike perhaps any other branch of the discipline, has depended on freedom-of-information legislation and the willingness of governments to make documents available to researchers. Unfortunately, the field has been plagued by government archival systems marred by neglect and government attempts to contest document releases.[23] Government efforts at hiding behind classification to prevent the release of material may temporarily hide embarrassing moments of the past, but such actions are a fool's errand. For not only will the material one day be released, but the damage done in the meantime can be substantial and cumulative, particularly to intelligence agencies – a vital component of statecraft. If the public is exposed only to past scandals that are forced out, perceptions are created about this crucial branch of government, perceptions that fuel debates, shape ideas, and create myth, some of which influence the creation of legislation. "Intelligence agencies are engaged in mass surveillance" and they often "abuse their powers" are common myths that appear in debates involving the creation of new national security laws because of the lack of historical knowledge available. What's more, perceptions of unchecked and secretive power and the lack of understanding of the history of intelligence services are now leading to growing conspiracy theories about the existence of a "deep state" that seeks to bring down presidents. The past matters to the present.

In closing out this volume on the Five Eyes and counter-intelligence history, Timothy Andrews Sayle examines how we can move forward in telling intelligence history. He examines how once-secretive signals intelligence (SIGINT) organizations like the National Security Agency (NSA), Government Communications Headquarters (GCHQ), and Canada's Communications Security Establishment (CSE), along with the governments that hold secret records, are coming to grips with their history. Focusing on CSE, Sayle attempts to explore the validity of a single "government line" on telling a secret past and reveals the multitude of ways different groups within government have examined and interpreted the pros and cons of releasing historical intelligence records. While London, Canberra, and Washington have increasingly allowed for more of their intelligence history to be told, Sayle notes how Canada lags behind in this regard. The book concludes with a postscript from Reid Morden, a former director of CSIS, who highlights the challenges faced by the FVEY community in the present and how the work of the contributors demonstrates how the intelligence community can benefit from the work of historians.

Ultimately this book stresses the complexity of the world of intelligence. The security services in the Five Eyes did engage in past activities that stigmatized individuals on account of their sexual orientation or political beliefs, but they were hardly the "rogue" agencies often portrayed in film and on television – trampling civil rights and ruining lives everywhere – but, in fact, they acted with much more restraint than is often alleged. The British didn't try to force themselves on smaller security services in the Commonwealth; the RCMP tried its best to remain within the law; the Australians treated their agents with respect and care; and the cautious Canadian government has, ever so gradually, begun to open up its own history.

It is hoped that this volume contributes to the understanding of past intelligence agencies and the world of counter-intelligence, and the recognition that, although flawed, this is a world that has still struggled to safeguard citizens from threats that are real. The use of intelligence has helped direct the course of history, in war and in peacetime. It is part of the history of any nation, and the inability to tell that history renders our understanding of the past, the present, and ourselves incomplete. The contemporary adversaries of the West rely on disinformation and subterfuge. The telling of history is thus not only a means of helping people understand and make sense of the present, but also a way to counter opponents in the wilderness of mirrors.

NOTES

1 Scott Shane and Charlie Savage, "In Ordinary Lives, U.S. Sees the Work of Russian Agents," *New York Times*, 28 June 2010, https://www.nytimes .com/2010/06/29/world/europe/29spy.html?rref=collection%2Ftimestopic %2FRussian%20Spy%20Ring%20(2010)&action=click&contentCollection =timestopics&region=stream&module=stream_unit&version=latest &contentPlacement=31&pgtype=collection.

2 Richard Norton-Taylor, "Russian Spies in UK 'at Cold War Levels,' Says MI5," *Guardian*, 29 June 2010, https://www.theguardian.com/world/2010 /jun/29/russian-spies-cold-war-levels.

3 Jennifer Rankin, "Skripal Poisoning Suspects Put on European Sanctions List," *Guardian*, 21 January 2019, https://www.theguardian.com/uk-news /2019/jan/21/skripal-poisoning-suspects-european-sanctions-list.

4 "Alexander Litvinenko: Profile of Murdered Russian Spy," *BBC*, 21 January 2016, https://www.bbc.com/news/uk-19647226.

5 Adam Goldman, Michael S. Schmidt, and Nicholas Fandos, "F.B.I. Opened Inquiry into Whether Trump Was Secretly Working on Behalf of Russia," *New York Times*, 11 January 2019, https://www.nytimes.com/2019/01/11 /us/politics/fbi-trump-russia-inquiry.html; Mark Mazzetti and Katie Benner, "Mueller Finds No Trump-Russia Conspiracy, but Stops Short of Exonerating President on Obstruction," *New York Times*, 24 March 2019, https://www.nytimes.com/2019/03/24/us/politics/mueller-report -summary.html.

6 Kara Scannell, David Shortell, and Veronica Stracqualursi, "Mueller Indicts 13 Russian Nationals over 2016 Election Interference," *CNN*, 17 February 2018, https://edition.cnn.com/2018/02/16/politics/mueller -russia-indictments-election-interference/index.html.

7 "Transcript: William Evanina Talks with Michael Morell on 'Intelligence Matters,' podcast, Sep. 4, 2018," 5 September 2018, https://www.cbsnews .com/news/transcript-william-evanina-talks-with-michael-morell-on -intelligence-matters-podcast-sep-4-2018/; Dustin Volz and Aruna Viswanatha, "FBI Says Chinese Espionage Poses 'Most Severe' Threat to American Security," *Wall Street Journal*, 12 December 2018, https://www .wsj.com/articles/senate-sifts-evidence-of-chinese-cyberespionage

-11544635251; Michael Pillsbury, *The Hundred-Year Marathon: China's Secret Strategy to Replace America* (New York: Henry Holt, 2016); Garrett M. Graff, "How the US Forced China to Quit Stealing – Using a Chinese Spy," *Wired*, 10 November 2018, https://www.wired.com/story/us-china-cybertheft -su-bin/; David E. Sanger, Nicole Perlroth, Glenn Thrush, and Alan Rappeport, "Marriott Data Breach Is Traced to Chinese Hackers as U.S. Readies Crackdown on Beijing," *New York Times*, 11 December 2018, https:// www.nytimes.com/2018/12/11/us/politics/trump-china-trade.html; Katie Benner, "Chinese Officer Is Extradited to U.S. to Face Charges of Economic Espionage," *New York Times*, 10 October 2018, https://www.nytimes.com /2018/10/10/us/politics/china-spy-espionage-arrest.html; Zach Dorfman and Jenna McLaughlin, "The CIA's Communications Suffered a Catastrophic Compromise. It Started in Iran," *Yahoo! News*, 2 November 2018, https:// in.news.yahoo.com/cias-communications-suffered-catastrophic-compromise -started-iran-090018710.html?guccounter=1.

8   Clive Hamilton, *Silent Invasion: China's Influence in Australia* (Richmond, Victoria: Grant – Chronicle Books, 2018), 154.

9   Ibid., 154–60.

10   Ann-Marie Brady, "Magic Weapons: China's Political Influence Activities under Xi Jinping," conference paper presented at conference on "The Corrosion of Democracy under China's Global Influence," supported by the Taiwan Foundation for Democracy and hosted in Arlington, Virginia, 16–17 September 2017), https://www.wilsoncenter.org/sites/default/files/for _website_magicweaponsanne- mariesbradyseptember2017.pdf; Eleanor Ainge Roy, "New Zealand's Five Eyes Membership Called into Question Over 'China Links,'" *Guardian*, 28 May 2018, https://www.theguardian .com/world/2018/may/28/new-zealands-five-eyes-membership-called -into-question-over-china-links; Eleanor Ainge Roy, "Campaign Calling for New Zealand to Protect China Expert Gathers Pace," *Guardian*, 6 December 2018, https://www.theguardian.com/world/2018/dec/06/campaign -calling-for-new-zealand-to-protect-china-expert-gathers-pace.

11   Robert Fife and Stephen Chase, "Trudeau Attended Cash for Access Dinner with Chinese Billionaires," *Globe and Mail*, 22 November 2016, https:// www.theglobeandmail.com/news/politics/trudeau-attended -cash-for-access-fundraiser-with-chinese-billionaires/article32971362/; Tom Blackwell, "How China Uses Shadowy United Front as 'Magic Weapon' to Try to Extend Its Influence in Canada," *National Post*, 28 January 2019, https://nationalpost.com/news/how-china-uses-shadowy-united-front -as-magic-weapon-to-try-to-extend-its-influence-in-canada; Terry Glavin, "Glavin: Learn from Australia – We Should Be Aware of Chinese Influence Peddling," *Ottawa Citizen*, 13 December 2017, https://ottawacitizen.com /opinion/columnists/glavin-learn-from-australia-we-should-be-aware-of

-chinese-influence-peddling; Clive Hamilton, "China's Influence Activities: What Canada Can Learn from Australia" (Ottawa: Macdonald-Laurier Institute, 2018), https://macdonaldlaurier.ca/files/pdf/201801026 _Commentary_Hamilton_FWeb.pdf; John Manthorpe, *Claws of the Panda: Beijing's Campaign of Influence and Intimidation in Canada* (Toronto: Cormorant Books, 2019); Tom Blackwell, "Activists Say New Canadian Group Supporting China's Control of Tibet Is a Front for Beijing," *Canada.com*, 24 April 2019, https://o.canada.com/news/activists-say-new-canadian-group -supporting-chinas-control-of-tibet-is-a-front-for-beijing/wcm/66fdd986 -897d-4952-8ad9-d6f239e04d80.

12   Paul Wells, "Who Lost China? And How Was Canada Supposed to Win It?" *Maclean's*, 3 January 2019, https://www.macleans.ca/politics/ottawa /who-lost-china-and-how-was-canada-supposed-to-win-it/.

13   Tom Blackwell, "MPP's Ties to China Raise Questions about How Close Canadian Politicians Should Get to Foreign Powers," *National Post*, 6 September 2019, https://nationalpost.com/news/mpps-ties-to-china -raise-questions-about-how-close-canadian-politicians-should-get-to -foreign-powers; Craig Offman, "The Making of Michael Chan," *Globe and Mail*, 17 June 2015, https://www.theglobeandmail.com/news/national /the-making-of-michael-chan/article24994796/; Robert Fife and Stephen Chase, "Senator Broke Ethics Rules By Accepting Free Travel to China," *Globe and Mail*, 18 February 2020; Terry Glavin, "Terry Glavin: As Chinese Money Corrupts Western Politics, Trudeau's Liberals Keep Cashing In," *National Post*, 3 December 2017, https://nationalpost.com/opinion /terry-glavin-liberals-not-keen-to-prohibit-foreign-read-chinese-money -from-influencing-canadian-voters; Steven Chase and Robert Fife, "John McCallum Fired as Canada's Ambassador to China amid Huawei Controversy," *Globe and Mail*, 26 January 2019, https://www.theglobeandmail .com/politics/article-john-mccallum-out-as-canadas- ambassador-to -china-trudeau-says/; Limin Zhou and Omid Ghoreishi, "The Man behind McCallum's Controversial Press Conference That Led to His Removal as Canada's Ambassador to China," *Epoch Times*, 28 January 2019, https:// www.theepochtimes.com/the-man-behind-mccallums-controversial-press -conference-that-led-to-his-removal-as-ambassador-to-china_2781522.html; Tom Blackwell, "How Chins Uses Shadowy United Front as 'Magic Weapon' to Try to Extend Its Influence in Canada," *National Post*, 28 January 2019.

14   Terry Glavin, "Terry Glavin: As Chinese Money Corrupts Western Politics, Trudeau's Liberals Keep Cashing In," *National Post*, 3 December 2017, https://nationalpost.com/opinion/terry-glavin-liberals-not-keen-to -prohibit-foreign-read-chinese-money-from-influencing-canadian-voters; Steven Chase and Robert Fife, "John McCallum Fired as Canada's Ambassador to China amid Huawei Controversy," *Globe and Mail*,

26 January 2019, https://www.theglobeandmail.com/politics/article
-john-mccallum-out-as-canadas-ambassador-to-china-trudeau-says/;
Limin Zhou and Omid Ghoreishi, "The Man behind McCallum's
Controversial Press Conference That Led to His Removal as Canada's
Ambassador to China," *Epoch Times*, 28 January 2019, https://www
.theepochtimes.com/the-man-behind-mccallums-controversial-press
-conference-that-led-to-his-removal-as-ambassador-to-china_2781522.html;
Tom Blackwell, "How Chins Uses Shadowy United Front as 'Magic
Weapon' to Try to Extend Its Influence in Canada," *National Post*, 28 January
2019, https://nationalpost.com/news/how-china-uses-shadowy-united
-front-as-magic-weapon-to-try-to-extend-its-influence-in-canada; Canada,
*National Security and Intelligence Committee of Parliamentarians 2019 Annual
Report*, (Ottawa: Her Majesty the Queen in Right of Canada, 2020) 59–66;
Robert Fife and Stephen Chase, "China, Russian Conducting 'Brazen' Interference Activity in Canada, Intelligence Committee Warns," *Globe and Mail*,
12 March 2020, https://www.theglobeandmail.com/politics/article-china
-russia-conducting-brazen-inference-in-canada-intelligence/; Alexander
Panetta, "Pandemic, an economic meltdown, now a 3rd crisis: China U.S.
tensions, *CBC News*, 16 April 2020, https://www.cbc.ca/news/world
/china-us-tension-1.5533509.

15 Tom Blackwell, "Alleged Mastermind of Lavish Mansion Casino Raided
by Police Met Twice with Prime Minister Justin Trudeau," *National Post*,
7 October 2020, https://nationalpost.com/news/canada/alleged
-mastermind-of-lavish-mansion-casino-raided-by-police-met-twice-with
-prime-minister-justin-trudeau; Sam Cooper, "Suspects in Alleged
Markham Illegal Casino Mansion Linked to B.C. Casino Suspects," *Global
News*, 26 October 2020, https://globalnews.ca/news/7416772/markham
-illegal-casino-mansion-b-c-casino-link/.

16 Sam Cooper, "United Front Groups in Canada Helped Beijing Stockpile
Coronavirus Safety Supplies," *Global News*, 30 April 2020, https://www
.globalnews.ca/news/6858818/coronavirus-china-united-front-canada
-protective-eqipment-shortage/; Kevin Breuniger, "China Hid Extent of
Coronavirus Outbreak, US Intelligence Reportedly Says," *CNBC*, 1 April
2020, https://www.cnbc.com/2020/04/01/coronavirus-china-hid-extent
-of-outbreak-us-intelligence-reportedly-says.html; Daniel Hurst, "Australia
Hails Global Support for Independent Coronoavirus Investigation,"
Guardian, 18 May 2020, http://www.theguardian.com/world/2020
/may/18/australia-wins-international-support-for-independent-coronavirus
-inquiry/; Andrew MacDougall, "Is Justin Trudeau Finally Showing Some
Backbone on China?" *Maclean's*, 14 May 2020, https://www.macleans.ca
/opinion/is-justin-trudeau-finally-showing-some-backbone-on-china/;
Alexander Panetta, "Pandemic, an Economic Meltdown, Now a 3rd Crisis:

China U.S. tensions, *CBC News*, 16 April 2020, https://www.cbc.ca/news/world/china-us-tension-1.5533509.

17 J.L. Granatstein and David Stafford, *Spy Wars: Espionage and Canada from Gouzenko to Glasnost* (Toronto: McClelland and Stewart, 1990); Amy Knight, *How the Cold War Began: the Gouzenko Affair and the Hunt for Soviet Spies* (Toronto: McClelland and Stewart, 2005); Mark Kristmanson, *Plateaus of Freedom: Nationality, Culture, and State Security in Canada, 1940–1960* (Don Mills, ON: Oxford University Press, 2003); J.L. Black and Andrew Donskov, *The Gouzenko Affair: Canada and the Beginnings of Cold War Counter-Espionage* (Manotick, ON: Penumbra Press, 2006); Reg Whitaker, Gregory S. Kealey, and Andrew Parnaby, *Secret Service: Political Policing in Canada from the Fenians to Fortress America* (Toronto: University of Toronto Press, 2012), ch. 7; Reg Whitaker and Gary Marcuse, *Cold War Canada: The Making of a National Insecurity State, 1945–57* (Toronto: University of Toronto Press, 1996); Reg Whitaker and Steve Hewitt, *Canada and the Cold War* (Toronto: James Lorimer, 2003); Jessica Wang, *American Science in an Age of Anxiety: Scientists, Anti-Communism and the Cold War* (Chapel Hill: University of North Carolina Press, 1999); Ross Lambertson, *Repression and Resistance: Canadian Human Rights Activists 1930–1960* (Toronto: University of Toronto Press, 2005), ch. 4; Dominique Clement, *Canada's Rights Revolution: Social Movements and Social Change, 1937–82* (Vancouver: University of British Columbia Press, 2008), ch. 3; Dominique Clement, "The Royal Commission on Espionage and the Spy Trials of 1946–9: A Case Study in Parliamentary Supremacy," *Journal of the Canadian Historical Association* 11 (2000): 151–72; Merrily Weisbord, *The Strangest Dream: Canadian Communists, the Spy Trials and the Cold War* (Toronto: Lester and Orpen Dennys, 1983); Dennis Molinaro, "How the Cold War Began … with British Help: The Gouzenko Affair Revisited," *Labour/Le Travail* (Spring 2017): 143–55.

18 Whitaker and Marcuse, *Cold War Canada*; Whitaker, Kealey, and Parnaby, *Secret Service*; Wang, *American Science*; Allen Weinstein and Alexander Vassiliev, *The Haunted Wood: Soviet Espionage in America – the Stalin Era* (New York: Random House, 1990); Reg Whitaker, "Cold War Alchemy: How America, Britain and Canada Transformed Espionage into Subversion," *Intelligence & National Security* 15, no. 2 (2000): 177–210; Kathryn S. Olmstead, "Blond Queens, Red Spiders, and Neurotic Old Maids: Gender and Espionage in the Early Cold War," *Intelligence and National Security* 1, no. 19 (2004): 78–94.

19 Gary Kinsman, *The Canadian War on Queers: National Security as Sexual Regulation* (Vancouver: University of British Columbia Press, 2010).

20 For more on these programs, see Whitaker, Kealey, and Parnaby, *Secret Service*, part 3.

21 Jefferson Morley, "Wilderness of Mirrors," *The Intercept*, 1 January 2018, https://theintercept.com/2018/01/01/the-complex-legacy-of-cia -counterintelligence-chief-james-angleton/; Dennis Molinaro, "'In the Field of Espionage, There's No Such Thing as Peacetime': The Official Secrets Act and the Picnic Wiretapping Program," *Canadian Historical Review* 98, no. 3 (September 2017): 457–82; Dave Seglins and Rachel Houlihan, "Federal Cabinet Secretly Approved Cold War Wiretaps on Anyone Deemed 'Subversive,' Historian Finds," *CBC News*, 15 December 2016, http://www .cbc.ca/news/investigates/ surveillance-cold-war-picnic-1.3897071; Jim Bronskill, "Ottawa Approved Secret RCMP Phone-Tapping during Cold War: Historian," *Canadian Press*, 15 December 2016, http://www .theglobeandmail.com/news/national/historian-uncovers-secret-rcmp -phone-tapping-program-during-cold-war/article33332518/; Dave Seglins, "'Secret Order' Authorizing RCMP's Covert Cold War Wiretapping Program Released after 65 Years," *CBC News*, 16 January 2017, http:// www.cbc.ca/news/politics/cold-warwiretapping-secret-order-1.3933589.

22 Frederick A.O. Schwarz Jr., " The Church Committee and a New Era of Intelligence Oversight," *Intelligence and National Security* 2, no. 22 (2007): 270–97.

23 See for instance, Dave Seglins and Jeremy McDonald, "Government Accused of Hoarding Canadian History in 'Secret' Archives," *CBC News*, 25 May 2017, http://www.cbc.ca/news/canada/government-records -archives-history-1.4129935.

1 After Gouzenko and "The Case": Canada, Australia, and New Zealand at the Secret Commonwealth Security Conferences of 1948 and 1951

GREGORY S. KEALEY AND KERRY A. TAYLOR

For the past five years we have been working on a project to study the three "junior" partners in the Five Eyes alliance on the human intelligence side of the intelligence equation. While much ink has been spilled on MI5 and the FBI, rather less attention has been paid to the history of the security services in Australia, Canada, and New Zealand.[1] And, of course, even less historical research has been devoted to the effort to compare the security experiences of these three settler colonies and to consider the interactions of the Five Eyes alliance, formal and informal.[2] We have chosen to focus on the immediate post–Second World War period because of the major changes that occurred in all three countries in the aftermath of the revelations of Soviet espionage, initially in Canada and subsequently throughout the other countries in the emerging Western alliance. In addition to the obvious historiographic advantages to be obtained by comparative study, we have also assumed that the difficulties of archival access to security records made a scouring of all pertinent national archives and a strategic use of the variant access to information regimes a necessity. We chose the Commonwealth Security Conferences of 1948 and 1951 as our first subject to test these methodological assumptions and approaches.

We commenced the research knowing very little about these conferences that have received only cursory mention in the standard works on the various national state security organizations of the Commonwealth. This historical vacuum was not a surprise given the limited archival access to security records in the pertinent countries until recent years. Each had different access to information regimes; moreover each service embraced a notion of "Glasnost" at different rates and with varying degrees of openness. Even now each regime subjects each release of information to an array of restrictions and redactions, but not the same array of restrictions. What was declassified in Canada or

Australia could still be classified in New Zealand. But we did know something from the history of the founding of the Australian Security Intelligence Organisation, a few things about New Zealand's later creation of its Security Intelligence Service, and a wee bit more from Christopher Andrew's official history of MI5.[3] Hence we set out with an expectation of a paternalistic, perhaps even domineering MI5 attempting to impose the "superior" British security and intelligence model on the naive colonials. Indeed, we were persuaded to some degree by the argument put forward by Philip Murphy that the "essential aim of the British appears to have been to centralize responsibility for security intelligence into the hands of a single agency modelled on MI5."[4] What we have discovered diverges from this expectation.

In October 1948, MI5 hosted the first Commonwealth Security Conference (CSC) in London in the aftermath of the Commonwealth Prime Ministers' (PMs') Meeting. Further advance discussions for the conference, first proposed by British Prime Minister Clement Attlee in May, took place that summer when Sir Norman Brook, the UK Cabinet secretary, toured Dominion capitals.[5] These discussions focused not on the subject matter of the proposed PMs' conference but rather on questions surrounding the invitation list. While the prime ministers of the new members of the Commonwealth – India, Pakistan, and Ceylon – were invited to attend the PMs' meeting, their security services were not even informed of the subsequent secret security conclave. For as Norman Robertson, Canada's high commissioner in London, explained to Lester Pearson, the undersecretary of state for External Affairs, "present security considerations ... set a limit on the exchange of confidential political and defence information between the government of the UK and the government of India."[6] The Labour governments of Australia and New Zealand, and their Liberal colleagues in Ottawa, raised no objections after Brook briefed them regarding the Attlee government's assessment of the new members. When Brook met with Prime Minister King, Pearson, and Minister of External Affairs Louis St. Laurent in Ottawa, the Canadians made it clear that their only concern was that "each member state of the Commonwealth must be left free to make whatever security arrangements with foreign states it deems essential."[7] In other words, Canada's primary concern both before and after the dual 1948 Commonwealth conferences (Prime Ministers and Security) was to ensure its freedom to pursue a continental defence partnership with the United States and to ensure that Commonwealth concerns did not impinge on its ability to do so. The issue of the new Asian members of the Commonwealth had far less profile for the Canadians. Their Australian and New Zealand colleagues apparently agreed. Although to be fair,

New Zealand Labour Prime Minister Peter Fraser did express concerns about the overall foreign policy directions of the Attlee government. Yet this "white" or "old" Commonwealth solution, as the participants described it, did not, of course, exclude South Africa or Southern Rhodesia, as their "white" governments passed the empire's peculiar colour line.[8]

We have written at some length about the prelude to the 1948 CSC elsewhere, so we shall only summarize its results here while incorporating some additional archival materials previously unavailable to us.[9] While British intentions are not absolutely clear in the available documentation, their primary aim appears to have been "educative" to ensure that the "old" Commonwealth countries recognized the threat of Soviet espionage and organized their domestic security services and internal security accordingly. PM Clement Attlee described this intent in his original invitation as "to counter the skillful and extensive infiltration measures which Russia is carrying on."[10] This was a lesson painfully, and openly, learned from the Canadian experience of Gouzenko's Ottawa defection, his purloined Soviet embassy documents, and the subsequent Star Chamber–like Kellogg-Taschereau Royal Commission.[11] In 1948 MI5 had also created a new overseas department to pay closer attention to its Commonwealth and colonial mandate.[12] The necessity of imparting such security lessons more widely in the Commonwealth became even more central to British foreign policy when the Venona decrypts began to bring strong US pressure to bear on the apparently porous Australian security system.[13] Recent works by Desmond Ball and David Horner have surveyed this crisis in loving (and excruciating) detail, so we shall not pursue its complexities here. We will say only that the British were placed in an impossible situation by the Americans' initial refusal to allow them to indoctrinate their Australian allies into the Venona project while simultaneously threatening and ultimately depriving Australia of intelligence-sharing status.[14] While New Zealanders Ian Milner and Wally Clayton did feature prominently in the Venona espionage conversation, it was in the context of their activities in Australia. There is no suggestion that Venona intercepts provided cause for concern within New Zealand itself.

The 1948 CSC met in secret in the shadows of the Commonwealth PMs' Meeting, and hence some of the senior delegates, such as Australia's Solicitor General Kenneth Bailey, New Zealand's External Affairs Secretary Alister McIntosh, and Canada's British High Commissioner Norman Robertson, were unable to attend many of the security sessions. Instead the duties fell to the "technical" security experts, as MI5 termed themselves and their colleagues. For Canada the experts were

George Crean, the External Affairs departmental security officer, and Superintendent George McClellan of the Royal Canadian Mounted Police (RCMP); for Australia Colonel Longfield Lloyd, the embattled and soon-to-be repudiated and replaced Director of the Commonwealth Intelligence Service; and for New Zealand Police Commissioner James Cummings and Sergeant E.A. Stephenson of Special Branch. Major du Plooy, the head of Special Branch, represented South Africa, and Police Commissioner Brigadier Ross, Southern Rhodesia.[15] It is worth noting here that with the exception of MI5, all the Commonwealth security services were then parts of domestic police forces.

In the opening session on 14 October, Sir Percy Sillitoe, the director general of MI5, took the chair and described the general purpose of the conference as the tripartite discussion of the Russian intelligence service and counter-espionage, communism and counter-subversion, and defensive security. In support of these themes, MI5 provided technical demonstrations of its Secret Service Registry, various technical aids (a euphemism for wiretaps and other bugs), and sabotage techniques.[16] In addition, MI5 supplied no fewer than seven papers as the basis for subsequent discussions.[17] Sillitoe indicated that these papers were for discussion only and were not presented for the conference's acceptance, but he did propose that MI5 seek a consensus at the meeting's conclusion on a set of recommendations for delegates to take to their home governments for approval.

At the end of the conference, delegates did agree to ten points that became the basis for their domestic security arrangements and for ongoing Commonwealth cooperation. While we have found no evidence in the archival records available to us to date, Christopher Andrew reports in his official history of MI5 that the Canadian delegation strongly resisted an effort by MI5 to centralize all work on the Russian intelligence service in its own hands, citing a lengthy memo from Roger Hollis to Percy Sillitoe.[18] Canadian resistance to the MI5 proposal as summarized by Hollis appears to be consistent with the position that the minister of External Affairs, Louis St. Laurent, who was acting in the place of an ill Prime Minister Mackenzie King, had taken at the Commonwealth PMs' Meeting on the question of increased Commonwealth defence cooperation. In both the defence and intelligence spheres, Canada had far more access to its continental neighbour than did either the UK or its Commonwealth partners and hence was uninterested in tying itself too tightly to further imperial commitments.[19]

The "Ten Points," which the Liberal government formally accepted in May 1949,[20] commenced with the general purpose of the meeting: "to discuss the general question of action in their respective countries to counter the skillful and extensive infiltration measures which Russia is now carrying on, and the way in which these security authorities could assist each other in relation to the Russian infiltration problem." The conference "reached the conclusion that this problem is twofold, involving both Russian espionage and Communist activities." "To counter these threats," point two called for the security services to deliver "a uniform standard of security throughout their countries" via the subsequent eight points. And the importance of point two cannot be overemphasized, as it represented the consensus on Commonwealth-wide security measures that MI5 had sought at the outset of the meeting.

Point three outlined the need for all Dominions to possess "counter-espionage organizations," "to identify the hostile intelligence organizations ... to discover any networks being run," and then "to control these networks by penetration or sterilization ... or by prosecution." The following point promoted "the fullest exchange among these security services of information on counter-espionage and upon the organization, personnel, methods, and targets of all hostile intelligence services" and encouraged exchange visits of personnel to other services. This phrasing, according to the Hollis memorandum, was a compromise to meet the Canadians' objection to centralization in London of materials related to Soviet espionage.[21] The next point demanded that all security services include a section "devoted to the study of the indigenous Communist Party," including "its structure, organization, and personnel," its "domestic and foreign policy," "its penetration of the Trade Unions," "the employment of Party members on industrial work of national importance," and its "penetration of the Civil Service and of the Armed Forces." A central registry containing "individual records of the total indigenous Communist Party membership," including both "sympathizers and 'fellow travellers,'" was mandated in point six. The next two points promoted departmental security and civil service vetting and purges, while point nine promoted close cooperation between the security service and "the Departments of Government responsible for travel control and for the control of aliens." The last point called for biannual Commonwealth Security Conferences to continue the dialogue.[22]

Hence the Ten Points represents an emerging Cold War consensus that blended counter-espionage measures against Soviet spying with new counter-subversion measures explicitly aimed at domestic communist parties. In all countries, however, the new counter-subversion efforts quickly encompassed the totality of the political Left, including pacifist, anti-nuclear, labour, and women's and gay movements, and in the latter case all citizens suspected of such "deviance." As David McKnight has written in the Australian context,

In my view the suspicions of espionage *added* to a campaign of anti-communism which began in 1917, they did not *originate* it [emphasis in original]. The recent confirmation of espionage doesn't change as much as one might think at first. Indeed it could be argued that the origin of anti-communism lay in hatred of the Industrial Workers of the World before 1917 and before that to hatred of any working class movement which sought to upset the existing exploitation and social arrangements.[23]

The Canadian delegation's post-conference commentary highlighted their view that MI5 regarded the conference's main purpose as "educative." They also noted:

Although the matter was never mentioned during the Conference, it was quite clear that the leakages which have taken place in Australia have given the UK some cause for concern, and the Conference was undoubtedly called in order to ensure that the Commonwealth governments concerned would realize the seriousness of the problem, and in the hope that they would take appropriate measures within their own Government services to protect information of a highly confidential character, passed to them by the UK government.

The Canadians were not sanguine about this outcome, because "it seemed questionable whether the Australian security service was in a position to cope with the political problem presented to them at the present time." After querying the structures under which Australian domestic security operated, they worried that there had "been a reluctance on the part of the Australian Government to take appropriate security measures within the Government service itself." Given that there was no discussion of these matters at the conference, one can only conclude that MI5 was the source for the Canadian concerns.[24]

The New Zealand delegates provided a more critical perspective than that of their Canadian counterparts. McIntosh wrote disparagingly to the acting secretary of the Prime Minister's Department, Foss Shanahan, from Paris, where he was attending United Nations meetings with Prime Minister Peter Fraser, that "the arrangements [the Ten Points] they [MI5] propose are satisfactory enough as far as they go." He continued, after complaining of MI5's security provisions regarding CSC documentation, "I do not think Mr. Cummings [New Zealand police commissioner] was particularly impressed, and, quite frankly, neither was I." Shanahan responded, concerning the Ten Points: "It is admittedly elementary but from my experience of the organization it is probably not a bad policy to emphasize the obvious and get established the organization we require." "The organization" referred to was undoubtedly the New Zealand Police, as he went on to express concern about Prime Minister Fraser's unwillingness to proceed with security changes. In closing, Shanahan worried that such security reform was key "to give us some measure of security against totalitarian infiltration."[25]

One recent historical commentator on the 1948 CSC summarized its achievements in a chapter titled "Creating a Commonwealth Intelligence Culture": "The resulting Conference discussed how intelligence could be shared securely between the participating countries and vetting procedures enhanced for detecting communists in government departments."[26] While Walton emphasizes throughout his work the influence of MI5 on the changing security services of the Commonwealth nations, he does so within a framework that emphasized the importance of local circumstances.[27] The phrase "Commonwealth intelligence culture" appears to have originated with Philip Murphy, who surveyed briefly "old" Commonwealth countries and their postwar relations with MI5 before turning his primary attention to Central Africa.[28]

In February 1951, PM Clement Attlee, acting on the advice of MI5 and the Commonwealth Relations Office, wrote to the Commonwealth prime ministers, carrying though with 1948's point ten, albeit a year later than anticipated.[29] As he noted in his invitation to a second CSC, the problems addressed by the 1948 CSC had "continued to increase in urgency." He also reversed the decision of 1948 to exclude the "new" Dominions (India, Pakistan, Ceylon), arguing that "in the present circumstances the balance of advantage lies in bringing them into such discussions."[30] The following month Prime Minister Louis St. Laurent accepted Attlee's proposal, indicating that the RCMP would represent Canada, agreeing with the participation of the "new" Commonwealth nations, and accepting that future communications on arrangements would be through the RCMP and MI5.[31]

In fact, however, External Affairs' Gordon Robertson accompanied the RCMP's McClellan to London in May. Both were tasked to make use of their time in London for additional work. McClellan would visit RCMP establishments in London and on the Continent that were engaged in immigration security screening, as well as meeting with Special Branch. Robertson was to "talk to some of the UK people about the organization and handling of emergency preparations such as those connected with censorship planning, national registration, the protective dispersal of government offices, war book preparations, etc."[32] Perhaps of even greater interest were the requests from the "secureaucrats" in the Privy Council Office (PCO) who gave Robertson a specific set of policy questions to be answered by their British colleagues. It is important to note that, as was generally the case in Canada, policy issues were primarily the domain of External Affairs and the PCO and were seldom left to the RCMP. As Norman Robertson explained to the prime minister, "I have suggested that Gordon Robertson [the two Robertsons were unrelated] might usefully accompany Supt. McClelland to the Security meeting … There are a number of policy aspects of these discussions on which it should be helpful to have a representative of the civil side of the Security Panel."[33]

The Security Panel's shopping list that Gordon Robertson carried to London included queries about the following: the UK "Security in Government Departments" document, details on UK vetting procedures in regards to file versus field checks, and issues surrounding agency workloads arising from the use of field checks. There was also a request for detailed information about the appeals procedures in cases of negative security reports. At their most mundane, the Canadian officials also sought information on the best locks and filing cabinets for security documents; on a higher plane, they wanted to know if the UK's Interdepartmental Committee on Security had executive or advisory power. But their major focus concerned the vetting process and especially how the appeals process worked. No doubt their curiosity arose from the fact that Canada had no appeals process in its vetting procedures, and this missing element caused periodic qualms of conscience about natural justice.[34] And, as usual, the anglophile officials of Canadian external looked first to British intelligence experience to provide guidance. Robertson's mandate concluded

> It would be useful also to have a general statement concerning the standards of assessment applied to facts turned up in a security investigation. For example, what associations or other connections would be considered to have a special significance if it were proven that a civil servant had been actively engaged in such activities.[35]

The 1951 CSC opened on 15 May in the Commonwealth Relations Office (CRO) and closed on 25 May. MI5's Sir John Shaw, the head of the Overseas Division since January 1950, chaired all nine plenary sessions.[36] They were held in the CRO Board Room, Whitehall, and for the three technical demonstrations the delegates moved to MI5 Headquarters at Leconfield House, Curzon Street.[37] The delegates from the eight Commonwealth countries included the head of the recently created Australian Security Intelligence Organisation, Colonel Charles Spry; New Zealand's P.J. Nalder of Special Branch; the veteran Lieutenant

Colonel du Plooy of South Africa; Brigadier Appleby of Southern Rhodesia; and the Secret Service heads of India (B.N. Mullik), Pakistan (Saiyid Kazim Raza), and Ceylon (S.W.O. de Silva). They were joined by Canadians McClellan (RCMP) and Robertson (External Affairs), as well as by MI5's leadership, including Sillitoe, his deputy director, Guy Liddell, and future directors Roger Hollis and Dick White, plus many others. On the first day, nine members of the UK's Joint Intelligence Committee (JIC) also participated in the opening event, but this did not recur.[38]

Sillitoe opened the conference with greetings (and regrets) from Prime Minister Attlee. Adding his own welcome, he reminded delegates of the Ten Points, which had now reached canonical status and were to form "the basis for our present discussions." He specifically extended a special warm welcome to the representatives of the "new" Commonwealth, and applauded "the wider exchange of experiences which their presence affords," which would "add much ... to the reality and point of the security problems we discuss." Citing the experience of the 1948 CSC and "the principles" of the Ten Points, he proposed that they eschew "the discussions of policy and the drafting of resolutions," and instead focus on "a practical examination of the job in hand." Finally, he summarized the seven main subjects for the ensuing sessions: security organization, communism, counter-espionage, departmental security, industrial security, counter-sabotage, and travel control. In closing, he reiterated the need for total secrecy and invited all to an informal reception at Leconfield House.[39]

Day two focused on the first topic, security organization, and was organized around a series of presentations by each delegation to provide a succinct survey of their security service and "salient developments" since 1948. For the purposes of this chapter, we shall focus on Australia, Canada, and New Zealand in these discussions. The Canadian delegates reported on the RCMP Special Branch as the responsible security agency and noted the highly ethnic nature of the Communist Party of Canada (CPC).

They emphasized that the Labour Progressive Party (LPP), the CPC's official name since the period of illegality in the Second World War, had lost roughly half its members since 1948 and now had between eight and ten thousand members. Front organizations were thought to contain another sixty to seventy thousand members, of whom some three to four thousand "it would be necessary to detain in time of war."[40] The RCMP Special Branch had a specialized unit to deal with counter-espionage and the "underground organization of the LPP." It maintained close liaison with the FBI, and the RCMP had a seat on the Canadian JIC. Protective Security had been stepped up since 1948 and all seamen were now vetted, and the RCMP cooperated with the Armed Services on an anti-sabotage school. The Security Panel received RCMP praise as "an excellent medium for keeping a proper standard of security within government departments." Finally, in a discussion of vetting and purge procedures, the RCMP made it clear that it provided only the security "facts" and left the final decisions about employment to the department concerned.[41]

Colonel Spry next described his newly created Australian Security Intelligence Organization (ASIO, 1949) as "on the lines of the UK Security Service," which, given the UK's role in general and MI5's in particular in ASIO's genesis, may represent the CSC's most profound understatement.[42] Spry then outlined the institutional organization, consisting of sections on communism, counter-espionage, and protective security, and a central registry in Melbourne, with all elements mimicked in each of the Australian states and in the country's overseas presence in Papua New Guinea. Given its MI5-like structure, ASIO depended on relations with state police forces and their Special Branches for any judicial proceedings. Spry estimated that the Communist Party of Australia (CPA) had declined in membership from a peak of twenty-three thousand in 1945 to only eleven thousand in 1949, and "probably today still less." His discussion of the Communist Party Dissolution Bill drew the most interest from other delegates and would continue to do so throughout the week. Although the Australian Supreme Court had declared the legislation ultra vires, he argued that it was necessary because of the CPA's "considerable disruption in industry."[43] He also noted that before the Supreme Court ruling, the CPA had "made extremely effective preparations for an underground organization." In the area of protective security, he pointed to ASIO's presence in Europe to screen potential immigrants and also noted that all Armed Forces personnel were now vetted by file and, if engaged in secret work, by field check as well. Such work kept ASIO's 250 members busy.[44]

P.J. "Jim" Nalder followed Spry with a description of New Zealand's security organization, based in the Special Branch (SB) under the commissioner of police. Nalder boasted with considerable pride that SB had files on all known members of the Communist Party of New Zealand (CPNZ). SB was also active in watching the Russian Legation and had witnessed "evidence that the Soviet Minister was endeavouring to build up a fifth column" among Slavic immigrants. SB also vetted all government departments for both the Public Service Commission and the Armed Forces and held the responsibility for alien registration. Finally, Nalder drew attention to the Interdepartmental Committee on

Security, on which all departments with security issues were represented. ASIO, however, were not so confident the Special Branch was up to scratch. A 1952 report noted their simple archive system and that internal security in their own offices was "no good."[45]

It is worth pointing out that neither Spry nor Nalder appear to have pointed to the various visits from MI5 officials to scrutinize their security systems. In addition the Australians harboured considerable suspicions of the inadequacies of SB.[46] Similar presentations were made by the South Africa, India, Pakistan, and Ceylon delegations. The issue that generated the most discussion in the aftermath of these narratives was South Africa's legal ban of the Communist Party. As du Plooy explained, the South African Communist Party's (CPSA's) dissolution in advance of the legislation "made the task of the SB more difficult." Nevertheless, he felt that on balance the banning of the CPSA gave "a slight advantage to the Security authorities."[47]

The next session of the CSC turned the delegates' attention to their Communist parties and to effective countermeasures. In the aftermath of MI5's description of their efforts, the delegates shared "best practices" with the Australians, claiming some success at penetration both at a top level and via placing typists inside the party apparatus.[48] Canada's contribution was to promote the use of penetration agents, "as there was no scope for subverting the leading members of the Party." The discussion then returned to the pros and cons of legal bans, with the South Africans claiming that their ban had led to "considerable disruption" of the party.[49]

In discussing the CPC, McClellan emphasized the party's considerable success during the wartime alliance with the Soviet Union. He also denounced "the complicity of leading members of the Party in the Russian espionage case." On the other hand, he noted its political setbacks in the labour movement, where he welcomed the purging of Communists from leadership positions in several unions. In addition, he noted that legislation was under development to allow the government to withdraw citizenship from naturalized Canadians.[50]

ASIO's Spry followed with an account of the CPA's decline to some ten thousand members and sixty thousand sympathizers from a 1945 peak of twenty-three thousand. The CPA's major successes in the labour movement, especially among seamen, dockers, and miners, had led directly to the Communist Party Dissolution Bill, which had unfortunately (in Spry's view) failed to survive a constitutional challenge. Of late, the CPA was devoting much effort to the peace movement. He praised the current (Liberal- Country, Robert Menzies) government for its "extremely tough line in suppressing communism."[51]

The fourth meeting on 18 May focused on sabotage, although all participants indicated that there had not been any cases to date. Nevertheless, a lengthy discussion ensued, and the afternoon demonstration at Leconfield House included a lecture on the protection of key points such as oil refineries and utilities.[52] The following day, attention shifted to counter-espionage. After MI5 discussed the atomic bomb spy cases arising from the Manhattan Project (May, Fuchs, Pontecorvo, and Gold), they shifted to their perception of changes in the Russian intelligence service.[53] The impact of the various spy cases had led the Russians to improve their spy tradecraft by minimizing actual contacts with agents, increasing their use of embassies and missions, and shifting from agents with ideological motivations to those with more venal aspirations.[54] In discussions dominated by the "old" Dominions, much emphasis was placed on watching the embassies and missions not only of the Soviet Union but also of its satellite partners. The possibility of restricting Soviet officials' travel was considered, as were concerns about immigrants from Soviet Bloc nations within Canada, particularly concerns about Ukrainian-language propaganda material. A tactic recommended by Canada received attention:

> Finally the Canadian delegate said that he had been informed by a prominent Soviet defector [Gouzenko?] that the best method for getting rid of any Soviet official accredited to a democratic country was to pick them up for a minor traffic offence and take him to the police station for half an hour to an hour and then return him to the Soviet Embassy with profuse apologies; the result invariably will be his immediate recall to Russia.[55]

It was not until the sixth meeting that the revised agenda provided the opportunity for New Zealand's Nalder to discuss the CPNZ in more detail. While the party had lost some influence in the labour movement, it remained their major area of influence. He too noted their activities in the peace movement. Special Branch's major technique was to place agents in the party, but to date they had succeeded only at a low level. They had been unable to penetrate the leadership of the party. He estimated membership at eight hundred to one thousand, with some four thousand sympathizers.[56]

Protective security, especially vetting, received lively attention on day seven. The UK purge procedure was described at length, but in discussion MI5 admitted to "many problems that arose in the assessment of doubtful adverse information about the individual under investigation" and emphasized "the need for just and accurate assessment in cases of this nature." The Australians complained that "vetting

for civilian firms employed on secret work had caused [their] organization embarrassment" because adverse reports had been revealed to
employees turned down for security reasons. The RCMP complained
bitterly, as they did constantly at home, about the massive human re-
source costs caused by vetting field checks. All agreed that the rapid
turnover of Communist Party membership also created significant vetting issues, as while many members left because of disillusionment,
others were simply concealing their relationship to the party. As MI5
pointedly asked, what does it actually mean to have been in the party?[57]

Day eight was dedicated to industrial security and included both the
vetting of personnel and the physical protection of key industries. The
Canadians expressed concern about how to deal with companies that
were not yet engaged on secret contracts but would be in the event of
war. They also sought MI5 advice on how to deal with unions, which in
the Canadian context were inclined to protect their members caught up
in security concerns. In response, the British explained that they never
revealed that such employment shifts were for security reasons and to
date unions had not contested the contract clauses concerning such personnel transfers.[58] Travel control and a Leconfield House lecture and
tour of the Central Registry filled day nine.[59] The Canadian delegates
absented themselves from the latter but were back the following day
for another lecture on "technical aids to security investigations," which
appears to be an MI5 euphemism for tapping, bugging, and other forms
of interception. A demonstration on telephone intercepts and their use,
and on the concealment and detection of microphones, followed.[60] The
agenda also contained a lecture on "agents," but if it was delivered it
went unrecorded in the minutes.[61]

Prime Minister Attlee and Undersecretary of State for the Commonwealth Sir Percivale Liesching attended the final meeting on 25 May.
The PM delivered a brief address, to which Canada, as the senior delegation, responded. After the dignitaries' departure, plans for a future
meeting in two years were discussed. A Pakistan proposal to meet in a
Commonwealth capital instead of London was given a polite hearing
but tabled, although concern was also expressed about the ability to
maintain the meeting's total secrecy elsewhere. The Australians proposed a visit to Scotland Yard if the next conference was held in London. The Australians also asked for additional time on "technical aids"
at the next meeting, while the Indians sought an MI5 technical course
for Commonwealth security officers. A proposal for bilateral personnel
exchanges and visits met with enthusiastic agreement.[62]

We know the Canadian reactions to the 1951 CSC thanks to a brief
summary prepared in June by Gordon Robertson only weeks after his

return to Ottawa from London. In it he outlined the organizational structure of MI5 in considerably more detail than was recorded in the CSC minutes. His most interesting comments concerned Division B2, Counter-espionage, under Dick White. The major insight he drew from White's comments was that

> it required very large resources to handle a single case because of the stead-
> ily increasing care that communists are using in covering all evidence of
> contacts and activity. He said that even with large resources available, it
> was impossible to deal with more than two or three major cases at a time.
> In most instances, a communist agent would not make contact with his
> principals more than once a quarter and there would almost never be an-
> ything in writing. Consequently the job of surveillance was enormous.[63]

Of C Division, Protective Security, under Roger Hollis, he noted that they were reconsidering their total reliance on vetting via file checks, as "the Fuchs case and others have shaken them a bit and they are about to institute field checks in some cases."

He then moved on to the Australian situation, where, after a brief description of the new ASIO structure, he focused his attention on the Communist Party Dissolution Act and Spry's views. Spry had argued that the bill's major aim was "to eliminate the control communists now had of the coal and shipping industries" and, through the for-mer, their "virtual control over the steel industry." The plan had been to "designate about 54 persons in the most relevant trade unions as communists" by way of a committee of senior civil servants making recommendations to a Cabinet committee consisting of the solicitor general, Spry, the defence secretary, and two judges. Individuals des-ignated as communists would be banned from trade union office and government employment. In the aftermath of the Supreme Court rul-ing that the legislation was ultra vires and the subsequent re-election of the Menzies government, Spry anticipated an attempt to amend the Constitution. He thought that "on balance it would be substantially helpful to the situation in Australia, if the communist party could be banned." Although he acknowledged that it would complicate security measures, he thought the disruption to the CPA would be greater.

Robertson then reported on the South African situation, where the Communist Party had dissolved itself in March 1950 in anticipation of the legislative ban of July. Colonel du Plooy argued that the ban had created many difficulties for the party and stopped their recent growth. Nevertheless, he felt that "the balance of advantage, taking into ac-count the increased complications for the security authorities, was only slight." After discussions of India and Pakistan, Robertson noted that "there was nothing of interest in connection with New Zealand, Ceylon, or Rhodesia," with New Zealand appearing "to have little but an ordinary police department and no special security service." Apparently, the similarities in structure of the Canadian RCMP Special Branch and its New Zealand equivalent were not evident to Robertson.[64]

We also know something of MI5's view of the meeting. On 8 June 1951, Sir John Shaw, representing Sir Percy Sillitoe at the JIC, reported that the meeting had been "successful" and characterized by "frank discussion." His major conclusion, however, concerned the new members:

A striking feature of the Conference was the atmosphere of cordiality and genuine friendship amongst the overseas delegates, in particular those from South Africa, India, and Pakistan who went out of their way, with seeming sincerity, to get together and understand one another. The presence of the new Commonwealth countries for the first time at a conference of this nature contributed to no small measure of its value and success.[65]

Naive perhaps, condescending certainly, but this was MI5 after all.

As we have argued elsewhere, MI5, throughout these two conferences and in their more important ongoing bilateral relations with Canada, Australia, and New Zealand, appeared to be wedded to no specific form of security service. They could deal with either a police-based service such as the RCMP or the newly minted civilian, MI5-like ASIO. Hence the two CSCs were devoted purposefully to ensuring suitable security outcomes rather than any attempt to impose a British-model security service on other Commonwealth countries. Frankly, because of the events surrounding the creation of ASIO in Australia and earlier suspect historical works on the New Zealand experience, these findings ran counter to our expectations.[66] What all three junior partners shared with their British colleagues, as evidenced in both the CSC discussions and in their behind-the-scenes domestic discussions, was an unambiguous anti-communism and a consequent significant confusion between espionage and subversion. Although all the security forces had been almost entirely focused on their home Communist parties throughout the 1920s and 1930s and yet totally failed to suspect, let alone prevent, international espionage appeared to give them little pause. Counter-espionage, in other words, simply provided a further excuse to return with renewed vigour to the same anti-communism that had dominated security service politics throughout the West from the Bolshevik Revolution forward.[67] Counter-subversion, with sad results for democracy and human rights, would dominate the worlds of the security services of the three junior partners as it did those of their senior partners in the UK and the United States until the demise of the Soviet Union and its Eastern Bloc allies.

NOTES

1 Selected major works include: on the United Kingdom, Christopher Andrew, *The Defence of the Realm: The Authorized History of MI5* (Toronto: Viking, 2009); on the United States, Tim Weiner, *Enemies: A History of the FBI* (New York: Random House, 2012); on Australia, David Horner, *Spy Catchers: The Official History of ASIO*, vol. 1 (St. Leonards: Allen and Unwin, 2014), and John Blaxland, *The Protest Years: The Official History of ASIO*, vol. 2 (Crows Nest: Allen and Unwin, 2015); on Canada, Reg Whitaker, Gregory S. Kealey, and Andy Parnaby, *Secret Service: Political Policing in Canada from the Fenians to Fortress America* (Toronto: University of Toronto Press, 2012), and Reg Whitaker and Gary Marcuse, *Cold War Canada: The Making of a National Insecurity State, 1945–1957* (Toronto: University of Toronto Press, 1994). New Zealand still lacks an equivalent scholarly study, but ongoing work by Richard Hill and Kerry Taylor should soon fill that vacuum.

2 Highly commendable early efforts at such comparative work include Reg Whitaker, "Fighting the Cold War on the Home Front: America, Britain, Australia and Canada," *Socialist Register* 21 (1984): 23–67; Reg Whitaker, "Cold War Alchemy: How America, Britain, and Canada Transformed Espionage into Subversion," in *American-British-Canadian Intelligence Relations, 1939–2000*, ed. David Stafford and Rhodry Jeffrey-Jones (London: Cass, 2000), 177–210; and Dominique Clement, "'It Is Not the Beliefs but the Crime That Matters': Post-War Civil Liberties Debates in Canada and Australia," *Labour History* 86 (May 2004): 1–32. Another useful study that wanders onto the signals intelligence turf is Scott Anderson, "The Evolution of the Canadian Intelligence Establishment, 1945–50," *Intelligence and National Security* 9, no. 3 (1994): 448–71.

3 Timothy Sayles's chapter in this volume shows just how complex the internal declassification processes can be. On the legislative context see for Australia, David McKnight, "How to Read Your ASIO File," in *Dirty Secrets: Our ASIO Files*, ed. M. Burgmann (Sydney: New South Press, 2014), 21–45. For Canada see, Suzanne Legault, *Striking the Right Balance for Transparency: Recommendations to Modernize the Access to Information Act* (Gatineau: Office of the Information Commissioner, 2015); James Brownlee and Kevin Walby, eds., *Access to Information and Social Justice* (Winnipeg: Arp Books, 2015); and Jim Bronskill and David McKie, *Your Right to Know: How to Use the Law*

to Get Government Secrets (Vancouver: Self-Counsel Press, 2014). For New Zealand see: https://www.nzsis.govt.nz/resources/records-and-archives/nzsis-archives-policy/; Andrew, *Defence of the Realm*; Horner, *Spy Catchers*; Michael Parker, *The SIS* (Palmerston North: Dunmore Press, 1979).

4 Philip Murphy, "Creating a Commonwealth Intelligence Culture: The View from Central Africa, 1945–1965," *Intelligence and National Security* 17, no. 3 (Autumn 2002): 131–62, at 137.

5 Clutterbuck to PM W.L.M. King, 2 August 1948, RG25, vol. 4481, file 50023-A-40, Library and Archives Canada (LAC). See also "Visits: Norman Brook, 1948–50," Archives New Zealand, R18870000.

6 Robertson to Pearson, no. 1291, 5 August 1948, RG25, vol. 4481, LAC. The Liddell diaries reveal ongoing MI5 concerns about the Indian high commissioner in London, Krishna Menon, whom MI5 had under surveillance from 1933 forward. Liddell Diaries, 12 May 1948, KV 4/470, National Archives (NA), Kew. In a discussion of Dominion security at the Commonwealth Relations Office, Liddell noted that "Menon was closely associated with the leaders of the CPGB [Communist Party of Great Britain]." Earlier that winter on 8 January, Liddell noted, "As regards to Hindustan and Pakistan nothing was passed to these Dominions which the British Government did not expect to reach the Russians." See similar comments regarding Menon by MI5's Martin Furnival Jones in Richard Aldrich, *The Hidden Hand: Britain, America, and Cold War Secret Intelligence* (Woodstock: Overland, 2002), 114. For general background on the Attlee government in the realm of foreign affairs and security, see John Bew, *Clement Attlee: The Man Who Made Modern Britain* (New York: Oxford University Press, 2017), ch. 18; Richard J. Aldrich and Rory Cormack, *The Black Door: Spies, British Intelligence and British Prime Ministers* (London: William Collins, 2016), ch. 6; and Daniel W.B. Lomas, "Labour Ministers, Intelligence, and Domestic Anti-Communism, 1945–51," *Journal of Intelligence History* 12, no. 2 (2013): 113–33.

7 Memo for the Prime Minister, "Changes in the Commonwealth since 1926," 13 August 1948, RG25, vol. 4481, LAC.

8 New Zealand Labour PM Peter Fraser did observe to the Canadian high commissioner in Wellington that "Foreign Secretary Bevin … is following a line in foreign policy which he [Fraser] feels repeats 'Tory blunders.' He feels that on a number of important matters of foreign policy since the War, standing with the UK has meant standing in the wrong." In addition, Fraser apparently indicated that while Nehru was "more suitable for the inner circle than South Africa," New Zealand would avoid issues "which would embarrass all of us." Canadian High Commissioner, New Zealand, to Secretary of State for External Affairs, no. 181, 24 September 1948, enclosed in Pearson to the Prime Minister, 2 October 1948. RG25, vol. 4481, LAC.

9 Gregory S. Kealey, "After Gouzenko: Commonwealth Security and Intelligence in the Early Cold War," and Kerry Taylor, "'A Uniform Standard
of Security': New Zealand and Empire Security, 1948–1951," unpublished
papers, Canadian Historical Association, Brock University, St. Catharines,
Ontario, 28 May 2014.

10 Memo for PM, 20 May 1948, RG2/15, vol. 245, file C-100-25, LAC. This
crucial file, obtained by an Access to Information request to LAC (A-2013-
00413), was not available to us when we wrote our 2014 papers.

11 The literature on Gouzenko is large and still growing, but for the most
recent accounts, see Amy Knight, *How the Cold War Began: The Igor Gouzenko Affair and the Hunt for Soviet Spies* (New York: Carroll and Graf,
2007); J.L. Black and Martin Rudner, eds., *The Gouzenko Affair: Canada and
the Beginnings of Cold War Counter-Espionage* (Manotick: Penumbra, 2006);
Dennis Molinaro, "How the Cold War Began ... with British Help: The
Gouzenko Affair Revisited," *Labour/Le Travail* 79 (Spring 2017): 143–55;
and Dominique Clement, "Canada's Integration into Global Intelligence
Sharing Networks: From Gouzenko to the Montreal Olympics," *Intelligence and National Security* 33, no. 7 (2018): 1053–69. See also the provoca-
tive Mark Kristmanson, *Plateaus of Freedom: Nationality, Culture, and State
Security in Canada, 1940–1960* (Toronto: University of Toronto Press, 2002).
Finally, specifically on the Alan Nunn May case, see Paul Broda, *Scientific
Spies: A Memoir of My Three Parents and the Atomic Bomb* (London: Trouba-
dor, 2011).

12 Calder Walton, *Empire of Secrets: British Intelligence, the Cold War, and the
Twilight of Empire* (London: Harper, 2013), 125.

13 Memo for the Acting PM, 18 September 1948, RG25, vol. 4481, LAC (un-
signed, but probably Arnold Heeney, the chair of the Security Panel):
"I gather that Mr. Attlee has been moved to raise the question as the result
of leaks which have taken place recently in Canberra. While I do not think
any leaks of UK information have taken place here, it seems to be in our
interest to do all we can to protect information passed to us by the UK and
other Commonwealth governments."

14 Desmond Ball and David Horner, *Breaking the Codes: Australia's KGB Net-
work, 1944–1950* (St. Leonards: Allen and Unwin, 1998), and Horner, *Spy
Catchers*. For an important discussion of Venona and Australia that acts
as a counter to the more blatant ideological argumentation in the previ-
ous two works, see David McKnight, "Reassessing the Rosenberg and
Petrov Affairs," *Labour History* 70 (May 1996): 182–90, especially 189; his
"The Moscow-Canberra Cables: How Soviet Intelligence Obtained British
Secrets through the Back Door," *Intelligence and National Security* 13, no. 2
(Summer 1998): 159–70; and his "Clear Thinking, Dogma, and the War on
Terror," *Sydney Papers* 16, no. 1 (2004): 96–101.

15 "Report by the Canadian Delegates to the Commonwealth Security Con-
    ference," 22 December 1948, RG2/15, vol. 245, LAC.
16 For reflections on the importance of the registry (archives) to security
    services, see Gregory S. Kealey, *Spying on Canadians: The Royal Canadian
    Mounted Police Security Service and the Origins of the Long Cold War* (Toronto:
    University of Toronto Press, 2017), ch. 8.
17 The papers covered (1) the Soviet intelligence service; (2) the organization
    of a counter-espionage division; (3) the security importance of a Commu-
    nist Party (CP); (4) the requirements of an intelligence section for the study
    of an indigenous CP; (5) the principles and organization of defensive se-
    curity; (6) control of entry into the UK; and (7) the Civil Service "purge"
    procedure.
18 Andrew, *Defence of the Realm*, 371–2.
19 St. Laurent at the end of the discussion at the Commonwealth PMs' meet-
    ing, Materials for Prime Ministers' Conference, RG25, vol. 4481, file 50023-
    A-40, LAC: "In view of the historic position of Canada, I wish to make it
    clear, so far as Canada is concerned, that in agreeing to recommend con-
    sultation between Commonwealth Governments to arrange co-operative
    action in matters of defence, it would be unreal for us to regard as effective
    either general or regional plans of defence which would comprise Com-
    monwealth countries exclusively, and which did not also include other
    peace-loving countries prepared to co-operate in resisting aggression." All
    this was, of course, preparatory to Canada's ever-increasing ties to North
    American continental defence, including NORAD.
20 King to Attlee, 20 May 1949, RG2/15, vol. 245, LAC: "I agree with them. In
    practice the authorities here have been following these principles for some
    time and, while there are improvements which might be made in carrying
    out the work, I do not think that there are any changes of principle which
    we would have to make in order to carry out the recommendations."
    King's confidence was supported by MI5 in December 1948, which when
    asked by the JIC to rank Commonwealth countries on their security pre-
    paredness gave Canada a first, while delivering seconds to Australia, New
    Zealand, and South Africa, and begrudging thirds to Ceylon, India, and
    Pakistan. Aldrich, *Hidden Hand*, 115.
21 Andrew, *Defence of the Realm*, 371–2.
22 The Ten Points can be found in NA, Kew, PREM 8/1343, LMV, "Note":
    "Sir Percy Sillitoe handed me this copy of the record of the discussions
    between the Security authorities of the UK and the Dominions. It will
    now be sent to the Prime Ministers through the Chief Security Officers. Sir
    Percy Sillitoe has shown it to Mr. Attlee." The Canadian commentary on
    the document can be found in "Report by the Delegates," 22 December 1948,
    prepared by Crean and agreed to by McClellan. The Canadians concluded

that for them "the chief value of the Conference was the opportunity it gave to discuss matters of detail with members of the United Kingdom Security Service."

23 Whitaker, Kealey, and Parnaby, *Secret Service*; David McKnight, *Australia's Spies and Their Secrets* (Sydney: Allen and Unwin, 1966); Gary Kinsman and Patricia Gentile, *The Canadian War on Queers: National Security as Sexual Regulation* (Vancouver: University of British Columbia Press, 2010). For the McKnight quotation, see his "Reassessing Rosenberg and Petrov," 187. For similar argumentation about the real "origins" of the Cold War, see Kealey, *Spying on Canadians*. For a supportive position, see Odd Arne Westad, *The Cold War: A World History* (New York: Basic Books, 2017). For New Zealand, see Graeme Dunstall, "Governments, the Police, and the Left, 1912–1951," in *On the Left: Essays on Socialism in New Zealand*, ed. P. Moloney and K.A. Taylor (Dunedin: Otago University Press, 2002), 87–101.

24 "Report," 22 December 1948, RG2/15, vol. 245, LAC. This surmise seems reasonable given that the only other possible source for the Canadians would have been the United States, and there is no evidence that even the existence of Venona, let alone its findings, was being shared in 1948.

25 For New Zealand Security Intelligence Service release of documents regarding CSCs of 1948 and 1951, see Dr Warren Tucker to Dr Kerry A. Taylor, 21 February 2014, 11 March 2014, and 9 April 2014. Documents released include McIntosh to Shanahan, 3 October 1948, and Shanahan to McIntosh, 18 November 1948. Discussions of tightening security certainly preceded the CSC, as MI5's Roger Hollis had visited Wellington in March 1948 with Sir Percy Sillitoe during their extended meetings in Australia. His five-page "Talk on Communism," delivered at Army Headquarters in Wellington, is also included in the above release. For more on the Hollis visit, see Taylor, "A Uniform Standard of Security."

26 Walton, *Empire of Secrets*, 146.

27 Ibid., 147.

28 Murphy, "Creating a Commonwealth Intelligence Culture." See also Daniel Lomas, *Intelligence, Security and the Attlee Governments, 1945–51* (Manchester: Manchester University Press, 2017), 237

29 P. Liesching, CRO, to Prime Minister, 31 January 1951, NA, Kew, PREM 8/1343.

30 Attlee to St. Laurent, 14 February 1951, RG2/15, vol. 245, LAC. Apparently South Africa objected to the presence of the "new" Commonwealth, but to no avail. See Andrew, *Defence of the Realm*, 444, and Walton, *Secrets of Empire*, 146.

31 St. Laurent to Attlee, 13 March 1951, RG2/15, vol. 245, LAC.

32 Norman A. Robertson to Dana Wilgress, 21 April 1951, RG2/15, vol. 245, LAC.

33 Norman A. Robertson to St. Laurent, 4 May 1951, RG2/15, vol. 245, LAC.
34 On vetting practices in Canada, see Reg Whitaker and Gary Marcuse, *Canada's Cold War: The Making of a National Insecurity State, 1945–1957* (Toronto: University of Toronto Press, 1994), and Larry Hannant, *The Infernal Machine: Investigating the Loyalty of Canada's Citizens* (Toronto: University of Toronto Press, 1995).
35 E.F. Gaskell to R.G. Robertson, "Security Items for Discussion in the U.K.," 7 May 1951, RG2/15, vol. 245, LAC. Such concerns preoccupied the Canadian Security Panel throughout the late 1940s and early 1950s. For examples, see Security Panel Minutes, RG2/18, vols 103, 188, 189, f. S-100, LAC. Our thanks to Reg Whitaker for access to copies of these documents. For Cabinet approval of the vetting process, see Cabinet Document No. 612 of 19 February 1948; Cabinet Conclusions, 25 February 1948; and Cabinet Directive, 5 March 1948, all in MG26J4, vol. 421.
36 Walton, *Empire of Secrets*, 125.
37 Leconfield House was the home of MI5 from 1945 to 1976, when it moved to Gower Street.
38 CSC, Minutes, 1st Meeting, 15 May 1951, RG2/15, vol. 245, LAC.
39 CSC, Draft, "Opening Address by the Director-General of the Security Service," attached to J.V.W. Shaw to C.G. Costley-White, CRO, 8 May 1951, NA, Kew, PREM 8/1343. See also CSC, Minutes, 1st Meeting, 15 May 1951.
40 Such internment plans for the CPC leadership have recently been studied in detail by Frances V. Reilly in "Controlling Contagion: Policing and Prescribing Sexual and Political Normalcy in Cold War Canada" (PhD thesis, University of Saskatchewan, 2016), and her chapter in this book, "Operation Profunc: The Cold War Plan to Intern Canadian Communists."
41 CSC, Minutes, 2nd Meeting, 16 May 1951, RG2/15, vol. 245, LAC.
42 For ASIO's roots, see Horner, *Spy Catchers*; McKnight, *Australia's Spies and Their Secrets*; and Frank Cain, *Terrorism and Intelligence in Australia: A History of ASIO and National Surveillance* (Melbourne: Australian Scholarly Publishing, 2008).
43 The literature on the Communist dissolution debate is voluminous, but see among others Phillip Deery, "Communism, Security, and the Cold War," *Journal of Australian Studies* 21 (1997): 162–75; S. Ricketson, "Liberal Law in a Repressive Age: Communism and the Law, 1920–1950," *Monash University Law Review* 3 (1976): 101–33; Laurence W. Maher, "The Use and Abuse of Sedition," *Sydney Law Review* 14 (1992): 287–316; and Roger Douglas, "Cold War Justice? Judicial Responses to Communists and Communism, 1945–55," *Sydney Law Review* 29 (2007): 43–84.
44 CSC, Minutes, 2nd Meeting, 15 May 1951.
45 CSC, Minutes, 2nd Meeting, 15 May 1951. Like Spry's Australian report, Nalder failed to note the extent of MI5 engagement with New Zealand

security organization, although PM Peter Fraser proved rather less suggestible than Australian Labor Party Prime Minister Ben Chifley, who of course had the Venona revelations and US threats urging, if not forcing, his compliance. On New Zealand developments, see Taylor, "A Uniform Standard of Security," and Susan Butterworth, *More Than Law and Order: Policing a Changing Society, 1945–1992* (Dunedin: University of Otago Press, 2005).

46 National Archives of Australia, Visit to New Zealand of Director, B1, A9108, ROLL 16/54.

47 CSC, Minutes, 2nd Meeting, 15 May 1951. Ceylon and Southern Rhodesia presented at the third meeting on 16 May. The order of presentation appears to be based on seniority of the nation's Dominion status.

48 This tactic had been employed with great success by MI5, which had an agent in an administrative role at CPGB headquarters for many years. See Andrew, *Defence of the Realm*, 179–85.

49 CSC, Minutes, 3rd Meeting, 17 May 1951, RG2/15, vol. 245, LAC.

50 On the politics of Canadian immigration policy, see Reg Whitaker, *Double Standard: The Secret History of Canadian Immigration* (Toronto: Lester and Orpen Dennys, 1987).

51 CSC, Minutes, 3rd Meeting, 17 May 1951.

52 CSC, Minutes, 4th Meeting, 18 May 1951, RG2/15, vol. 245, LAC.

53 On Pontecorvo, see the excellent study by Frank Close, *Half-Life: The Divided Life of Bruno Pontecorvo, Physicist or Spy* (New York: Basic Books, 2015).

54 This last point is of considerable interest, as some scholars have argued that the failure of Western intelligence agencies owed much to a fixation on communist ideology as a basis for espionage. See, for example, Whitaker, "Cold War Alchemy."

55 CSC, Minutes, 6th Meeting, 21 May 1951.

56 CSC, Minutes, 6th Meeting, 21 May 1951, RG2/15, vol. 245, LAC. For a rare account of one such Security Intelligence Service penetration agent, see George Fraser, *Seeing Red: Undercover in 1950s New Zealand* (Palmerston North: Dunmore Press, 1995).

57 CSC, Minutes, 7th Meeting, 22 May 1951, RG2/15, vol. 245, LAC.

58 CSC, Minutes, 8th Meeting, 22 May 1951, RG2/15, vol. 245, LAC.

59 CSC, Minutes, 9th Meeting, 23 May 1951, RG2/15, vol. 245, LAC.

60 For recent work outlining early RCMP wiretapping "arrangements," see Dennis Molinaro, "'In the Field of Espionage, There's No Such Thing as Peacetime': The Official Secrets Act and the PICNIC Wiretapping Program," *Canadian Historical Review* 98, no. 3 (September 2017): 457–82.

61 CSC, Minutes, Demonstration, Leconfield House, 24 May 1951, RG2/15, vol. 245, LAC.

62 CSC, Minutes, 10th Meeting, 25 May 1951, RG2/15, vol. 245, LAC. Gordon
    Robertson, "Memo for Norman A. Robertson re Commonwealth Security
    Conference, May 1951," 4 June 1951, RG2/15, vol. 245, LAC.
63 Robertson "Memo," 4 June 1951.
64 JIC Minutes, 8 June 1951, NA, Kew, CAB 159/9.
65 Parker, *The SIS*, and Graeme Hunt, *Spies and Revolutionaries: A History of
    New Zealand Subversion* (Auckland: Read, 2007).
66 In John le Carré, *The Secret Pilgrim* (Toronto: Viking 1991), 116, Smiley re-
    flects: "In the Cold War, when our enemies lied, they lied to conceal the
    wretchedness of their system. Whereas when *we* lied, we concealed our
    virtues. Even from ourselves. We concealed the very things that made us
    right. Our respect for the individual, our love of variety and argument, our
    belief that you can only govern fairly with the consent of the governed,
    our capacity to see the other fellows' view – most notably in the countries
    we exploited, almost to death, for our own ends. In our supposed ideo-
    logical rectitude, we sacrificed our compassion to the great god of indif-
    ference. We protected the strong against the weak, and we perfected the
    art of the public lie. We made enemies of decent reformers and friends of
    the most disgusting potentates. And we scarcely paused to ask ourselves
    how much longer we could defend our society by these means and remain
    a society worth defending." On le Carré himself, and especially his own
    role as an informant and later as an agent of MI5, see Adam Sisman, *John le
    Carré: The Biography* (Toronto: Knopf, 2015). For le Carré's quasi-rejoinder,
    see his *The Pigeon Tunnel: Stories from My Life* (Toronto: Viking, 2016).
67 We are aware that we have not addressed the important arguments ad-
    vanced by David McKnight in his "Rethinking Cold War History," *Labour
    History* 95 (November 2008): 185–96, concerning the complicity of the CPA
    in their own demise. See also his, we feel rather less persuasive, *Espionage
    and the Roots of the Cold War: The Conspiratorial Heritage* (London: Frank
    Cass, 2002). In a similar vein, we note Phillip Deery's "'A Very Present
    Menace?': Attlee, Communism and the Cold War," *Australian Journal of
    Politics and History* 44, no. 1 (1998): 69–94, although we would challenge
    his reading of the Canadian Seamen's Union strike of 1948, which he ap-
    pears to view as similar to his version of the London Dockers' strike as the
    CPGB complying with Stalinist foreign policy. We shall pursue these issues
    in future work.

2 American Communism, Anti-Communism, and the Cold War: The Case of Carl Marzani, 1947–1951

MARCELLA BENCIVENNI

On 17 January 1947, about two months before US President Harry Truman announced his war on communism, Carl Marzani, a former employee of the State Department and the wartime Office of Strategic Services (OSS), was indicted on fraud charges against the government under Title 18, Section 80, of the US criminal code.[1] More specifically, he was accused of having lied about his communist affiliations to investigative authorities in order to keep his government job, thereby "fraudulently" receiving his pay. The original indictment included eleven counts: the first nine went back to sworn statements that Marzani made to FBI and Civil Service Commission officials investigating his fitness for government employment between 1942 and 1943; the last two related to an informal interview he had with a State Department superior on 1 June 1946. All related essentially to the same offence: that Marzani had concealed his "red tie" on separate occasions, denying that he had been a member of the Communist Party; that he had attended, contributed to, or participated in any of the party's activities; that he had used an alias while in the party; and that he had spoken against the Conscription Bill.[2]

As Attorney General Tom Clark revealed in a press conference announcing the indictment against Marzani, the charges were part of an intensive inquiry of federal workers suspected of subversive affiliations that would later grow into the country's first general loyalty program.[3] Out of three thousand initial investigations, 314 employees were said to need further checking: of these, 202 had left their positions and 59 were cleared of suspicions, while the other 53 continued to be investigated.[4] Marzani was the first of these "dubious" civil servants to be tried and convicted. The trial opened with great anticipation on 12 May 1947 and received close press coverage for its entire eleven-day duration. Marzani was eventually found guilty on all eleven counts and sentenced to one to three years in prison – an unusually harsh sentence for cases involving false statements.[5]

On 2 February 1948, the appellate court dismissed the first nine counts on the ground that they were barred by the statute of limitations, but it sustained the last two.[6] Dragging on for another two years, the case then went twice to the Supreme Court. Marzani recalled that during the oral arguments feelings among the justices ran high as they discussed the case for three hours, with the most liberal justices questioning whether the government was exceeding its power.[7] The court decision came down a few days before Christmas: it was a tie vote – four to four, with one justice, William O. Douglas, abstaining.[8] The split decision upheld the earlier conviction, but Marzani petitioned for, and, unexpectedly, won a rehearing.[9] It is rare for the Supreme Court to grant a second review; it was then only the eighth time in its 160-year history that it had agreed to reconsider its verdict – a fact clearly underlining the significance of the Marzani case.[10] But for the second time Douglas recused himself, and the justices deadlocked again, splitting the verdict four to four.[11] That left the conviction standing, and Marzani went to prison on 22 March 1949, serving almost three years, with parole repeatedly denied despite many pleas for clemency from a variety of activists and intellectuals, including eminent figures such as Albert Einstein, Eleanor Roosevelt, Thomas Mann, and Henry Wallace.[12]

The circumstances of Marzani's prosecution were far from ordinary. The case coincided with mounting tensions between the United States and the Soviet Union, as the two countries fell from being wartime allies to staunch adversaries following the end of the war. As public fear and anxiety grew, so did domestic repression and surveillance. Reflecting growing political pressures to eradicate communism from American society, Marzani's indictment was a prelude to the massive purge of federal workers suspected of subversive affiliations ordered by President Truman under Executive Order 9835 on 21 March 1947. Also known as the "Loyalty Order," this program required that all civil service employees (over three million) be screened for loyalty to root out any communist influence in the US government, especially in sensitive positions in the State Department.[13]

Unlike other suspected communists, however, Marzani was not accused of treason, sabotage, or disloyalty. No evidence was ever produced that he had passed secret information to the Soviets, endangered in any way national security, or conspired against the United States. In fact, he had served his country diligently during the war, gaining frequent praise by his superiors. To complicate the case even further, Marzani had resigned from his government job on 12 November 1946, well before his indictment. What, then, was the actual objective of his conviction? What accounts for the zeal of the prosecution and severity of the sentence? What was the Marzani case really about?

Despite the government's claim that Marzani was being charged with "simply" lying to the federal authorities, it was clearly the political nature of Marzani's lie – his denial of his membership in the Communist Party – that lay at the heart of the matter. As this chapter will show, Marzani's indictment served three main goals: it supplied the Department of Justice with a potentially new legal weapon to prosecute undesirable government employees; it helped Truman to rally public opinion behind his Cold War policies and counter-intelligence programs; and, finally, it warned radicals and progressive-minded persons "to keep out of Washington" for fear that they might be recklessly charged with being subversive.[14] As the *Daily Worker* remarked, the Marzani affair was "one of the most notorious cases in the witch-hunt drive of the government."[15]

The indictment was meant to test whether loyalty investigations that had already been closed by the FBI and the Civil Service Commission could be reopened and other ex-government employees suspected of subversive affiliations or ideas sent to jail, establishing a legal precedent for similar prosecutions. Technically, the accusations against Marzani had to do with perjury, not fraud. However, the government could not prosecute him for perjury because the alleged false statements he had made to federal investigators went back to 1942 and were barred by the three-year statute of limitations. Therefore, the Justice Department sought to convict him under a wartime provision enacted by Congress in 1944 suspending the statute of limitations in fraud cases for the duration of the war.[16] The question that Marzani's case was meant to test was whether the suspension of the statute of limitations applied only to war contracts and other matters in which the government was defrauded financially or could be extended, as the prosecution contended, to any misstatement made to federal officials where there was no financial loss, as in the Marzani case.

Investigative journalist I.F. Stone, a vocal critic of secret surveillance and domestic purges, had no doubts that Marzani's indictment was politically motivated and that the anti-communist hysteria had "infected" the American judicial system.[17] Between 1947 and 1949, Stone wrote a stinging series of articles in defence of Marzani, describing his case as a cautionary tale – a carefully orchestrated government frame-up designed to ignite fear and conformity. "This test prosecution of an obscure ex-government employee" – he wrote in *The Nation* – "cast a lengthening shadow over past and future loyalty purges," providing a way in which "old charges, true, dubious or false, can be rehashed in an atmosphere of growing hysteria." The Marzani case, he concluded, "may give the witch hunters a new and formidable weapon."[18]

Mainstream newspapers seemed to concur: "Small wonder," *Newsweek* candidly wrote after the guilty verdict was announced, "that Marzani's conviction brought joy to the Department of Justice: although every high official in Washington has long known that Communist penetration into the government has attained serious proportions, this trial was the first of its kind." The door was now "wide open to press the Administration's $25,000,000 program to eliminate Communists from the Federal payroll."[19] In a similar vein, the *New York Post* presaged that "additional loyalty prosecutions are expected soon as a result of the conviction of Carl Aldo Marzani."[20]

The case's high stakes were evident from the extensive public attention and press coverage it received at the time. Taking place after the "*Amerasia* Affair," the first public espionage drama of the postwar era, Marzani's incident escalated partisan controversy, arousing deep and fierce passions that still dominate popular, as well as scholarly, perceptions of the Cold War.[21] From the onset, liberals and conservatives fought bitterly over the truth, constructing two diametrically opposed narratives about the case in which Marzani stood either as a prime victim of the growing Red Scare that was destroying civil liberties, or, by contrast, as powerful evidence that communists had effectively infiltrated and betrayed the nation.

But despite the enormous publicity it generated in its time, Marzani's case has received surprisingly little attention from scholars of the Cold War. A charismatic and important figure of the American Left, Marzani too has been largely forgotten. Recently, however, his name has resurfaced in a number of books uncovering the secret world of Soviet espionage during and immediately following the Second World War.[22] The main source of these investigations comes from decoded messages in the "Venona Project," a secret counter-intelligence program set up by the National Security Agency (NSA) in 1943 to decipher telegraphic cables between Soviet intelligence agencies in Moscow and their American stations. Declassified in 1995 and totalling more than five thousand pages, these documents, along with newly opened Soviet archives, have bolstered a spate of sensational spy stories and reignited debates over high-profile trial cases. John Earl Haynes and Harvey Klehr were among the first and most prolific authors to mine the Venona files to contend that what historians had characterized as anti-communist hysteria was in fact a "legitimate" response against a real threat to American security.[23] Building upon their findings, other scholars have reached similar conclusions, with some going so far as to justify the red witch-hunt (and its concomitant assault on civil rights) and even to exonerate Senator Joseph McCarthy from any wrongdoing.[24]

Of the approximately three thousand Venona translations that have been made public, Marzani appears in only one message (#1354), dated 22 September 1944. This cable listed twenty-six OSS employees suspected of communist affiliations but, obviously, not all those whose names were mentioned were necessarily guilty of treason. Several scholars, nevertheless, have alleged that Marzani may have had compromising relationships with Soviet intelligence. Haynes and Klehr, for instance, believe he is one of the unidentified sources of the Soviet ring operating in the OSS, which according to their findings sheltered at least fifteen covert agents.[25] Two neoconservative writers, Herbert Romerstein and Eric Breindel, have also speculated that the code name "Kollega," which appeared in a Venona message reporting the names of covert Soviet spies in the OSS and which NSA analysts were unable to identify, was possibly Marzani.[26]

Adding more fuel to these allegations, two retired KGB agents, Oleg Kalugin and Vasili Mitrokhin, in their sensationalized autobiographies have claimed that Marzani was a Soviet agent operating under the code name NORD during the 1960s and that he was probably recruited before the Second World War. More specifically, they maintained that in the early sixties he accepted KGB funds to support his publishing venture, Marzani & Munsell, which ran the Liberty Book Club and Prometheus Book Club, by printing books deemed useful to Soviet propaganda.[27]

That Marzani rubbed shoulders with communists was hardly a secret, but the claim that he was a spy remains disputable. There is no hard evidence, other than smuggled KGB documents by Soviet intelligence defectors, indicating that he assisted the Russians, and, as Christopher Andrew notes in the Foreword to his acclaimed history of the KGB, *The Sword and the Shield*, "although certain individuals were targeted by the KGB, and may have been given codenames, this does not mean that persons named were conscious or witting agents or sources – or even that they were aware that they were being targeted for recruitment or political influence operations."

Marzani coincidentally died in 1994, a year before the opening of the Soviet and American archives. We will never know how he would have responded to the espionage charges against him, and we might never resolve completely all the puzzles of his life and the precise nature of his association with Moscow. From oral interviews I conducted with three members of his family, it is clear they consider the accusations ludicrous. Exonerating Marzani is beyond the scope of this chapter but, guilt or innocence aside, his story points to a far more complicated picture than hitherto suggested. Espionage, in other words, is not the whole story, nor the most important part of the story. There are other questions that have been completely overlooked; they deserve more attention.[28] The Marzani case, indeed, speaks to the core of the complex and murky relationship between secrecy, surveillance, and national security that, as this volume argues, loomed large during the Cold War years. A detailed account of his indictment, trial, and imprisonment not only offers a rare insight into the inner world of Washington (particularly the political and bureaucratic struggle over intelligence between Truman, Hoover, and Donovan), but it also reveals the full depth and breadth of American anti-communism and police spying.

Fears of internal communist subversion in the United States reached a nearly hysterical pitch by the early 1950s, fuelled by several high-profile spy cases and Senator Joseph McCarthy's sensational claims, but Marzani's prosecution shows that attempts to fend off a growing "red menace" were well underway by 1946. It is also important to note that the anti-communist crusade extended well beyond the threat of Soviet infiltration. As Frances Reilly recounts in chapter 5, by 1948 Canada had established a secret communist internment preparedness plan called "Operation Profunc" that put tens of thousands of civilians under police surveillance "for fear that they would lead an uprising, sabotage vital industries in wartime, and, most concerning, subvert Canadian society with communist ideology." Concerns over national security similarly led to the criminalization of homosexuality and the purge of gay men from government positions, as in the case of diplomats in the British Foreign Office discussed in the next chapter.

Who Was Carl Marzani?

The first of two children, Marzani was born on 4 March 1912, in Rome, Italy. As he details in the first book of his memoirs, he grew up a beloved son in a happy, prosperous, close-knit family. His world and security, however, began to falter after the Great War, with the rise of fascism.[29] Unlike other Italians who underestimated Mussolini, Marzani's father, a utopian socialist and civil servant, sensed from the start that fascism was a new, potent, and dangerous movement and decided to leave Italy. In 1923 he fled to the United States, settling in Scranton, Pennsylvania, where his oldest brother had already migrated; the rest of the family joined him a year later.[30]

Adjustment to the new land was not easy. Carl was only twelve when he arrived in America; he spoke no English and initially felt alienated and ashamed. Other kids made fun of him, calling him "wop," and he got often into fist fights with them. A precocious learner, he quickly mastered English, and within seven years from his arrival in the new land, went from elementary school to high school, excelling in all subjects and eventually winning a scholarship to Williams College. As the "most brilliant" student of his class, upon graduation he was awarded a fellowship to Oxford University.[31]

Planning to become a playwright, he immersed himself in theatre at Oxford, writing, directing, and producing plays. World events, however, quickly catapulted him into the political scene, propelling him to become, in his own words, "a reluctant radical." When the Spanish Civil War broke out in 1936, he crossed the border into Spain to see what was going on. Although his original intention was to report on the war for the *Daily Herald* of London, he ended up in the Aragon front, fighting for several months along with the legendary Durruti Column, the war's most important anarchist brigade. While brief, the front experience altered his life forever, reinforcing his radical bent and pushing him towards communism.[32]

In fact, in June 1937, upon his return to England to complete his studies, Marzani joined the British Communist Party along with his wife, actress Edith Eisner, whom he had met while at Williams College and had married on 12 March 1937. They began to attend party meetings and study Marxism, and Marzani became treasurer of the South Midlands district. When the two returned in the United States in May of 1939, following a long trip in Asia, they joined the CPUSA, assuming the names of Tony Wales and Edith Charles. They became active organizers in New York's Lower East Side, where they had settled, working particularly around local problems and election campaigns of local progressive councilmen. Marzani was the section's educational director for well over a year. He ran classes, wrote leaflets, and spoke frequently – on street corners, at settlement house forums, and in storefront African American churches.[33]

The Lower East Side had been a lively radical enclave since the early twentieth century. Overwhelmingly ethnic and working class, it was "the only place in the entire United States where New Deal Democrats were the right wing of the political spectrum, and Republicans hardly visible ... There was a commitment, a way of life," recalled Marzani, "that was extraordinary."[34] In the late 1930s, the district boasted 3,200 communist members organized into more than forty branches. Far from subversive, they were, as many other party activists have recounted, "a humane, democratic force," which functioned largely as the left wing of the New Deal. Most of their work revolved around local problems and election campaigns of local progressive council members, most notably Congressman Vito Marcantonio, for whom Marzani also did a political campaign documentary in 1948.[35]

While as a party organizer Marzani found intellectual excitement, he grew dissatisfied with the party "establishment," which he considered too doctrinaire, rigid, and bureaucratic. On 23 August 1941, he allegedly resigned to help organize a local community council spearheaded by the American Labor Party to support the war efforts – the "East Side Conference to Defend America and Crush Hitler." Although he had embarked upon this leadership position at the party's request, he agreed to do it only on the condition he would have complete independence of action, and, albeit reluctantly, the party ultimately consented to his resignation. At the time, however, he did not make public his break, and, to this day, the question of his membership in and relationship to the Communist Party remains ambiguous.[36]

The East Side Conference to Defend America and Crush Hitler, later renamed the East Side Defense Council, was part of a carefully organized response by the Popular Front to Hitler's invasion of the Soviet Union on 22 June 1941. With headquarters on the second floor of a building on Avenue B, directly across from Tompkins Square, it was composed of hundreds of organizations, groups, societies, and clubs active in Lower Manhattan. The group's official chairman was New York City councilman Meyer Goldberg, and its board of directors included Alan Hall of the Henry Street Settlement and Harry Schlacht, editor of the East Side News. The secretary was Ethel Rosenberg; this was her first volunteer job for the party.[37]

Marzani poured all his energies into the conference planning and its day-to-day operations, culminating in two spectacular parades in support of President Roosevelt's war preparations, on 24 September and 27 October 1941, along with a blood donor drive for the Red Cross, which many newspapers hailed as the first of its kind in the country.[38] Once the United States entered the war following the Pearl Harbor attack in December 1941, the East Side Conference affiliated with the Civilian Defense Volunteers Organization, becoming de facto the official branch of the United States civil defence operations. For Marzani, America's entry into the war not only marked a positive political alliance to wipe fascism off the face of the earth, but it was also a turning chapter in his life. Determined to further the war efforts, he resigned from the teaching position in the economics department he had assumed at NYU in 1939 and, despite his wife's objections, went to Washington looking for government jobs.

He immediately received a job offer from the Board of Economic Welfare, established by President Roosevelt to develop policies and programs related to the war efforts and postwar reconstruction.[39] Meanwhile, he received a letter from a friend from Oxford, Guy Nunn, advising Marzani to get in touch with a friend of his, Hubert Barton, at a newly created agency: the Coordinator of Information (COI), headed by Colonel William ("Wild Bill") Donovan.[40]

Barton was chief of the Editorial Section, Economic Division, Research and Analysis Branch. After a brief interview, impressed by Marzani's credentials, he offered him a position at $3,600 a year, $400 more than the job offer from the Board of Economic Welfare. Barton's superiors, Emile Despres, chief of the Economic Division, and his deputy, Chandler Morse, also enthusiastically approved Marzani's appointment. The head of the branch, who was directly responsible to Donovan, was James Phinney Baxter III, the president (on leave) of Williams College. He naturally welcomed Marzani, recalling that the school had awarded him a Moody Fellowship to study at Oxford. Marzani did not mention that he had been a member of the Communist Party, but made it clear he was very much on the Left. In addition, he was certain that Baxter's assistant, Paul Birdsall, who had been his professor of history at Williams and knew him very well, had warned his superior of his radical tendencies.[41]

His communist past notwithstanding, Marzani had on his side a strong letter of support by Italian anti-fascist Gaetano Salvemini, a professor of history at Harvard who was well known and highly respected among American scholars and public intellectuals.[42] Salvemini had known Marzani for many years: while attending Williams College Marzani had helped him with his book *Under the Axe of Fascism*, and later at Oxford, upon Salvemini's request, Marzani had sheltered Marion Rosselli and her son for two weeks after her husband Carlo and his brother Nello were murdered in France by Mussolini's emissaries. Marzani later described the letter as "a gem of political persuasion," noting that it was a decisive factor in getting him hired. In fact, it had apparently completely won over Edward Mason, a Harvard professor of economics who represented the Research and Analysis Branch on the Joint Intelligence Committee of the Joint Chiefs of Staff and who had a final say on all appointments. "What went on behind the scenes," wrote Marzani in his account of how he was hired, "I do not know. I do know that Despres consciously avoided the imprimatur of an FBI clearance by getting Baxter and Mason to agree to a check by G-2 and ONI, the Army and Navy Intelligence."[43] The ploy worked, and Marzani formally joined the OSS on 4 March 1942. It was his thirtieth birthday.

The Office of Strategic Services (OSS)

President Franklin D. Roosevelt initiated the Office of Strategic Services during the Second World War upon the suggestion of General Donovan to improve, coordinate, and provide intelligence needed for wartime activities. Donovan had won early renown as the most decorated American officer of the First World War and by the early 1940s had gained the respect and trust of President Roosevelt despite belonging to the opposite party. After the Second World War broke out, Roosevelt asked Donovan to undertake a series of overseas missions to assess the military situation and evaluate American intelligence needs. Donovan concluded that the country did not have an "effective service" for developing accurate, comprehensive, and long-range information, and suggested the creation of "a central enemy intelligence organization which would itself collect either directly or through existing departments of government, at home and abroad, pertinent information" on the total resources and intentions of the enemy. Acting upon his recommendation, on 11 July 1941, Roosevelt created the Office of the Coordinator of Information (COI) and named Donovan its director.[44]

After the United States became involved in the war, in June 1942 the COI was reorganized as the Office of Strategic Services (OSS), with Donovan still in charge. It quickly became the chief American intelligence agency in the war and the predecessor to the contemporary Central Intelligence Agency. As many scholars have pointed out, the OSS consisted of men and women from many areas and backgrounds – lawyers, historians, bankers, baseball players, actors, and economists. Their main task was to conduct espionage activities and to collect and analyze strategic information required by the Joint Chiefs of Staff on the nation's enemies and their capabilities.[45]

Like other intellectuals and academics in the OSS, Marzani maintained that he was drawn into the US government mainly by his desire to annihilate fascism and Nazism. All the people involved in his hiring, as discussed earlier, were most likely aware of his past involvement in the Communist Party since, as Hugh Barton told Marzani, they had been warned by Paul Birdsall, Marzani's history professor at Williams.[46] His radical views in the OSS were far from unique. Despite being a conservative Republican, Donovan despised the head of the FBI, J. Edgar Hoover, and hired anyone of ability who could help his intelligence efforts, including many well-known communists. "With remarkable boldness," wrote political scientist Barry M. Katz, "Donovan recruited New Deal economists from Washington, Marxist philosophers from the German refugee community, socialite adventurers from the Ivy League; and a motley assortment of American labour activists, European social democrats, White Russians monarchists, and some two-hundred and fifty veterans of the Abraham Lincoln Brigade." When others warned him that Marzani was a "Red," he quickly overruled them, saying that he "would put Stalin himself on the OSS payroll if it would help to defeat Hitler."[47] Marzani later said that his superiors, Emile Despres and Edward Mason, specifically instructed him to "not give an inch" in the FBI interview needed to approve his appointment and to deny his previous party membership.[48]

From 1942 to 1945, Marzani played a significant role in the OSS as a deputy chief of the "Presentation Division," which did research and analysis for General Marshall and the joint chiefs and general staff of the War Department. His primary responsibility was the preparation of war reports and data for military leaders – compiling, evaluating, and presenting complex statistics visually using all kinds of media: texts, charts, slides, and films. He was first stationed in Washington, but in 1944 and 1945, spent several months in England and Italy supervising US military projects there. His most noteworthy contributions to the war effort included picking the targets for the raid on Tokyo by General Doolittle on 18 April 1942 – the first air operation to strike the Japanese home islands – and producing documentaries such as *The United States Army*, *War Department Report*, and *Air Force Report* that brought him direct accolades from General Marshall's deputy, Lieutenant McNarney, and General Edwards, assistant chief of staff for G-3.[49]

Following the end of the war, in the early fall of 1945, the OSS was dissolved: one half became the nucleus of the future CIA; the other half was transformed into the Office of Intelligence in the State Department. The branch in which Marzani worked was transferred to the State Department and reorganized as the Office of Research and Information. Marzani was tasked with modernizing the department's communications and with preparing for the first session of the United Nations Security Council in London on 17 January 1946, where, as he recalls in his memoirs, he witnessed the Soviet–American confrontation over Iran. That event, followed by Churchill's famous speech at Westminster College in Fulton, Missouri, in which he introduced the phrase "Iron Curtain" to describe the increasing division between Western powers and Eastern Bloc countries, convinced Marzani that the political climate was quickly shifting and that radicals and progressives in the US government would become increasingly vulnerable to attack.[50]

He began to consider leaving his post and went on leave in August. Together with other OSS colleagues dissatisfied with the restructuring of the department, Marzani decided to start a film-making company.[51] Almost immediately they were commissioned to produce two films: one for the United Electrical, Radio and Machine Workers union (UE-CIO) – one of the largest and most radical unions in the CIO, with over six hundred thousand members – the other for the Federal Reserve

Board, winning a contract in competition with Paramount Pictures and the March of Time. His superiors were apparently saddened by his intention to resign and urged him to stay. Confident that he could make a new living by producing films, Marzani nevertheless forwarded them his resignation from the State Department on 9 October 1946, with an effective date of 12 November 1946.[52]

The film for the UE was *Deadline for Action*. Forty minutes long, it analyzed the postwar economic situation through the experience of one UE worker. Focusing on the celebrated strike wave of 1945–6, when over two million workers went out in protest over wage cuts, it exposed American corporations like General Electric for price-fixing and their connections with Nazi and Japanese corporations and accused Harry Truman of betraying Roosevelt's legacy and starting the Cold War. The documentary was released in September 1946 and quickly created a sensation: allegedly, millions of workers saw the film. Socialist economist Leo Huberman said it was "the best educational weapon that labor has ever gotten out."[53] The *Saturday Evening Post* conceded it was "worth seeing, both as a technical *tour de force* and as a masterful piece of propaganda."[54] But the film infuriated big business, and conservative papers viciously attacked it as communist propaganda.[55] The *World Telegram*, for instance, published an eight-column story about it, with the headline "*Deadline* Wins an Oscar in Moscow," implying that the film was paid for by the Soviets.[56] The movie was apparently one of the topics of discussion at the annual executives' meeting of the National Association of Manufacturers (NAM). As Julius Emspak, the secretary of the UE, said to Marzani: "They were mad when they saw it; believe me they are still mad."[57]

Four months later, without warning, Marzani was indicted by the federal government for making false and fraudulent statements against the US government. He was the first casualty of what would become known as the second Red Scare.

The Marzani Case

Throughout the entire trial and in the course of the various appeals, Marzani loudly proclaimed his innocence – insisting that he was not, and had never been, a member of the Communist Party. Obviously, that was a lie. As he admitted in his memoirs, he had joined the Communist Party together with his wife first at Oxford and then in New York City, assuming, as the prosecution contended, the party name of Tony Wales.[58] Marzani also claimed, however, that he had left the party at the end of the summer of 1941, well before starting his job at the OSS. As discussed earlier, while he did not mention specifically that he had been a member of the Communist Party, he had made no secret of his radical tendencies, and his superiors did not seem particularly concerned about his past.

Even though Marzani passed intelligence screenings upon his hiring, he ran into trouble a few months later after J. Edgar Hoover submitted an FBI report on his prior communist activities to senior officials at the OSS, in response to the implementation of a Roosevelt administration task force directive authorizing immediate discharge of communists from government service. The FBI memorandum, dated 13 May 1942, was largely based on confidential information obtained in the course of investigations conducted by the Work Projects Administration during 1940–1, when the Marzanis applied for relief, and by the New York City Police Department. Evidence against Marzani relied for the most part on oral testimonies of Lower East Side residents and police informants advising that the subject "was formerly a section organizer of the Communist Party in New York under the name Tony Whales [sic]"; that his wife, "who is known as Edith Charles, is also a member of the Communist Party"; and that he "fraudulently obtained relief money from the New York Department of Welfare based on false statements made by him relative to his financial means and the status of his wife's parents." A subsequent FBI report also noted that Marzani had signed a Communist Party nominating petition for Earl Browder, the general secretary of the CPUSA, that he read the *Daily Worker*, and that he had been in touch with communists while attending Oxford University.[59]

Marzani was interrogated about these matters on two separate occasions in 1942: by FBI agents on 29 July, and by Civil Service Commission representatives on 23 November. Both times, he denied all earlier connections with the Communist Party but admitted signing a nominating petition for Earl Browder and addressing communist organizations in his official capacity as director of the East Side Defense Council. He also admitted to making false statements to the New York City Department of Welfare, but stated that he did so simply to get on relief rolls as quickly as possible so that he could be eligible for a Workers Party of America research job. Eventually, on 9 January 1943, in a letter setting forth the results of the investigation, the Civil Service Commission informed the OSS that Marzani had been rated "unfit" and requested that his services be terminated.[60]

The commission decision apparently caused distress among Marzani's superiors, with many trying to intercede in his favour. In fact, William Langer, the head of the Research and Analysis Branch, quickly advised Donovan that the decision to fire Marzani should be appealed.[61]

While I could not find any record of Donovan's explicit orders, it is obvious from subsequent exchanges that he tried to appease Marzani's supporters. In fact, a few weeks later, in a letter to the executive director of the Civil Service Commission confirming Marzani's intention to appeal, James Opeata, the OSS director or personnel, requested that Marzani be allowed to continue working in his present position until the results of the appeal were known.[62] Though in limited capacity, without access to confidential or secret material, Marzani did continue to work pending appeal.[63]

A dozen memos were consequently exchanged in the course of 1943–4 between OSS officials, Hoover, and the Department of Justice regarding the Marzani case, illustrating the secret struggle for control of foreign intelligence that was unfolding between Hoover and Donovan. Eventually, the Civil Service Commission cleared Marzani on 19 July 1943, as noted in this letter to him:

Dear Mr. Marzani:

Reference is made to your personal appeal from the action taken in requesting the Office of Strategic Services to terminate your services as Economic editor because of apparent unsuitability for Government employment. Careful consideration has been given to your entire record, including the representations made by you and for you at the hearing before the Board of Appeals and Review of this Office. The conclusion has been reached that you meet the standards of suitability maintained for appointment in the Federal service. The Commission is pleased to advise you that you have been rated eligible for Government employment.[64]

In a confidential memorandum on the Marzani case, it was noted that during the appeal hearing "very favorable testimony as to the subject's ability, character, loyalty and political attitude was received from OSS employees H.C. Barton, Emil Despres, Professor Edward D. Mason, and Majors D.T. Thompson and S. Gerard of the Army Service Forces" and that the subject himself had produced "a very strong, well supported and logical appeal."[65] Donovan consequently communicated with the Department of Justice on several occasions and personally notified Herbert E. Gaston, chairman of the Interdepartmental Committee on Employee Investigations in the Department of Justice, that "no action should be taken by this agency to terminate Mr. Marzani's services."[66]

However, Marzani's "suitability for responsible government employment" continued to be a matter of discussion and dispute, as evidenced by a 4 November 1943 "summarization of Marzani's record" sent by Weston Howland, the OSS security chief officer, to Duncan Chaplin Lee, special assistant to Donovan and, according to Haynes and Klehr, a Soviet spy. After rehashing the main findings about Marzani's earlier communist affiliations, Howland concluded that

> there are ample arguments and much information to substantiate a decision either way, i.e., that Subject is a Communist, or that Subject is not a Communist but merely a liberal thinker who enjoys argumentative political discussions along any line … It is realized that Subject has very pronounced capabilities along certain lines and that to date he had indisputably done excellent work for OSS. There is no doubt that Subject can make a substantial contribution to the war effort along certain lines, but there is also little doubt that under an easily conceivable different International situation a Communist having access to highly confidential military secrets could cause serious if not irreparable damage to the war effort of this country. In view of the foregoing, this office feels that it is a matter for Executive determination as to whether Mr. Marzani is terminated or permitted to continue in the employ of the O.S.S. and if the latter, as to the type of work that he is permitted to engage in, i.e., confidential in nature, or non-confidential.[67]

Memos indicate that the OSS executive had indeed met on 5 October 1944 to consider the cases of three persons suspected of being communists by the Security Office: Carl Marzani, David Zablodowski, and Virginia Boyle Gerson. While all present voted to recommend that the latter two be terminated, they decided to retain Marzani, who in the meantime had been inducted into the army, agreeing that "some method of transferring him should be worked out which would not affect his record or reputation, and would, if possible, permit the Army to use his abilities in a position in which there is no security problem."[68]

Marzani was discharged after seven months of theatre service and assigned to work overseas as chief of the Presentation Unit in the United States Group Control Council upon recommendation of Major General Otto L. Nelson. Although he was highly commended for the "valuable work" he had done along varied lines – "research, planning, editing, and establishing contacts for Visual Presentation" – the issue of his "loyalty" arose once again after he was transferred to the State Department during an interview on 1 June 1946, with a State Department representative, Anthony Panuch. Marzani claims that the meeting was informal and not transcribed, and there is indeed no record in the

OSS file that it even took place. The interview lasted three hours, and when the issue of Marzani's relation to the party came up, among other things, he denied any affiliation, as he had done before with the Civil Service Commission and the FBI.[69] His negative answers to what essentially was the same question became the substance of the eleven counts of his 1947 indictment.

A conviction was politically important. As I.F. Stone remarked, "The State Department and Panuch personally had been under fire in Congress for protecting Reds." A guilty verdict was "to demonstrate the political purity of the Truman administration and the efficiency of his Attorney General."[70] In addition to fending off growing concerns among Republicans that Truman was "soft" on communists, Marzani's prosecution also provided a justification for the loyalty oaths, the McCarran Act, and other repressive measures, all then still in the drafting stages. And the exposure of Marzani's communism helped to give credibility to the FBI suspicions of Soviet penetration, its cleaning out opposition to Truman's Cold War foreign policy (including people like Donovan), and its discrediting of the Popular Front. It was the beginning of the anti-communist crusade, fanned by growing concerns about Soviet espionage at home and the spread of communism in other parts of the world (China, and later on Korea). The Marzani case only added to such a culture of fear: the mounting confusion and anxiety, the reckless accusations, and the convenient criminalization of communism. But why Marzani, specifically? Sure, he had lied to the FBI and government officials, but as OSS documents indicate, he was not considered a security threat. On the contrary, his superiors, including Donovan, considered him a valid addition to war efforts and repeatedly dismissed the charges against him as part of what they clearly saw as a bureaucratic struggle between the FBI and OSS for control of foreign intelligence, rather than evidence of disloyalty. One of the puzzles left unresolved is why he was cleared in earlier investigations, though the undercover police reports that were used as evidence against him in the trial were already available at the time. Was the indictment a carefully thought-out government response to real national security concerns, supported by secret information that was not disclosed during the trial and that would have involved other people in the OSS? Or was it, as the defence argued, a politically motivated test case designed to open the door to similar prosecutions in order to purge the country of all undesirable subversives – whether real spies or simply activists associated with the American Left? But if the government's objective was the dismissal of public servants deemed a security risk, then why go after Marzani, who had already resigned from the OSS?

Marzani, it should be recalled, was not being tried explicitly for being a communist. As Judge Keech cautioned the jurors, his political beliefs were not on trial: "The simple issue is whether the defendant knowingly, willfully, and feloniously made false statements to Government loyalty examiners."[71] Yet, as soon as the conviction was secured, Senator Taft was quick to declare in the debate on the Taft-Hartley bill that "union officers shall file statements to the effect that they are not Communists. If a man who files such as statement tells the untruth he is subject to the same statute under which Marzani was convicted last week."[72] Attorney General Clark similarly affirmed Marzani's a "test case to show how subversives could not only be purged from Government employment but sent to jail for having denied that they were Reds."[73]

The mainstream press quickly hinted at treason, sensationalizing the case as irrefutable evidence of a growing "red menace." As the *Daily News* wrote the day after Marzani's conviction, "this case illustrates the Communist pattern of intrigue, deceit and infiltration into key positions in countries which the Kremlin wants to break down with within ... It is to be hoped that the Marzani case will open some eyes here and there to what kind of people these practicing Reds are and what designs they have on the liberties of all the rest of us."[74] In another article entitled "Reds in Our Government," J. Parnell Thomas (a New Jersey Republican representative and a staunch conservative opponent of President Roosevelt and the New Deal, later appointed chairman of the House Committee on Un-American Activities) used the Marzani case to press for the need to curb the government of its subversive elements. After noting that "the Communist Party's members and followers have no loyalty to the United States," he pompously declared the nation's obvious duty "to clear the communists and pro-Communists out of government and keep them out ... The country must realize that it involves the protection of our national sovereignty against a creeping invasion."[75]

According to Marzani, however, besides providing a weapon for the witch-hunting of government employees deemed dangerous, there was another more personal reason to indict him: his production of *Deadline for Action*. The intent was to undermine the film's success and cripple radical unions like the UE by branding them "communist."[76] The case, as he put it, was a "harbinger of domestic repression."[77]

Despite its political overtones, legally Marzani's case was risky. First, the prosecution had little evidence to discredit Marzani: in fact his trial was marked by conspicuous absence of any attempt by the prosecution to question his good record at OSS and the Army. Several prominent figures, including a former general, Ed Greenbaum, testified on Marzani's behalf, asserting that there was never any doubt about his loyalty and integrity, and the government did not contest these accounts.[78] There was also the fact that Marzani had resigned from his post on 15 November 1946, but the government sent him a letter saying that he had been fired on 20 December. Marzani was able to prove that the government had altered the date and changed the word "resignation" to "removal," but the judge dismissed the evidence. And, finally, there was the issue of the statute of limitations, which stated that crimes must be prosecuted within three years, but that in the case of fraud had been suspended by Congress for the duration of the war.

Marzani later explained that he would have preferred to plead guilty to the 1942–3 counts and not guilty to the 1946 counts for which the government had no evidence – as there was no hearing, notice, transcript, or witness. But as his lawyer, Allan Rosenberg, explained to him, "they'd drop the two counts and you'd be up for sentencing without a trial." He also worried that if he had pleaded guilty, he would have caused harm to people at OSS who had shielded him, including Donovan, and he feared that this would have been way more harmful as it would have played exactly into the hands of people like Hoover who wanted to oust anyone with progressive ideas.[79]

The trial focused almost exclusively on circumstantial evidence related to Marzani's activities during 1940–1. Using inflammatory language, the prosecuting attorney, John Kelly, told the jury that Marzani had advocated revolution, opposed the conscription, and "sowed resentment and discontent among the Negroes" before he entered government employment.[80] But when the defence tried to obtain the records of the Civil Service Commission investigations to show that those accusations had been dismissed, as either non-credible or irrelevant, Judge Keech granted the government the privilege to not submit them to the court. In addition, the court dismissed a request of the Defence to subpoena Secretary of State George Marshall, Secretary of War Robert Patterson, FBI Director Hoover, and General Donovan, after they failed to appear in defence of Marzani.[81]

Perhaps the strangest thing about the case was the jury that tried it. It consisted of six men and six women; nine were black. This was highly unusual; in fact it might have been the first time a jury in a southern city was made up by a majority of black people. The defence did not object to their selection, as they thought the black jurors, being persecuted themselves, might have proven sympathetic towards Marzani given that he had worked on African American causes and that communists had been active in denouncing segregation and fighting for racial equality.

What Marzani and his lawyers did not know was that the three main witnesses for the prosecution, George Hewitt, Louis O. Harper, and Archer Drew, were also black. As was disclosed during the trial, Drew was an undercover cop who had been recruited for a special "secret sabotage squad" created by Major Fiorello LaGuardia in 1939 to infiltrate subversive groups, including the National Negro Congress, with which Marzani had often collaborated. Assuming fake names and false identification cards, squad members "were instructed to try to get positions in organizations under scrutiny and gain access to membership rolls and records."[82] Drew had operated as such a spy first in Harlem and then in the Lower East Side under the name of Bill Easley until his real identity was uncovered in 1943; he was the confidential source mentioned in the Marzani FBI reports to OSS security agents. Drew testified that he knew Marzani as a Communist Party member under the name of Tony Wales and that he had heard him saying at a communist meeting in 1941, among other things, "that now is the time for revolt."[83] Marzani's defence hoped to destroy Drew's credibility by exposing his lurid tactics as an agent provocateur engaged in political espionage. Drew indeed had organized a branch of the National Negro Congress, drawing many Black communists into its work, and then turning them in to the police department for subversive activity that he himself had encouraged.[84] But as Marzani lamented, "Judge Keech not only prevented our access to the reports, but refused to allow any cross examination or any discussions of Negro matters on the ground that it would inflame the jury."[85] He made rulings that fatally handicapped the defence. The prosecution, noted Stone, "could lug in inflammatory matter to show how Marzani served the communists, but the defence was limited to character witness and Marzani's denials."

The other two witnesses the prosecution had "on tap" were even less credible than Drew. George Hewitt was an ex-communist, who had been expelled by the Communist Party in 1945 and had subsequently served on other cases against radicals. He falsely testified that Marzani had attended his meetings to receive party directives; Marzani had never seen or heard of him before the trial. Hewitt's deceitfulness was eventually exposed in 1949 in a case against a professor at the University of Washington, Melvin Rader. Hewitt claimed Rader had attended a communist class he was running in Kingston, New York, but Rader was able to prove that he was in the west coast at the time of the alleged class. Hewitt was indicted for perjury; the FBI hustled him out of the state and after the prosecutor refused to drop the indictment as the FBI had requested, Hewitt disappeared, surfacing years later in a mental hospital in New York.[86]

Louis Harper, the third star witness for the prosecution, was an organizer of the African American branch of the Lower East Side section of the Communist Party, where Marzani was active. A postal employee, he was under the same threat of prosecution as Marzani. He did not accuse Marzani of being a communist, but testified that he had seen Marzani speaking at the National Negro Congress. Marzani admitted knowing Harper, but when he alluded to a discussion he had at his home about the "beating of two Negroes on the east side, Justice Keech winced, shook his head and said: I am not interested in that."[87] Again and again, as many radical reporters noted, when Marzani and the defence witnesses were on the stand the court ruled out questions that would have shown Marzani's ideas and time spent helping people and advising them on their problems – police brutality, discrimination, and housing. The government, on the other hand, was allowed to ask questions of a political and personal nature, such as whether Marzani's wife had been a communist.

The unusual number of blacks on the jury panel may well have been sheer coincidence, but as communist journalist Virginia Gardener commented for the *People's Voice* in 1947: "It is fair to assume that a chauvinistic concept common in the South was at play: namely the theory that a predominantly white jury would not find a white man guilty on the testimony of three Negro witnesses."[88]

Conclusion

The significance of the Marzani case extends well beyond the obvious subject matter of the Red Scare, illuminating both the tumultuous times he lived in as well as the timeless struggle over the meaning of American freedom. Marzani still commands our attention, not because of whether he was a Soviet spy or not, but because he challenged the Cold War consensus by believing that there could have been a better pathway to postwar politics – that, as he wrote in a book while in prison, the Soviet Union and the United States "could be friends."[89] The overarching theme emerging from the case and, in my view, its most important lesson, is the repression of dissent that began under the anti-communist crusade. Certainly Soviet espionage created a troubling and frustrating security challenge. But the hunt for spies led to a wide, indiscriminate net and to the abrogation of constitutional rights that criminalized not only communists but also other people of presumed "questionable" character, such as homosexuals and feminists. Whether justifiable or not, the purge of federal radical employees like Marzani forever diminished America as an idea: blacklisting and loyalty-security programs might have been considered necessary steps to protect the nation, but they also led to increased American anti-intellectualism and the marginalization of radicals from both the political and public arena. Loyalty-security programs were just a way to trap people like Marzani, helping to shift political power and, more importantly, building up a peacetime spy apparatus that did not exist before and expanding Hoover's domestic surveillance.

The criminal convictions against the leadership of the Communist Party deprived it of legitimacy in the eyes of most Americans. Fear galvanized consensus and discouraged dissent. The events of 9/11 and continued world terrorism make it easy to draw some present-day lessons from the case of Carl Marzani, showing how, in times of national fear and insecurity, dissent is easily confused with disloyalty. Espionage and terrorism should, of course, not be condoned, but neither should political repression. As Eleanor Roosevelt wrote in her column ("My Day") after reading about Marzani's case:

> As to his innocence or guilt I know nothing, but on reading the article I feel that our civil liberties are being endangered. Through fear and undisciplined prejudice, we are becoming the very thing which we have condemned other people for being ... Either we are strong enough to live as free people or we will become a police state.[90]

NOTES

I wish to thank Charlotte Pomerantz Marzani, Tony Marzani, Gabrielle Marzani, and Bob Murtha for sharing their stories and memories of Carl Marzani with me. I am also very grateful for various funding I received to conduct research on this project from my University: a PSC-CUNY Award (2015), a Distinguished CUNY Fellowship (2016), and a Chancellor's Research Fellowship (2017).

1 Originally an act of 18 June 1934, 18 U.S.C.A. § 80 provided that "whoever shall make or cause to be made any false or fraudulent statements or representations in any matter within the jurisdiction of any department or agency of the United States shall be fined not more than $10,000 or imprisoned not more than ten years, or both."

2 *United States v. Marzani*, 71 F. Supp. 615 (D.D.C. 1947). See also Lewis Wood, "Indict Ex-State Department Aide, Accused of Hiding Red Membership," *New York Times*, 18 January 1947, 1; "Statement of the Case" and "Summary of Indictment of Carl Marzani," in Carl Aldo Marzani Papers (c. 1890–1994) box 1, Tamiment Library and Robert F. Wagner Labor Archive, New York University.

3 Clark was appointed attorney general by Truman in 1945 and was responsible for developing and implementing a number of the Truman administration's aggressive anti-communist policies, including the List of Subversive Organizations (AGLOSO). See "Tom C. Clark, Former Justice, Dies; on the Supreme Court for 18 Years," *New York Times*, 14 June, 1977, 1

4 Wood, "Indict Ex-State Department Aide," 1.

5 See "Marzani Trial Opens: U.S. Charges Red Tie," *New York Times*, 13 May 1947, 8, and "Marzani Guilty of Hiding Red Link; Ex-Government Man Faces Prison," *New York Times*, 23 May 1947, 1.

6 *Marzani v. United States*, 168 F.2d 133 (D.C. Cir. 1948).

7 Carl Marzani, *The Education of a Reluctant Radical*, book 4: *From Pentagon to Penitentiary* (New York: Topical Books, 1995), 252–3.

8 *Marzani v United States*, 334 U.S. 858 (1948), cert. granted 21 June, 1948. The case was argued on 8–9 December 1948 and decided 20 December 1948. The justices who voted in favour of Marzani were Hugo Black, Felix Frankfurter, Frank Murphy, and Wiley Blount Rutledge, while Fred Vinson, Robert J. Jackson, Stanley Forman Reed, and Harold Hitz Burton voted against him. See *Marzani v. United States*, 335 U.S. 895 (1948).

9 *Marzani v. United States*, 336 U.S. 910 (1949).

10 "Review Is Granted in Marzani's Case," *New York Times*, 8 February 1949. See also "High Court Grants Marzani Rehearing," *Washington Post*, and "Supreme Court Grants Rehearing to Marzani in Communist Case," *Washington Star*, both also published on 8 February 1949.

11 *Marzani v. United States*, 336 U.S. 922 (1949). The case was re-argued on 28 February 1949 and decided 7 March 1949. The Supreme Court appeals and decisions were reported by the *New York Times* and other newspapers: see, for example, the *Times* articles published on 15 May 1947, 20; 16 May 1947, 44; 21 May 1947, 4; 23 May 1947, 1; 28 June 1947, 1; 3 February 1948, 16; 22 June 1948, 12; 21 December 1948, 20; 8 February 1949, 5; 8 March 1949, 22; 26 March 1949, 3; and 21 May 1949, 6.

12 Copies of the letters of support for Marzani are available in Carl Marzani Papers, box 3, folder 5, Tamiment Library and Robert F. Wagner Labor Archive, New York University.

13 Executive Order no. 9835, 12 Fed. Reg. 1935 (March 25, 1947).

14 I.F. Stone, "Last Chance for Justice," *New York Star*, 7 January 1949.

15 "Canny Justice Douglas," *Daily Worker*, 22 December 1948, 1.

16 Contract Settlement Act of 1944, 58 Stat. 651; 41 U.S.C. 104 (1 July 1944).

17 Generally admired for his provocative investigative reports, Stone has been, like Marzani, a target of posthumous accusations of espionage by neo-revisionist scholars. See above all, John Earl Haynes, Harvey Klehr, and Alexander Vassiliev, *Spies: The Rise and Fall of the KGB in America* (New Haven: Yale University Press, 2009). For a counter-narrative see Myra

MacPherson, *All Governments Lie: The Life and Times of Rebel Journalist I.F. Stone* (New York: Scribner, 2006).

18 The first quote is from "The Unresolved Marzani Case," *Nation*, 8 January 1949, 36–8; the second from "A New Weapon for Witch Hunters," *PM*, 3 July 1947. Other important articles Stone wrote on the Marzani case were: "The Witch Hunters Lose a Round," *PM*, 4 February 1948; "Nine-Negro Jury in Jim Crow City," *New York Star*, 27 December 1948; "Was Perjury on Tap in the Marzani Case?" *Daily Compass*, 30 November 1949.

19 "What Communists Are Up To: Intrigue and Infiltration," *Newsweek*, 2 June 1947, 22.

20 "More Loyalty Probes Seen," *New York Post*, 24 May 1947.

21 Harvey Khler and Ronald Radosh, *The Amerasia Spy Case: Prelude to McCarthyism* (Chapel Hill: University of North Carolina Press, 2000).

22 Herbert Romerstein and Eric Breindel, *The Venona Secrets: Exposing Soviet Espionage and America's Traitors* (New York: Regnery, 2000); Richard Adrich, "CIA History as a Cold War Battleground: The Forgotten First Wave of Agency Narratives," in *Intelligence Studies in Britain and the US: Historiography since 1945*, ed. Christopher Moran and Christopher J. Murphy (Edinburgh: Edinburgh University Press, 2013); Oleg Kalugin, with Fen Montaigne, *The First Directorate: My 32 Years in Intelligence and Espionage against the West* (New York: St. Martin's, 1994).

23 John Earl Haynes and Harvey Klehr, *Venona: Decoding Soviet Espionage in America* (New Haven, CT: Yale University Press, 1999), and *Early Cold War Spies: The Espionage Trials That Shaped American Politics* (Cambridge, MA: Harvard University Press, 2006).

24 See above all Stanton Evans, *Blacklisted by History: The Untold Story of Senator Joe McCarthy and His Fight against America's Enemies* (New York: Crown Forum, 2007).

25 Earl Haynes and Harvey Klehr, "Arthur J. Goldberg and the Reds in OSS: A Soviet Espionage Cable Redacted, Revealed and Confirmed," *Washington Decoded*, 11 September 2011, http://www.washingtondecoded.com/files/venona.pdf.

26 Venona No. 880 (8 June 1943), cited in Romerstein and Breindel, *The Venona Secrets*, 295. "Kollega," however, was noted to be working in the "Photographic Section Pictorial Division" of the OSS, while Marzani worked in the "Presentation Branch."

27 See Vasili Mitrokhin and Christopher M. Andrews, *The Sword and the Shield: The Mitrokhin Archive and the Secret History of the KGB* (New York: Basic Books, 1999), 226–7. It should be noted, however, that the provided evidence simply points to the fact that Marzani may have taken money from the USSR, not that he was a spy. Additionally, Marzani's KGB file information cited in the Notes (chapter 14, note 16, p. 615) of

The Mitrokhin Archive contains several mistakes, most notably Marzani's alias (which was Tony Wales, not Well) and other inaccuracies regarding his case, suggesting that these files should not be regarded as absolute truths.

28 For a more subtle approach to the study of espionage see, for example, K.A. Cuordileone, "The Torment of Secrecy: Reckoning with American Communism and Anticommunism after Venona," *Diplomatic History* 35, no. 4 (September 2011): 615–42.

29 Carl Marzani, *The Education of a Reluctant Radical*, book 1: *Roman Childhood* (New York: Topical Books, 1992), 123. Marzani wrote his memoirs in five separate volumes covering his entire life up to the early sixties.

30 Ibid., 131.

31 His encounter with American society is the subject of book 2 of his memoirs, *Growing Up American* (New York: Topical Books, 1993).

32 For more information on his experience in the Spanish Civil War, see book 3 of his memoirs, *Spain, Munich and Dying Empires* (New York: Topical Books, 1994).

33 Marzani recounts in great detail his communist activities in the Lower East Side in the second chapter of book 4 of his memoirs, *From Pentagon to Penitentiary*.

34 Ibid., 22.

35 Ibid., 36–7.

36 Ibid., 38–58. Marzani also discussed his relationship to communism in an interview with Vivian Gornick for her book *The Romance of American Communism* (New York: Basic Books, 1977), 116–25, 248–55.

37 Ilene Philipson, *Ethel Rosenberg: Beyond the Myth* (New Brunswick, NJ: Rutgers University Press, 1993), 137–43.

38 Marzani, *From Pentagon to Penitentiary*, 63, and Philipson, *Ethel Rosenberg: Beyond the Myth*, 137.

39 Seejames Ciment, ed., *Home Front Encyclopedia: United States, Britain and Canada in World War I and II* (Santa Barbara, CA: ABC CLIO, 2007), 787–8.

40 Marzani, *From Pentagon to Penitentiary*, 67–8.

41 Ibid., 69–71.

42 A copy of Salvemini's reference letter is reproduced in full in ibid., 72.

43 Edward Mason corroborated Marzani's account on the circumstances of his hiring in a personal letter he wrote to Marzani in 1986. See ibid., 74.

44 "Memorandum of Establishment of Service of Strategic Information," dated 10 June 1941, cited in "Donovan's Original Marching Orders," Central Intelligence Agency, Historical Review Program. https://www.cia .gov/library/center-for-the-study-of.../kent.../v17i2a05p_0001.htm.

45 There are several studies of the OSS. See above all Barry M. Katz, *Foreign Intelligence: Research and Analysis in the Office of Strategic Services, 1942–1945* (Cambridge: Harvard University Press, 1989), and Michael Warner, *The Office of Strategic Services: America's First Intelligence Agency* (Washington, DC: Central Intelligence Agency, 2001).

46 Marzani, *From Pentagon to Penitentiary*, 71.

47 Barry Katz, "The Arts of War: 'Visual Presentation' and National Intelligence," *Design Issues* 12, no. 2 (Summer 1996): 4–5.

48 Marzani, *From Pentagon to Penitentiary*, 73–5.

49 "Letter by General McNarney to Marzani" (22 October 1942) reprinted in ibid., 94–5.

50 Marzani, *From Pentagon to Penitentiary*, 166–7.

51 "Union Films: An Interview with Carl Marzani," *Cineaste* 7, no. 2 (Spring 1976): 33. Marzani would go on to produce several documentary films in the late forties: *Deadline for Action* (1946), *The Great Swindle* (1947), *Dollar Patriots* (1948), *Our Union* (1949). For a detailed discussion of these documentaries see Charles Musser, "Carl Marzani and Union Films: Making Left-Wing Documentaries during the Cold War, 1946–1953," *Moving Image* 9, no. 1 (Spring 2009):104–60.

52 Marzani, *From Pentagon to Penitentiary*, 193–4.

53 Cited in James McLeish, "The Man Who Made a Movie," *March of Labor* no. 4 (November 1950): 12.

54 J.A. Livingston, "CIO Prestige Hurt by Dubious Statistics," *Saturday Evening Post*, 22 March 1947

55 Roger Stuart, "Reveal State Dept. Aid Made Pro-Red Movie," *World Telegram*, 20 January 1947, 1

56 Frederick Woltman, "CIO Electrical Union's Pro-Red Film Is Given Wide Distribution," *World Telegram*, 29 October 1946, 3. The title of the original article was changed in the journal's later editions to: "CIO Electrical Union Pro-Red Film Is Given Wide Distribution." See also James Walter, "Marzani Revealed as Director of Soviet Propaganda Movie," *Washington Times-Herald*, 27 July 1947, 1

57 Cited in Marzani, *From Pentagon to Penitentiary*, 213.

58 The government, and later the press, actually incorrectly referred to Marzani's alias as Whales, rather than Wales, a mistake suggesting that they did not have any written proof of his communist activities.

59 Cited in an FBI "Memorandum for the Interdepartmental Committee on Employee Investigations," 8 June 1943, Marzani FBI file. This memo and all other FBI documents cited hereafter are included in the Marzani Papers, Series II (Trial/Prison Papers), box 3, Tamiment Library.

60 Letter from James Opeata to Marzani, 10 February 1943, Marzani FBI file.

61 Memo from James Opeata to William Donovan, 27 January 1943, Marzani FBI file.

62 Letter from Opeata to Mr. Moyer, executive director of the US Civil Service Commission, 10 February 1943, Marzani FBI file.

63 See letter from Edward Buxton to Herbert E. Gaston, 30 June 1943, Marzani FBI file.

64 Letter by William C. Hull to Marzani, United States Civil Service Commission, 29 July 1943, Marzani FBI file.

65 Summarization of Carl Marzani case, 5 (n.d.), Marzani FBI file.

66 See Donovan's memo to Herbert Gaston dated 9 March 1944, Marzani FBI file.

67 Interoffice confidential memo dated 4 November 1943, page 3, Marzani FBI file.

68 Confidential memo by Lieutenant William H. Miley dated 7 October 1944, Marzani FBI file.

69 Marzani, *From Pentagon to the Penitentiary*, 175–6.

70 "Was Perjury on Tap in the Marzani Case?," 5.

71 "Marzani Guilty of Hiding Red Link; Ex-Government Man Faces Prison," *New York Times*, 23 May 1947, 1.

72 Cited in "The Case of Carl Marzani," published by the Committee in Defense of Carl Marzani (n.d., ca. 1947), 10, in the Marzani Papers.

73 "Was Perjury on Tap in the Marzani Case?," 5.

74 "How the Reds Do Business," *Daily News*, 24 May 1947.

75 J. Parnell Thomas, "Reds in Our Government," *Liberty*, 19 July 1947. He was later convicted of corruption in 1948 for putting friends on his congressional payroll and paroled after serving nine months in Danbury, Connecticut, where Marzani too was held.

76 See, for example, the article written by Frederick Woltman, a red-baiter, for the *New York World Telegram*, 29 October 1946: "*Deadline* Wins an Oscar in Moscow."

77 Marzani, *From Pentagon to Penitentiary*, 234.

78 Fred Vast, "Marzani on Stand: Gov't Fails to Shake Story," *Daily Worker*, 21 May 1947, 2.

79 Marzani, *From Pentagon to Penitentiary*, 217.

80 Fred Vast, "Trial Opens, Charge Ex-Gov't Man with Perjury," *Daily Worker*, 13 May 1947.

81 William Flythe, "Marzani to Take Stand Today," *N.Y. Journal-American*, 17 May 1947.

82 "Secret City Police Fought Sabotage," *New York Times*, 15 May 1947, 20.

83 "Marzani Calls Patterson, Marshall," *New York World Telegram*, 5 May 1947.

84 Stone, "Dirty Business," *The Daily Compass*, 9 February, 1947.

85 Marzani, *From Pentagon to Penitentiary*, 221.

86 "Hewitt – Informer on Call – Well Protected from the Law," *Sunday Compass*, 27 November 1949, 13; and "Hewitt, Pet U.S. Informer, Found in Bellevue," *Daily Compass*, 2 December 1949.

87 Virginia Gardner, "Two Negroes Stand Out in Marzani Persecution," *People's Voice*, 31 May 1947.

88 "Marzani Made a Movie," *NM*, 10 June 1947.

89 *We Could Be Friends: Origins of the Cold War* (New York: Topical Books, 1952).

90 "This Column Deals with a Very Serious Subject," reprinted in *The Case of Carl Marzani*, 11.

3 Security or Scandal? Homosexuality and the Foreign Office, 1945–1991

DANIEL W.B. LOMAS AND CHRISTOPHER J. MURPHY

Cold War concerns about Soviet espionage activity in the West forced counter-espionage officials to turn their attention to the security of government departments and the screening of civil servants for their political views and private lives. In Britain, this work was not the sole responsibility of the Security Service (MI5); government departments also had their own security staff to guard against Soviet spies, which represents a wholly neglected aspect of Britain's Cold War secret state. This chapter looks at two important strands of Whitehall history: the evolution of sexuality as a security risk across government, and the first serious study of Whitehall departmental security at the start of the Cold War, looking at the example of the Foreign Office. Like the security scares in the United States – a subject touched upon in Bencivenni's earlier chapter on the Marzani affair, questions of loyalty even extended into sexuality. In the aftermath of the defection of the Foreign Office officials Guy Burgess and Donald Maclean in 1951, it has been suggested that homosexuality came to be increasingly associated with the issue of national security in the UK, largely on account of pressure exerted by the United States, resulting in a purge of gay men from positions in the diplomatic service.[1] Through the use of documents previously withheld as part of the Foreign Office "special collections," it is now possible to study the departmental aftermath of the defection of the two men and to test such claims against the official archival record.[2] The results of such a study challenge some of our previous assumptions. Homosexuality was certainly considered to be the "central theme of the affair Burgess-Maclean," and the fallout from the defection of

Note: the chapter uses the term "Foreign Office" to cover "diplomatic service" and, since 1968, the Foreign and Commonwealth Office (FCO).

these two men saw the beginnings of screening for so-called character defects, which would shape the landscape of postwar security vetting in the Foreign Office for the following four decades. However, there is little evidence to support the view that the perception of homosexuals as a security threat had its origins in pressure from the United States.[3] Indeed, the extent to which the Foreign Office viewed homosexuality as constituting a *security* problem is also open to reinterpretation; concerns over the reputation of the department, and the possibility of a public homosexual scandal impacting upon this, appear to have been just as prominent in official minds as security matters.

The subject of homosexuality and security in postwar Britain has been influenced by the work of Peter Wildeblood, journalist and campaigner for homosexual decriminalization. In 1954, Wildeblood was convicted and sentenced to eighteen months for conspiracy to incite acts of gross indecency.[4] He lost his job as the diplomatic correspondent of the *Daily Mail* and went on to write an account of his experiences titled *Against the Law* in 1957, describing "oppressive police behaviour, harassment, public humiliation, distorted evidence." The book was influential and fed into the creation of the Departmental Committee on Homosexual Offences and Prostitution.[5] In his book, Wildeblood maintained that homosexuals charged with gross indecency were the victim of an overtly political McCarthyite witch-hunt. Britain's willingness to clamp down on homosexuality was, in Wildeblood's view, a "political manoeuvre, designed to allay American fears that people susceptible to blackmail were occupying high positions in Britain."[6] This purge, he suggested, had spread from the United States, where concerns about communists in government, fuelled by Joseph McCarthy's sensational claims, resulted in the removal of hundreds of homosexuals from the State Department. Security concerns about homosexuals were certainly rife in North America during the 1950s. As early as June 1947, the US State Department had started a drive to root out suspected communists and individuals exhibiting character weakness, focusing on "habitual drunkenness, sexual perversion, moral turpitude, financial irresponsibility or criminal record." In the first years of the purge, the department removed thirty-one homosexuals in 1947, twenty-eight in 1948, and thirty-one in 1949.[7] By the 1950s, gay men were considered "emotionally unstable" and the cause of a "morale" problem that was incompatible with "the folkways and mores of our American society." The zeal of the State Department's campaign against the "lavender lads" even reached overseas, with US diplomats told to be "continually on alert" to "ferret out" gay men before they posed a risk.[8] By the 1960s, the State Department had removed an estimated one thousand gay or lesbian employees.[9]

Wildeblood's claims of a homosexual witch-hunt have since been echoed elsewhere, the screening of gay men being interpreted as an essential step in order to secure Washington's continued cooperation in the Cold War.[10] Stephen Jeffrey-Poulter suggests that "the American security agencies put strong pressure on their British counterparts to weed out known or suspected homosexuals in sensitive government posts" to prevent future security lapses, while Leslie Moran dates the start of this homosexual purge to 1952, shortly after the defection of Burgess and Maclean, arguing that the issue of homosexuality as a security risk was quickly taken up to "secure American co-operation, to enable the U.K. to be a party, not only to important alliances, but also to have access to secret, particularly atomic research."[11] Elsewhere this interpretation has been questioned; Patrick Higgins suggests that the Whitehall witch-hunt was a "myth" fuelled by developments on Fleet Street, where newspapers, feeding 1950s Britain's prejudice about gay men, reported on homosexuality more than ever.[12] The defection of Burgess and Maclean "did not trigger a witch-hunt," and the British government did little to tighten security, engaging in a cover-up to limit the repercussions of the affair on the "special relationship" with Washington.[13] Higgins also argues that the committee of "three wise men" set up to investigate security inside the Foreign Office did not see homosexuality as a security issue: "Despite a careful combing of the archives in Washington there is little evidence to suggest that the British government took any action that might have appeased American fears."[14]

Foreign Office material now in the public domain offers a more nuanced picture, which draws together certain aspects of the existing, opposing perspectives on the subject outlined above. While there is little to suggest that the Foreign Office was consciously acting in response to pressure, or the threat of pressure, from the United States, the department acknowledged that homosexuality could cause a security risk. However, at the same time it can be suggested that the main driving force that lay behind these changes in the screening of prospective employees was not security, but concern for the reputational damage that the Foreign Office would suffer as a result of a homosexual scandal breaking in public. On the basis of available material, it appears that the issue of departmental reputation, set within the context of the prevailing societal attitudes of the day, was a more significant driver for the introduction of new policies to prevent the employment of homosexuals than security. The reforms that followed were significant, as they saw the beginnings of a move away from purely political vetting into the screening for sexual and other character "defects" that was gradually adopted elsewhere in Whitehall in the mid-1950s.

On the night of 25 May 1951, Foreign Office diplomats Guy Burgess and Donald Maclean left Britain, bound for the Soviet Union. Both men were already known to the security authorities. Prone to outlandish behaviour, Burgess had been investigated as the source of unauthorized leaks and had been recalled home from his position at the British embassy in Washington pending disciplinary action. Maclean, a former first secretary at Britain's Washington embassy and recently appointed as the head of the Foreign Office's American Department, had fallen under suspicion as the source of a series of leaks to Soviet spies and had been placed under surveillance by MI5. The initial response of the Foreign Office to their disappearance was to play down the story, but leaks from French sources led to reports that two officials had fled London with "important papers," forcing the release of an official statement that the missing diplomats were believed to be in France, having been suspended by their department. The release did little to quell speculation, and attention quickly turned to Burgess's reported communist leanings and drinking habits. Britain's Labour prime minister, Clement Attlee, wrote to Foreign Secretary Herbert Morrison about the "unsatisfactory" characters of both men[15] and questioned during Cabinet on 11 June whether the "standard of conduct" in the Foreign Office was high enough.[16] That afternoon, speaking in the House of Commons, Labour backbencher George Wigg raised the subject of "widespread sexual perversion in the Foreign Office," which gave the press free rein to add a sexual dimension to the ongoing speculation.[17]

In response to the unfolding crisis, Morrison appointed a committee of inquiry to investigate the disappearance and its broader implications for the Foreign Office. On 21 June, nearly a month after the disappearance, Morrison wrote to Attlee, explaining that an inquiry would consider the security checks applied to members of the Foreign Service and the "existing regulations and practice of the Foreign Service in regard to any matters which have a bearing on security."[18] As Morrison had already told Attlee, events highlighted the problem of how to "adequately check" an individual's career without adopting a system of screening "repugnant to our traditions."[19] The task of chairing the review was given to Sir Alexander Cadogan, a former permanent undersecretary at the Foreign Office, recently retired as Britain's representative to the United Nations. Cadogan's Foreign Office experience made him the ideal candidate to chair the review. In addition, he was unlikely to rock the boat, being, as one former official recalled, "'sound' in judgement."[20] Cadogan was also joined by Cabinet Secretary Sir Norman Brook and Sir Nevile Bland, a former Foreign Office junior official and British ambassador to the Hague. It was clear, as former Foreign Office official

Robert Cecil later observed, that "no outsider was to be allowed to peep behind the curtain while the Foreign Office washed its dirty linen."[21]

It appears that the Foreign Office knew what it wanted from the inquiry at the outset, and this was to stop the employment of homosexuals. Writing in his diary on 7 July, the day the Cadogan committee was formed, MI5's deputy director general, Guy Liddell, wrote, "I had a talk with Dick [White], who tells me that there is to be a highly confidential enquiry in the Foreign Office about the security risks of employing homosexuals."[22] A further indication of Foreign Office thinking in the area is provided by a confidential memorandum prepared by the Personnel Department during this period, entitled "The Problem of Homosexuality in Relation to Employment in the Foreign Service." Here, concerns over sexuality in relation to security were made clear, as was the fact that the department was clearly aware of how such issues were dealt with in the United States. Same-sex attraction was considered a medical problem with "psychological and physical" dimensions, and, at home and overseas, because homosexuality was illegal, gay men would find themselves subject to "criminal proceedings." The paper claimed that homosexuality had "long been" considered a possible security risk by both MI5 and the Foreign Office's own Security Department, with gay men "subject to greater psychological stresses than the normal individual," adding:

(ii) Abnormality in one direction is often symptomatic of instability in others; and it may be that homosexuals have a greater tendency to extreme and unbalanced political views than normal persons. Their feeling that they are different from others may lead to a feeling of rejection by society, and give them a grudge against it.

(iii) There is a solidarity between homosexuals which may in certain circumstances override other loyalties.

(iv) They are open to blackmail. This may lay them open to direct pressure by hostile intelligence agents. (The State Department believe that Soviet and satellite agents collect information about the sexual habits of the U.S. Foreign Service for precisely this purpose.) They may also fall into the hands of an ordinary criminal blackmailer, and commit acts of disloyalty in order to get money to satisfy the blackmailer's demands.[23]

Security was not, however, the Foreign Office's sole concern. In addition, it was concerned about the department's reputation and the potential for embarrassment. It was observed in the memo that members of the

Foreign Office were "representatives of their country," and any risk of "effeminate appearance" was likely to undermine their role. Given the strong British diplomatic presence across the globe, this was a serious issue, nowhere more so than in the United States, which was, the paper noted, "strongly anti-homosexual." The report suggested that, even though most homosexuals were of "high intelligence and ability" and the Foreign Office was not a "court of morals," there was an argument to be made that gay men were unsuited to the diplomatic service, a result of a combination of their "unstable" mindset, the security issues raised by the opportunity for blackmail, and the increased chance of bringing "discredit on the service." The paper concluded that these factors, taken together, meant that policy should "aim at eliminating homosexuals from the Foreign Office."[24] A further undated Foreign Office report similarly outlined the underlying prejudices against homosexuals and related security matters:

> The central theme of the affair Burgess-Maclean [sic] is homosexuality. Out of that theme arise the mental and moral disequilibrium which perversion produces or predicates, as well as the vulnerability it creates, and to grasp its importance it is necessary to understand its peculiar and rather paradoxical status in Britain. Homosexuality could be said to have almost respectable antecedents in the country of Wilde and Byron. It was only recently realised how widespread the vice was, especially among young men of the better families. From a security point of view, this state of affairs would not be dangerous in, say, Paris or Rome. Frenchmen and Italians have different moral standards, and a French pervert in an official position would not be generally blackmailable because public opinion in his country would not be sufficiently concerned about his morals to make him go to great lengths to avoid exposure. But in Britain, along with the tolerance in certain circles, there remains a strong national puritanical streak which even the biggest figures in public life can ill afford to ignore. (Homosexuality is also a criminal offense.)[25]

During the course of its inquiries, Cadogan's committee held thirteen meetings and heard evidence from six Foreign Office and four other officials.[26] The cross-examination of officials started on 20 July, when the committee spoke to Robin Hooper, the head of the Foreign Office's Personnel Department, followed by discussions with the head of the Security Department, George Carey-Foster, on the relationship between the Foreign Office Security and Personnel Departments.[27] At the end of the month, the committee met again with Carey-Foster and the director of MI5's B Division, Dick White, who revealed that MI5 knew of Burgess and his "weaknesses, including his indiscretions and his homosexual tendencies." He added that Burgess was not regarded as a member of the Communist Party or as a Soviet agent, as he was, in MI5's view, incapable of operating as a KGB mole.[28] Homosexuality was also discussed during the committee's eighth meeting, when it heard from Assistant Commissioner Ronald Howe. When questioned about "Scotland Yard's attitude and practice in the matter of homosexuality,"[29] Howe explained that the police, while prosecuting cases that caused scandal or a public nuisance, did not actively "seek out and prosecute homosexuals." Nevertheless, it had "a considerable volume of records" on the subject, mostly tip-offs from informers. It was easy for the police's Criminal Investigation Department (CID), Howe reported, to search this material, and, if a member of the Civil Service was arrested for a criminal offence, the news would always be reported to the department concerned.[30]

Cadogan's final report was completed in November 1951. In a covering letter to the new Conservative foreign secretary, Anthony Eden, Foreign Office permanent undersecretary Sir William Strang noted that Cadogan and his committee had "not found anything radically wrong with the arrangements in the Foreign Office," which was, he told Eden, a "great relief to my mind."[31] Running to twenty-eight pages, the report provided background information on the Burgess and Maclean case and outlined current Foreign Office security procedures. It also considered the "personal conduct" to be expected from members of the Foreign Service. Cadogan and his committee felt that the conduct of officials "must be of a very high standard," as they held "positions of trust and responsibility" and represented Britain's overseas interests, with members of the Foreign Service being "persons of character and integrity." The report noted that there were certain character defects that posed a risk to security, making reference to a recent circular by Strang to the heads of missions overseas mentioning "drink, drugs, sex or money troubles" and "sexual abnormality, bad company, undue extravagance, unexplained overstrain or nervous trouble."[32] Particular attention was paid to the issue of homosexuality, since, the report stated, "both Mr. Burgess and, to a much lesser extent, Mr. Maclean are alleged to have had homosexual tendencies."[33] While the report explained how the "moral issues" raised by homosexuality were of no concern to the Foreign Office, it highlighted two areas where it was felt to be of significance. First, the report highlighted how the "homosexual behaviour" of a member of the foreign service had the potential to "bring discredit on the Service," making the individual "no longer ... fit to discharge the representational side of their duties," with the result that they would be required to resign. Second was the matter of security:

> In this and some other countries some forms of homosexuality involve offences under the criminal law. A practicing homosexual is therefore especially liable to blackmail, and on this account represents a serious security risk. We therefore consider that any member of the Foreign Service who is suspected of indulging homosexual tendencies should be carefully watched, even though his conduct has not occasioned any public scandal, and that his appointments within the Service should take account of this risk.[34]

Rather than set "hard and fast rules," the committee left it open for officials to decide how individual cases would be dealt with.[35]

Cadogan was ambivalent about the ultimate value of his report, confiding to his diary his belief that it "doesn't help much very effectively."[36] The report was, however, an important step in the development of British vetting, marking the start of a shift away from purely political vetting into screening for personal "character defects." Eden thought that the report was "very well done" and the "recommendations ... practical."[37]

Despite Cadogan's calls for the issue to be considered on a case-by-case basis, Foreign Office officials proceeded to set down further guidance on how cases of homosexuality should be dealt with during a meeting in February 1952. The officials recognized that, in the future, "practicing homosexuals [would be] regarded as generally unsuitable to be members of the Foreign Service."[38] Three categories were set out where action should be taken. The first, Category 1, where an individual was clearly guilty of misconduct and had brought public discredit on the Service, should be dealt with under normal disciplinary procedures; the second, Category 2, where rumours suggested an individual was involved in homosexual activity, would result in the individual being be warned to change their ways or their "usefulness for the Service would inevitably be diminished" and future appointments "carefully considered in light of all the circumstances of the case"; and finally, Category 3, where guilt was established, but there was no evidence of public discredit, would see individuals asked to leave the Foreign Office if a further case of homosexuality occurred.[39] None of the categories referred to the security issue of blackmail, which had been raised by Cadogan's report. Instead, the focus was wholly upon protecting the department's public image and credibility. This guidance was approved by Eden in May and proceeded to form the basis of future Foreign Office policy.

Almost as soon as the new guidelines had been approved, the Foreign Office found itself coming under increased scrutiny from journalists. In May 1952, Carey-Foster warned officials that the editor of the *Daily Express* had appointed reporter Donald Seaman to "spend as much time and money as was necessary to get an exclusive story." Seaman had interviewed one of Burgess's former lovers, who "revealed names of other men who had 'shared' him," including Anthony Blunt, a former MI5 officer who had attracted attention as a "Communist sympathiser" and who would later admit to being part of the so-called Cambridge Five. Carey-Foster reported that Seaman believed that officials were "primarily concerned with protecting the Foreign Office from scandal ... and only secondarily with the realities of security" – a perceptive observation.[40]

The ultimate impact of the Foreign Office's shift in policy is hard to assess. Certainly, as with the development of "negative" and "positive" vetting, the number of individuals concerned was certainly smaller than in the United States, where the screening of homosexuals had resulted in 425 "homosexual separations" in the State Department alone by 1953.[41] Figures on the Foreign Office "purge" are hard to find, but during the first three years of the department's new approach to homosexuality, the head of the Security Department, Arthur de la Mare, recorded that twenty-six cases had come to the attention of the Personnel and Security Departments.[42] Few of these resulted in the officials concerned being removed from their posts. In his paper, de la Mare categorized twenty-six of the current homosexual cases under the three categories set out under the Foreign Office guidelines. Once again, the omission of blackmail as an important issue underlines the emphasis placed on maintaining the public standing of the Foreign Office. Of all the cases considered, only two were classed as Category 1 – "clear evidence of guilt which has involved public discredit upon the Foreign Service." The first example, that of P.S. Stephens, who had served in the British embassy in Washington, was known to the local vice squad and the FBI, but had not yet brought public discredit.[43] More embarrassing for the Foreign Office was the case of Sir Douglas Howard, British ambassador to Uruguay (1949–53). Howard had a distinguished war record and had received the Military Cross in November 1918 during an action in the closing days of the First World War, before going on to join the diplomatic service in 1922. He had served in Oslo, Bucharest, Rome, and Sofia and was appointed chargé d'affaires to Madrid in 1946 before moving to Uruguay, where, in July 1953, he had been arrested "wearing female attire in a house known to be the haunt of male prostitutes," though he strenuously denied any charges of impropriety. "No doubt because of his then position as H.M. [Her Majesty's] Representative no formal complaint was made," although, as de la Mare recorded, "the story was said at the time to be common property in Montevideo."[44] It was also common knowledge in the embassy itself. The stepdaughter of "Toby" Hildyard, then a junior diplomat in the mission, recalled that Howard "was accustomed to leave the residence on a Friday evening wearing full ambassadorial finery … carrying a small suitcase" but one evening "was returned to the residence in an unmarked police van wearing seamed stockings, high heels and a skirt."[45] As a consequence of this behaviour, Howard was removed from Uruguay and appointed as minister to the Holy See, a relative diplomatic backwater, prior to his retirement in 1957.

Only one case, that of Mr. A. Goodison, was described as a Category 2, where guilt was "confessed but … there is no evidence that the conduct of the officer concerned has brought public discredit." Goodison confessed "to a homosexual past including a relapse while posted to Khartoum in 1953," with the details of the case known only to "medical advisors" and the Security Department. The remainder were considered Category 3, "where there is gossip among colleagues, within H.M. Missions or among the local British community to arouse suspicion of homosexuality or to cause a risk that public scandal may arise,"[46] even if evidence was lacking. The report suggested that evidence against Frederick Archibald Warner, who had transferred to the diplomatic service in 1946, having served with the Royal Navy in wartime, was mostly gossip; despite Warner's denials, senior officials had "grave" suspicions about his sexuality, with his bachelor status and links to "exotic as well as distinguished social circles" leading to "Fleet Street" gossip and public naming by Kenneth de Courcy, the editor of the *Intelligence Digest*, a politically motivated private subscription newsletter, based on leaks and de Courcy's own fantasies.[47] Warner was said to have been involved in "drunken brawls" and to be guilty of "moral crimes" and leaks of sensitive papers – the latter, a serious allegation which had little basis.[48] To make matters worse, Warner had worked alongside Burgess in the Foreign Office, sharing a room overlooking Downing Street, "between the minister and a room with clerks, acting as gatekeepers" between Foreign Office officials and the Secretary of State, before a posting to the embassy in Moscow.[49] Warner had come to the attention of George Carey-Foster and the Security Department after Maclean's disappearance. In September 1952, officials had also received from the CIA the text of a magazine article containing allegations that Warner and another unnamed diplomat had had "homosexual relations with Burgess." The article had been suppressed by the publishers "because of the damage it would do to Anglo-American relations," but

Carey-Foster had subsequently interviewed Warner, who gave a "categorical assurance that he never indulged in homosexual practices," an assertion "fully accepted" by the Security Department.[50] Nonetheless, with question marks now over his reliability, Warner was posted as head of chancery in Burma in June 1956, served in Athens before an appointment as the head of the Foreign Office's South-East Asian Department, married in 1971, and ended his career as ambassador to Tokyo in 1975.[51] Another "serious" case was Samuel Hood, 6th Viscount Hood. The son of Rear-Admiral Samuel Hood, who had been killed at the Battle of Jutland in May 1916, Viscount Hood had a distinguished diplomatic career despite nearly "giving rise to a public scandal" as a junior official, later serving as chargé d'affaires to Madrid and subsequently becoming undersecretary, minister in the Washington embassy in 1957, and deputy undersecretary for Western European affairs until his retirement in 1969. He remained a bachelor until his death in 1981. A further official identified as Category 3 was John Hughes Wardle-Smith, who had served in South America and who was reported for his "alleged conduct" in Buenos Aires. This led to the "immediate break-up of his marriage to the daughter of the Canadian Ambassador there," resulting in "something very close to a public scandal."[52] Once again, Wardle-Smith continued in the diplomatic service, ending his career in Brazil in 1966.[53] In two other cases, one official had come to the Security Department's attention after an incident in New York giving "rise to some comment both in and out of the Office but not ... amounting to a public scandal," while another "became involved in a homosexual affair against his own wishes and because of his youth and inexperience." In each case, the officials were vetted by the Foreign Office and cleared, as the rumours were not "sufficiently strong to warrant refusal."[54] In all such cases, Foreign Office security officials appeared to have differed with their US counterparts. Suspicion of homosexuality did not lead to automatic removal, even if the allegations remained on file. Even in the worst-case situations, likely to undermine the Foreign Office's much-prized reputation, officials were allowed to continue their career paths – some of those identified here went on to have distinguished careers, though the rules on homosexuality and the Foreign Office's deep-rooted conservatism on such issues would continue to impinge upon the lives of gay officials until the end of the ban in 1991.

The disappearance of Burgess and Maclean in May 1951 brought the issue of homosexuality into sharp focus as a matter of both security and reputational concern. While the Foreign Office was quick to develop in-house guidelines, the rest of Whitehall reacted more slowly. Beyond the Foreign Office's new reforms carried out independently of

US concerns, American officials siting on the transatlantic Tripartite Security Working Group were critical of British standards generally, forcing ministers to agree to a "stiffening of the standard of investigation."[55] This drive to improve government security, starting with the Ministry of Supply and other departments dealing with atomic research, was divorced from the Foreign Office's own focus on sexuality, which came from the fallout of the Burgess–Maclean disappearance and attempts to protect the department from exposure to any further public scandals. Pressure from Washington had little impact upon the Foreign Office. US influence can be seen, however, shaping attitudes to security in Whitehall more generally, even if officials were reluctant to act. During a meeting of the Personal Security Committee in February 1954, officials agreed that political bars were "relatively straightforward" but that further criteria referring to the vetting of alcoholics and drug addicts, individuals who were discreet and dishonest, and homosexuals were difficult and lay outside of the terms of the vetting rules first outlined in March 1948 by the Attlee government. Homosexuality was a particular issue, as "embarrassment might arise in dealing with cases ... unless there was sufficient evidence to justify a prosecution, which was improbable, dismissal might give rise to an action for defamation, and was not therefore practicable," with suspected gay men "moved elsewhere ... without the true reason for the move being disclosed." As has been illustrated, such concerns were not shared by the Foreign Office.[56] In 1955, Prime Minister Anthony Eden appointed an ad hoc "council" of privy counsellors to recommend changes in vetting, including the study of character defects, across the public services.[57] Here, the Foreign Office appears to have taken a hawkish stance, describing gay men as a "particular problem" and suggesting that "if an individual showed such instability in character and conduct that he could not be trusted, he should be dismissed."[58] In discussions on the findings of the privy counsellors, homosexuality was quickly identified as the most significant "character defect" even if, officials admitted, "more defections to the Russians" had been caused by "misconduct with women." The final recommendations, despite finding little wrong with the vetting generally, recognized the need to watch for "character defects as factors that might make a man unreliable or expose him to blackmail ... There is a duty on Departments to inform themselves of serious failings such as drunkenness, addiction to drugs, homosexuality or any loose living."[59] In private, however, homosexuality was seen as the key threat, with one Admiralty official writing,

It seems ... that by "serious character defect" the Conference have particularly in mind homosexuality ... Awkward questions might then be asked: would mere suspicion of homosexuality be taken into account, or if not, what would be the Government standard of proof? I think before any public statement is made which might lay the Government open to such questions they should consider how far homosexuality is to be taken into account for this purpose. For example, is it only to be taken into account to the extent that it might lay a person open to blackmail ... Or is homosexuality on the other hand to be regarded as creating a security risk not only because of the probability of blackmail but because it is held to be an indication of a character particularly liable to be untrustworthy.[60]

Having interviewed Foreign Office officials, the privy counsellors concluded that "serious failings" would be a bigger issue there than in the Home Civil Service, since homosexual diplomats would lose the "confidence of foreigners," with known or suspected homosexuals "unlikely to be fully trusted by the Americans."[61] By the 1960s, Foreign Office officials were planning to raise the screening of homosexuals with the introduction of a "Special Investigator" who would head an "Elite Squad" of officials to screen the private lives of new entrants and warn of "danger signs."[62] Beyond the fear of scandal, internal security guidelines made it clear that gay men were unsuited as diplomats, as "infamous, immoral or disgraceful conduct" would expose individuals to blackmail by "hostile intelligence services."[63] The decline of "ideological spies" such as Burgess and Maclean, following Nikita Khrushchev's denunciation of Stalin and the brutal suppression of the Hungarian uprising in 1956, meant that Soviet intelligence had to increasingly rely on sexual "honey traps" or the gathering of *kompromat* to pressure Western officials. The Foreign Office was already aware of the risk; in 1962 Admiralty clerk John Vassall was arrested, having been blackmailed into spying for the KGB while stationed at the British embassy in Moscow, when he was secretly photographed having sex with "a number of different men."[64] The *Daily Telegraph*'s Moscow correspondent Jeremy Wolfenden, the son of Lord Wolfenden, was similarly blackmailed with images of sexual encounters with other men.[65] Heterosexual diplomats were also vulnerable; in 1968, the British ambassador to Moscow Sir Geoffrey Harrison "let his defences drop" and had an affair with a Russian maid who, it turned out, worked for the KGB, with Harrison forced to admit the affair and recalled to London.[66]

The decriminalization of homosexuality under the 1967 Sexual Offenses Act changed attitudes across the Home Civil Service, with the majority of departments having no formal discrimination for the appointment or promotion of gay men.[67] Yet despite changes elsewhere, the Foreign Office, in line with the intelligence services and

Armed Forces, maintained its sexuality bar. In December 1967, the Official Committee on Security ruled that, despite a change in the law, the "risk of blackmail or pressure in homosexual cases" remained significant, while "importuning in public" was still a criminal offence, and the "social stigma" of homosexuality meant there were still significant reputational risks in coming out. Concern over the vulnerability of gay men overseas also continued. The committee noted, "the law in communist countries is almost inevitably more restrictive than our own, and staff at Missions in or on visits to those countries are therefore no less liable to pressure or blackmail than before: indeed they are more liable, since they may no longer be on their guard to conceal this aspect of their behaviour."[68]

As in the 1950s, security was secondary to the importance to maintaining the Foreign Office's carefully cultivated image overseas. Officials believed that gay men and women serving overseas could damage Britain's diplomatic ties, especially in the United States, while at home the Foreign and Commonwealth Office (FCO, as the FO was renamed in 1968)[69] wished to conform with prevailing public attitudes to homosexuality, despite legalisation. Even as recently as 1981, one senior official believed it was important to "discourage homosexuals from joining the Service [and] to encourage them to leave once identified," arguing that homosexuality was "probably regarded by most British people as immoral." Another official went further, signalling his preference for "a notice, 'No homosexuals should apply.'"[70] Tasked to look at Whitehall security in the early 1980s by Prime Minister Margaret Thatcher, following the publication of a book by journalist Chapman Pincher alleging wider penetration of MI5 and the Civil Service, Lord Diplock reiterated that homosexual relationships, even if admitted, would "continue to be a bar to recruitment to the Diplomatic Service and, if undiscovered upon initial PV [positive vetting], should result in removal ... when it does come to light," with the Foreign Office beginning yearly reviews of its policy from 1984.[71] Cabinet Secretary Sir Robert Armstrong stated the FCO's position in August 1987, writing "Male homosexuality should be regarded as an absolute bar to posts in the Diplomatic Service or any other post which might involve a posting outside Great Britain on the grounds that there were many countries where homosexual behaviour was still a criminal offence."[72]

Once again, the impact of the bar on serving diplomats is hard to assess, even if the number of cases was "very small." In September 1987, the head of the Foreign Office's Security Department reported "a Grade 7D officer who will leave us next year at the end of his current overseas tour ... Certain other cases which came to light in previous years are still causing administrative difficulties, eg one officer is still on sick leave after over a year, having had a mental breakdown; and another, who was given the chance to serve overseas after an isolated homosexual incident, has had to be withdrawn as his behaviour was giving rise to an unacceptable level of gossip."[73] Between 1979 and 1986, a total of thirty-five officials had their positive vetting certificates withdrawn; "eleven (31%) were homosexual/lesbian, or had admitted previous homosexual experiences" – a "high proportion," officials believed – due to a "rigid interpretation, and heightened awareness" of Diplock's recommendations.[74] Another official, a "Home Civil Servant in the FCO," was allowed to remain, as they were based in London, while another was "seeking transfer to the Home Civil Service."[75] The bar undoubtedly placed significant strain on officials, likely contributing to the suicide of diplomat Robert Facey, who had come out during a posting in Latin America and had been left without a job.[76] Facey had been a "quirky, brilliant diplomat who talked in non-stop Oscar Wildeish epigrams," yet, recalled colleague Charles Crawford, "his life and career dissolved, and he committed suicide in June 1989."[77] By the late 1980s, the Foreign Office's policy was growing increasingly out of line with allies and the rest of government. While an internal review found that "male homosexuality contravenes the law in 63 countries, female in 50," attitudes towards gay diplomats varied from country to country, with even the strictest taking a lenient stance towards Western diplomats, even if some laws "might impede the ability of a homosexual diplomat to do his or her job."[78] Certainly the Foreign Office was the "odd man out in taking so strict a line against homosexuality," officials admitted, with the US State Department, West German, Belgian, Netherlands, Australian, and Canadian governments now taking a more relaxed view.[79] Ironically, the State Department had ended discrimination on grounds of sexuality after a Civil Service Commission announcement in 1975 that sexual orientation alone could not be used to terminate the careers of federal officials, though gays and lesbians in the US Armed Forces continued to face discrimination.[80] Indeed, the Foreign Office's strict stance created its own problems, as D.C. Walker of the Personnel Policy Department recognized. Under the policy, homosexuals were "in a Catch 22": if they admitted their sexuality, they would be removed, while those who hid their sexuality would similarly be removed, should it be discovered.[81] By 1990, the Foreign Office permanent undersecretary, Sir Patrick Wright, hoped ministers would review policy, as "our analogue Services appear to find little difficulty with security considerations, and I note that our closest intelligence partners (the Americans) are quoted as saying that homosexuals are no more open to blackmail than others." Wright went on: "It is admittedly a striking fact that male homosexuality is still illegal in 63 countries, but this does not seem to have caused problems for most of our allies and partners; and in one of the 'illegals,' namely the Soviet Union, I believe that there have been at least as many attempts at compromise in recent years on the basis of heterosexual misbehaviour as homosexual. Furthermore, Saudi Arabia's legal constraints on alcohol and Christian worship do not affect our postings policies."[82] By the 1990s, officials considered gay amnesty on a case-by-case basis, with the end of the bar finally announced in July 1991 by Prime Minister John Major, who announced that "there should be no posts involving access to highly classified information for which homosexuality represents an automatic bar to security clearance, except in the special case of the armed forces where homosexual acts remain offences under the service disciplinary Acts."[83]

NOTES

1 See, for example, David Vincent, *The Culture of Secrecy: Britain, 1832–1998* (Oxford: Oxford University Press, 1999), 245; Stephen Jeffery-Poulter, *Peers, Queers and Commons: The Struggle for Gay Law Reform from 1950 to the Present* (London: Routledge, 1991), 25; Jeffrey Weeks, *Sex, Politics and Society: The Regulation of Sexuality since 1800* (London: Longman, 1993).

2 Copies of documents on Burgess and Maclean were released in January 2012 following a Freedom of Information (FOI) request to the FCO. Where possible, references have been made to the documents as subsequently released to the National Archives (NA), Kew. Where it has not proved possible to locate FOI material at Kew, "FOI" denotes material that has been deposited at the University of Salford's FOI Intelligence and Security Archival Collection, where it is available for consultation. Access to the archive is by appointment only, through the university's Archives and Special Collections coordinator (Library-archives@salford.ac.uk). The online catalogue for the collection can be found at http://www.salford.ac.uk/__data/assets/xml_file /0006/776886/IntelligenceSecurityStudies.xml (accessed 14 February 2019). Details of the Burgess and Maclean file release can be found in Richard Dunley and Andrew Holt, "Burgess and Maclean: Revelations," National Archives blog, 23 October 2015, http://blog.nationalarchives.gov.uk/blog /burgess-maclean-revelations/ (accessed 12 February 2019).

3 FOI: Annex A: The Burgess-Maclean Case [undated].

4 See Robert Aldrich and Garry Wotherspoon, *Who's Who in Contemporary Gay and Lesbian History: From World War II to the Present Day* (London: Routledge, 2000), 445.

5 Matthew Parris, "Wildeblood, Peter (1923–1999)," *Oxford Dictionary of National Biography*, online ed., May 2006, http://www.oxforddnb.com/view/article/70643 (accessed 13 July 2018); and Patrick Higgins, *Heterosexual Dictatorship: Male Homosexuality in Post-War Britain* (London: Fourth Estate, 1996), 231.

6 Peter Wildeblood, *Against the Law* (London: Penguin, 1957), 69.

7 David K. Johnson, *The Lavender Scare: The Cold War Persecution of Gays and Lesbians in the Federal Government* (Chicago: University of Chicago Press, 2006), 21.

8 Ibid., 74–5.

9 Ibid., 166.

10 See Reg Whitaker, "Cold War Alchemy: How America, Britain and Canada Transformed Espionage into Subversion," *Intelligence and National Security* 15, no. 2 (2000): 199–201.

11 Jeffery-Poulter, *Peers, Queers and Commons*, 25; L.J. Moran, "The Uses of Homosexuality: Homosexuality for National Security," *International Journal of the Sociology of Law* 19 (1991): 157.

12 Higgins, *Heterosexual Dictatorship*, 249–50.

13 Ibid., 263–5.

14 Ibid.

15 Attlee to Morrison, 10 June 1951, PREM 8/1524, NA, Kew.

16 Cabinet Secretary Notebook, 11 June 1951, CAB 195/9, NA, Kew; C.M. (51) 42nd Conclusions, 11 June 1951, CAB 128/19, NA, Kew.

17 House of Commons Debates (HC Deb.), 11 June 1951, vol. 488, col. 1672; "Morrison Says 'No' to Weekly Security Check," *Daily Mirror*, 12 June 1951; "The Words That Started It All," *Daily Express*, 12 June 1951, 2.

18 Morrison to Attlee, 21 June 1951, PREM 8/1524, NA, Kew.

19 Morrison to Attlee, 13 June 1951, PREM 8/1524, NA, Kew.

20 Paul Gore-Booth, "Cadogan, Sir Alexander George Montagu (1884–1968)," rev. G.R. Berridge, *Oxford Dictionary of National Biography*, online ed., January 2011, http://www.oxforddnb.com/view/article/32234 (accessed 8 May 2018). See also David Dilks, ed., *The Diaries of Sir Alexander Cadogan, 1938–1945* (London: Cassell, 1971).

21 Robert Cecil, *A Divided Life: A Biography of Donald Maclean* (London: Coronet, 1990), 224.

22 Liddell diary, entry for 7 July 1951, KV 4/473, NA, Kew.

23 FOI: "The Problem of Homosexuality in Relation to Employment in the Foreign Office," 2.

24 Ibid.

25 FOI: Annex A: Burgess-Maclean Case [undated].

26 The committee heard evidence from Sir William Strang, Ashley Clarke (chief clerk), Roderick Barclay (parliamentary private secretary to secretary of state), Patrick Reilly, George Carey-Foster (head of Security

Department), and R.W.J. Hooper (Personnel Department). It also heard
from Stewart Menzies (Secret Intelligence Service), Dick White (MI5),
A.J.D. Winnifrith (Treasury), and R.M. Howe (Metropolitan Police).
Cadogan Report, CAB 301/120, NA, Kew.

27 Cadogan diary, entries for 20 and 25 July 1951, ACAD 1/22, Churchill
Archives Centre (CAC), Cambridge.

28 FOI: Record of 4th meeting, 31 July 1951.

29 Cadogan diary, entry for 16 August 1951, ACAD 1/22, CAC.

30 FOI: Record of 8th meeting, 17 August 1951. Rather than homosexuality,
Howe believed that the "surest" sign to detect the unreliability of an individual was when "a married man in the public service … [was] found to be
spending a good deal of money on a woman or women other than his wife."

31 FOI: Strang to Eden, 3 November 1951.

32 Report of Committee on Enquiry, 19, CAB 301/120, NA, Kew.

33 Higgins, *Heterosexual Dictatorship*, 265.

34 Report of Committee on Enquiry, 20, CAB 301/120.

35 Report of Committee on Enquiry, 21, CAB 301/120.

36 Cadogan diary, entry for 11 October 1951, ACAD 1/14, CAC.

37 FOI: Minute by Eden, 21 December 1951.

38 FOI: Summary of meeting held in the Clerk's room on Friday, February
1st at 3 p.m. to consider action to be taken on the recommendations of the
Cadogan Committee.

39 FOI, Strang to Secretary of State, 9 May 1952.

40 FOI, Report by Carey-Foster, May 1952.

41 Whitaker, "Cold War Alchemy," 157.

42 De la Mare later published details of his role as head of security in the
Foreign Office in his memoir, *Perverse and Foolish*. See Arthur de la Mare,
Perverse and Foolish: A Jersey Farmer's Son in the British Diplomatic Service
(Jersey: Le Haule Books, 1994); "Homosexuality in the Foreign Service,"
10 October 1955, FCO 158/177, NA, Kew.

43 See F.J. Thompson, *Destination Washington* (London: Robert Hale,
1960), 176–7, 205–6. Stephens may have been one of those identified by
Washington-based security officer Francis "Tommy" Thompson, who
worked alongside local law enforcement and the FBI in rooting out gay
British diplomats from the embassy and took pride in sending officials
home to be removed from the Foreign Office.

44 "Homosexuality in the Foreign Service," 10 October 1955. Details on
Howard can be found in "Howard, Sir Douglas Frederick (1897–1987),"
in *Who Was Who* (A & C Black, 1920–2008); online ed., Oxford University
Press, Dec. 2007, https://doi.org/10.1093/ww/9780199540884.013.U165499
(accessed 13 February 2019).

45 Elisabeth Luard, *My Life as a Wife: Love, Liquor and What to Do about Other
Women* (London: Bloomsbury, 2013), 23. In another passage Luard recalls

that "when, halfway through his tenure, the British sent a cruiser and two destroyers to celebrate the hundredth anniversary of Uruguay's liberation from the colonial power ... Ambassador Howard disappeared into the innards of the cruiser as soon as it docked and didn't reappear till it left. Unsure of what this strange behaviour might mean, I passed the information on to Nanny" (23).

46 "Homosexuality in the Foreign Service," 10 October 1955.

47 Ibid. On de Courcy, see Christopher Moran, *Classified: Secrecy and the State in Modern Britain* (Cambridge: Cambridge University Press, 2013), 117–19.

48 FOI: Foreign Office Letter, 5 September 1952.

49 Andrew Lownie, *Stalin's Englishman: The Lives of Guy Burgess* (London: Hodder and Stoughton, 2015), 158.

50 FOI: Foreign Office Letter, 5 September 1952.

51 John Ure, "Warner, Sir Frederick Archibald [Fred] (1918–1995)," *Oxford Dictionary of National Biography*, online ed., May 2014, http://www .oxforddnb.com/view/10.1093/ref:odnb/9780198614128.001.0001/odnb -9780198614128-e- 60056 (accessed 4 October 2018). See also Alan Campbell, "Obituaries: Sir Fred Warner," *Independent*, 3 October 1995, https://www .independent.co.uk/news/people/obituaries-sir-fred-warner-1575741.html (accessed 4 October 2018).

52 "Homosexuality in the Foreign Service," 10 October 1955.

53 British Diplomats Directory: Part 2 of 4, 507, https://issuu.com /fcohistorians/docs/bdd_part_2_with_covers/212 (accessed 13 February 2019). While a summary of his diplomatic career does not mention service in South America before 1950, Wardle-Smith's work there is referred to in Marcelo de Paiva Abreu, "Brazil as a Creditor: Sterling Balances, 1940–1952," *Economic History Review* 43, no. 3 (August 1990): 461.

54 "Homosexuality in the Foreign Service," 10 October 1955.

55 Positive Vetting Procedure, 26 January 1954, S. (P.S.) (54) (3), CAB 134/1165, NA, Kew.

56 2nd meeting, 12 February 1954, S. (P.S.) (54), CAB 134/1165, NA, Kew.

57 Ian Beesley, *The Official History of the Cabinet Secretary, 1947–2002* (Oxon: Routledge, 2017), 125; Peter Hennessy, *The Secret State: Preparing for the Worst, 1945–2010* (London: Penguin, 2010), 103; Mark Hollingsworth and Richard Norton-Taylor, *Blacklist: The Inside Story of Political Vetting* (London: Hogarth Press, 1988), 29–30.

58 Meeting held in Sir Edward Bridges' room, 18 November 1955, CAB 21/4035, NA, Kew.

59 Cmd. 9715, *Statement of the Findings of the Conference of Privy Councillors on Security* (London: HMSO, March 1956), 3.

60 Report of Security Conference on Privy Councillors – Comments by the Secretary of the Admiralty, April 1956, CAB 21/4035, NA, Kew.

61 Report of Security Conference of Privy Councillors, April 1956, 9.
62 James Southern, *Homosexuality at the Foreign Office, 1967–1991*, FCO Historians, History Notes, Issue 19, Foreign & Commonwealth Office, July 2017, 9.
63 "Security Implications of the Sexual Offences Act, 1967," SM(O)(67)19, CAB 134/3256, NA, Kew.
64 John Vassall, *Vassall: The Autobiography of a Spy* (London: Sidgwick & Jackson, 1975), 67. On the Vassall case, see Christopher Andrew and Oleg Gordievsky, *KGB: The Inside Story* (London: Hoddor & Stoughton, 1990), 363–4.
65 Jon Kelly, "The Era When Gay Spies Were Feared," *BBC News*, 20 January 2016, https://www.bbc.co.uk/news/magazine-35360172 (accessed 12 February 2019).
66 Dan Lomas, "All the Precedent's Men: Russia's History of Using Sex for Spying," *Independent*, 18 January 2017.
67 Rodney Lowe, *The Official History of the British Civil Service: Reforming the Civil Service*, vol. 1: *The Fulton Years, 1966–81* (Oxon: Routledge, 2011), 513.
68 "Security Implications of the Sexual Offences Act, 1967," SM(O)(67)19, CAB 134/3256.
69 See Richard Smith, "1968 and All That: The Creation of the Foreign & Commonwealth Office," History of Government Blog, 17 October 2018, https://history.blog.gov.uk/2018/10/17/1968-and-all-that-the-creation -of-the-foreign-commonwealth-office/ (accessed 13 February 2019).
70 Southern, *Homosexuality at the Foreign Office*, 12.
71 Cmnd. 8540, *Statement on the Recommendations of the Security Commission* (London: HMSO, 1982), 8.
72 FOI: Letter by Sir Robert Armstrong, August 1987.
73 FOI: A. Ford to Deputy Chief Clerk, 16 September 1987.
74 FOI: P. Cooper to A. Ford, 14 July 1989.
75 FOI: "Homosexuals in the Diplomatic Service," 24 October 1988.
76 FOI: D.C. Walker to Ford, 5 July 1989.
77 See Charles Crawford, "The Love That Dared Not Speak Its Name in the Foreign Office," *Independent*, 30 March 2010, https://www.independent.co .uk/news/uk/this-britain/the-love-that-dared-not-speak-its-name-in-the -foreign-office-1931127.html (accessed 11 May 2018).
78 FOI: Peter Cooper [Security Department] to Ford, 30 October 1989.
79 FOI: Cooper to Ward, 8 September 1989.
80 See Judith Adkins, "Congressional Investigations and the Lavender Scare," *Prologue Magazine* 48, no. 2 (Summer 2016), https://www.archives.gov /publications/prologue/2016/summer/lavender.html (8 March 2018).
81 FOI: Walker to Ford, 5 July 1989.
82 FOI: Patrick Wright to Lord Brabazon, Minister of State, 28 February 1990.
83 Crawford, "The Love That Dared Not Speak Its Name"; HC. Deb., 23 July 1991, vol. 195, col. 474W.

4 "Our No. 1 Spy": Counter-Subversion in Cold War Australia

PHILLIP DEERY

It is the first duty of a Security Service to counter subversive activities by Communists.

> – Report of Enquiry by Sir Norman Brook into the Secret
> Intelligence and Security Services, 1951[1]

In contrast to countries such as the United States, where FBI undercover agents became government witnesses before congressional hearings and then published their stories,[2] Australian penetration agents are obscure. They remain shrouded in mystery with their anonymity preserved and protected. However, there is one significant exception. The Australian Security Intelligence Organisation (ASIO), through the National Archives of Australia, released 2,664 pages on the operational career of an undercover agent, Anne Neill. For no other agent has anything like this occurred. These files include the agent's reports and the case officers' assessments. They permit revealing insights into ASIO's counter-subversion priorities and tradecraft in the early Cold War. There is a limited scholarly literature on the employment of female spies, mainly by the Central Intelligence Agency,[3] but nothing on ASIO's recruitment of women. The literature on ASIO's modus operandi in running agents who penetrated the Communist Party of Australia (CPA) in the 1950s is similarly sparse. Both McKnight and Horner have briefly discussed Operation Sparrow – initiated in July 1956 with the aim of penetrating every branch of the Communist Party with an ASIO agent – and in this context Neill is referred to.[4] I have also examined the penetration of communist organizations by a Czechoslovak informant, the unreliable "walk-in," Maximilian Wechsler, in the 1970s.[5] But that is all. It is only recent public access to these unique files that has enabled this historical reconstruction of counter-subversion agent running. Such access echoes the 2017 release of previously secret Orders-in-Council that enabled the Canadian security service's wiretapping program, discussed by Dennis Molinaro in chapter 7 of this book.

ASIO was concerned with counter-intelligence, both its product and as an activity. Indeed, its formative years were devoted to "The Case": the exposure of Soviet espionage operations in Australia, especially in the Department of External Affairs. On this, the literature is rich and extensive.[6] As a domestic counter-intelligence service, ASIO also sought to nullify the influence of organizations, deemed subversive, that supported the Soviet Union. The counter-subversion branch of ASIO relied on the infiltration of local organizations and, to be effective, required stable, committed, and long-serving penetration agents. This chapter examines the operational history of one such agent. Through its analysis of ASIO's handling of Anne Neill by three case officers throughout the 1950s, the chapter will suggest that, at least in this instance, agent management was shrewd, sensitive, and competent. The chapter draws a conclusion contrary to the widely held view that "as an organization, the intelligence service has lost contact with feeling and humanity and has become an anonymous bureaucracy that makes decisions without considering the consequences for the individual agent."[7]

Recruitment: ASIO and the CPA

Born on 17 June 1898 in Mount Torrens, South Australia (SA), Freda Bennett Parsons (known as "Anne") was raised a devout Christian. Her parents instilled strong Wesleyan religious doctrines in her from an early age, accompanied by political values that were deeply conservative and imperial minded.[8] She married Wilfred Roy Neill soon after he divorced his first wife in April 1945 on the grounds of desertion.[9] They had no children. Her occupation was listed on her 1952 passport application as "home duties." Roy Neill had served overseas for three years with the 50th Battalion of the First Australian Imperial Force, contracted a long-term, incapacitating war-related illness, and died on 9 March 1949.[10] Through living with this bitter, personal legacy of war, Anne Neill was predisposed to believe in the importance of peace between all nations.

In 1949, her cousin May Parsons told her about a new peace organization formed in July, the "Women's Peace Crusade."[11] Neill filled in a membership form and subsequently received a pamphlet, *The Woman Crusader*. However, because the Menzies government had published a list of peace organizations affiliated with the CPA in early 1950, she believed that the Women's Peace Crusade, one of those listed, had been infiltrated by the CPA. She took the next two copies of *The Woman Crusader* to the chief secretary in the Liberal Country League (LCL) government and explained how she "had been caught up with the organisation." Shortly afterwards, a senior ASIO officer, Rod Allanson, made contact. Allanson was a Second World War veteran and one of ASIO's first recruits when he joined the organization in July 1949.[12] He was the sole agent runner in the Adelaide office, and Anne Neill was his first agent. Allanson asked Neill if she would attend a forthcoming peace conference in Adelaide as a credentialed representative of the Women's Peace Crusade. Her task was to ascertain and report on "just how strong Communist influence was at the Conference." Thus, on 23 June 1950, she attended the first of innumerable peace conferences and gatherings and simultaneously embarked on an eight-year working relationship with ASIO.

Why was the peace movement of special interest to the newly elected Menzies government? By the early 1950s, it had access to abundant evidence from the Department of External Affairs and the British Foreign Office that the peace movement was "subversive." This evidence elaborated and validated the links between the World Peace Council, a Cominform (Communist Information Bureau) creation, and the establishment of local peace committees.[13] In 1949 a Cominform resolution directed that peace "should now become the pivot of the entire activity of the Communist Parties." All Western communist parties faithfully responded and injected the "struggle for peace" into both their doctrines and their strategies. The postwar peace movement took shape at the first World Peace Congress, held in Paris in April 1949. The Congress recommended the creation in every country of "national peace committees"; accordingly, the Australian Peace Council was formed the following month. It was a short step to argue that the Australian peace movement was assisting the so-called "Peace Offensive" and ipso facto the foreign policy of the Soviet Union. Prime Minister Menzies argued that the communist-controlled peace movement was designed to "prevent or impair defence preparations in the democracies."[14] In this sense, then, the South Australian (SA) Peace Council was seen as part of a larger and formidable plan of communist subversion and must, therefore, be closely monitored. Counter-subversion was necessary. To achieve this, a recruit like Anne Neill was essential.

When ASIO recruited Anne Neill in June 1950, it had, nationwide, a total of two agents inside the Communist Party.[15] Its tradecraft in running agents was embryonic. Certainly, it had inherited some operational procedures, as well as personnel, from military intelligence and the state police forces, while institutional knowledge, as well as considerable guidance, was also provided by visiting officers from Britain's MI5, on which ASIO was modelled.[16] It had also inherited

46,200 files, transferred incrementally from the Commonwealth Investigation Service (CIS) by May 1950.[17] However, in its first year, as the internal history of ASIO noted, "the new organization had very few assets with which to commence operations."[18] Its relationship with the CIS was testy and, despite attempts to clarify the distinctions between the two security agencies, confusion existed over the specific roles and functions of each.[19] This began to change after the appointment in July 1950 of Colonel Charles Spry, formerly the wartime director of military intelligence, as director general (DG), a position to which he brought administrative discipline and bureaucratic order. Fortuitously for Anne Neill, her recruitment coincided with his appointment.

Neill was driven overwhelmingly by a sense of patriotism. Pecuniary benefit was not a motivation. (Her remuneration was £5.10.0 per week, with £2 per week for allowable out-of-pocket expenses.) To help preserve the freedoms for which she believed her husband and so many Australian soldiers had fallen, and which were now allegedly imperilled, she "accept[ed] this particular work solely as a duty to my country." ASIO was convinced of these motives, assessing them as "patriotism and deep-seated loyalty to [the] British Crown."[20] She did not fail to see the difficulties of her new role, which she described as "formidable": "I recognised the paradoxical nature of this kind of work ... I would have to assume a dual personality." But such compartmentalization, required of her role, was for her a necessary if not noble sacrifice.

Once she joined the South Australian Peace Council, Neill worked unpaid, five days a week, in its offices. The secretary of the Peace Council was Elliott Frank Johnston, a lawyer and member of the Central Committee of the CPA, and it was he who recruited her to the Communist Party.[21] As his secretary, Neill controlled the correspondence between the council and the CPA (when relevant to Johnston), and acquired knowledge of Johnston's associates and out-of-hours activities.[22] As we shall see, it was her prolific work for the council that enabled her trip behind the Iron Curtain.

It was not only the Peace Council in which Neill became prominent. In the following years she joined, and extensively reported on, another eight CPA front organizations in Adelaide. She was secretary of the Women's Peace Crusade; assistant secretary of the Australian–Soviet Friendship Society (ASFS); executive committee member of the New Theatre; management committee member of the Union of Australian Women (UAW); SA representative of the Eureka Youth League; vice-president of the Committee for Self-Determination for Cyprus; member of the International Film Society; and CPA fraction committee member of the Realist Writers Group. She was also secretary of the Women's

International League for Peace and Freedom (WILPF), which was not a front organization, but monitored by ASIO because of its international connections. "There were times," she later wrote, "when I was out at meetings every night of the week, Sunday not excepted."[23]

But it was joining the Communist Party in September 1951 that was the biggest coup for ASIO and Neill's case officer. According to Neill, John Sendy, a State Committee member (later secretary of the SA branch and CPA national president, 1972–74) approached her in late 1950 and "started discussions with me about Party policy" and gave her a copy of the party's constitution.[24] Sendy found her "well mannered, unassuming and quite charming."[25] Her unthreatening, benign affability created a "natural" cover; she didn't have to assume a persona. On 25 July 1951 Elliott Johnston, now a full-time party organizer, having relinquished his law practice,[26] met Neill and told her that Sendy had asked him "before he went away"[27] to discuss membership with her. He encouraged her to join the CPA as a secret member, since "saying you are a member of the Party wouldn't get us anywhere." Neill was concerned her Christian and Liberal Party background would be a barrier, but "Elliott said, 'although they [the CPA] have to be careful because Security recruits its agents from the middle-class,' the work [she] had done in the Peace Council would be 'enough' for them." If she agreed, Johnston continued, "the Party would be pleased to welcome you." Neill was both daunted by an "unpleasant awareness" of what her future role would involve and bemused by "a Security Agent being *welcomed* into the Communist Party."[28]

The CPA security procedures in place when Neill was admitted to membership were extremely lax. This is surprising given this was a period in which heightened vigilance and self-protection against "Menzies' secret police" could be expected,[29] in which the party was under siege, with its very legality being threatened, and in which a senior party member, Horace Pile, was transferred by the CPA Central Control Commission's Wally Clayton (then in hiding) to Adelaide in 1951 to prepare an illegal apparatus in the event of the CPA being banned.[30] Indeed, Neill's two conversations with Johnston about joining the CPA, in July and August 1951, occurred during the referendum campaign to outlaw the CPA (June–September). Furthermore, Neill had made no secret of her conservative political allegiances. In February 1950 she was still the secretary of a women's branch of the LCL,[31] which she had joined in 1937, and her blatant anti-Labor bias was evident in a recent signed letter to the *Adelaide Advertiser*.[32] Yet after merely a matter of months undertaking secretarial duties for the peace movement, she joined the party with little or no rigorous scrutiny of her background.

Undoubtedly, her gender helped. In fact, according to John Sendy, comrades "laughed" at the "far-fetched" idea of "this middle-aged, matronly, ex-Church worker, so kindly, willing and polite, being a security copper."[33] While they were laughing, Neill was providing her case officer, whom she met weekly, with highly detailed reports on all the organizations she had infiltrated.

Operation Hunter

Neill became highly active for both the CPA and ASIO in 1952. In March, she travelled to Sydney to attend the CPA-initiated Youth Carnival for Peace and Friendship. She met with a contacting officer on no fewer than nine occasions between 14 and 24 March and supplied, inter alia, signatures of delegates.[34] In Sydney Neill learned of a planned Pacific Peace Congress to be held in Peking in October. After a briefing by her case officer, she reported to the SA branch of the CPA that the Sydney experience had "inspired and enthused" her and, if it could be arranged, she was keen to attend the conference in Peking. Owing, at least in part, to her stated intention to pay her own way (ASIO had in fact provided £400), a meeting of the SA Peace Council Executive on 18 May officially nominated Neill as one of its two representatives to the main conference.[35] It was in this context of Neill assuming an international role that ASIO initiated Operation Hunter and began employing its nascent tradecraft. Only the DG and five ASIO officers were aware of this top-secret operation, and Spry issued instructions not to discuss the case with any other ASIO officer; "the utmost security is vital to safeguard the individual [Neill] concerned."[36] Her imminent attendance represented a breakthrough. ASIO had closely monitored delegates to the Peking Congress and advised the Menzies government on the issuing of passports.[37] But as a source *within* the delegation – especially one who then believed she was on "very friendly terms" with the CPA state secretary and "more popular [with leading CPA members] than ever before"[38] – Neill could provide invaluable intelligence. ASIO tasked its agent with several priorities, including reporting on the congress itself and on "delegates using the Congress as a cover means for other meetings."[39]

But Operation Hunter had another aim: "the long-term penetration of THORNTON." Ernie Thornton, a powerful member of the Central Committee of the CPA,[40] was then based in Peking (1950–3) as the representative of the Australian and Asian liaison bureau of the World Federation of Trade Unions. Spry suggested that Thornton "might brief subject [Neill] to undertake missions in ports along the return sea route."[41] Neill was instructed to remain in Peking after the congress to establish contact with Thornton "either direct or through his wife" and to "give him any assistance he might ask of her."[42] Because she would be contacting a station officer, most likely from the overseas agency, the Australian Secret Intelligence Service, in Hong Kong (for limited debriefing, the copying of congress documents, and any financial assistance if required), "Notes for Contacting Officers" were compiled. In these notes, Neill was described as

> of genteel background and probably enjoys the feeling of importance this type of work gives her. She has a natural veneer of a "fluttery old lady" behind which lies a shrewd and intelligent mind. A contacting officer must be prepared to withstand with patience and interest an hour's minor feminine utterance to obtain one-half hour's intelligence.[43]

The DG was more generous and clear-sighted than his ASIO subordinate when he drew attention to the all-important relationship between the agent and the contacting officer, implicit in the last sentence:

> I would like to stress that this lady has, out of the best motives, done a magnificent job on our behalf and should not be treated as an experienced paid agent. The point of a contacting officer withstanding with patience and interest extraneous utterances to obtain intelligence is most important.[44]

In the end, however, only eight delegates (several with British passports) managed to reach Peking. Anne Neill was not one of them. The Menzies government reversed its policy and announced it would deny passports and/or order return all passports issued to delegates seeking to attend this congress.[45] Afterwards, Neill was bedridden with pleurisy, caused, so her case officer believed, "by the terrific strain imposed on her by the Peking operation." The controller, Special Services Section (SSS), Bob Rodger, recommended to Spry that he write a personal note expressing his appreciation of both her efforts to get to Peking and how "awful it must be to deal with the wretched people in the Communist Party," parenthetically adding, "she really hates these people and only associates with them on our behalf."[46]

Operation Elmtree

Neill's undoubted worth to ASIO was confirmed by her next major assignment: a visit behind enemy lines. This was the very first time an ASIO operative, embedded in a communist delegation, not only had access to the international peace movement but entered countries that were the "denied areas" for Western intelligence. Operation Elmtree was ASIO's code for Neill's attendance at the Third World Peace Congress (WPC) in Vienna, her visit to Moscow, and her return to Australia via communist China. It was an operation fraught with danger. If her cover were blown and she was arrested, she would probably have suffered the same fate as 104 informers, mainly Austrian: they were sentenced to death and executed in Vienna and Moscow between 1950 and 1953.[47]

A meeting of the state executive of the SA branch of the CPA on 1 October 1952 decided that two delegates from SA should go to the Vienna conference, to be held on 12–20 December 1952. It recommended that Neill (after being nominated by the SA Peace Council) be one of the delegates on the proviso that she pay her own expenses. Her willingness to do so was a factor in the CPA leadership's approval of her nomination. The DG approved the transfer of £350 from the SSS to the SA regional director (to cover ship, train, and accommodation expenses, later increased to £500) on 10 October. [48] Her case officer believed that she had "the sincere backing" of the senior members of the Communist Party; as Elliott Johnston told a special council meeting of the SA Peace Council executive, "We are very happy to have Mrs. NEILL going; she has done splendid work for the Council." This was reiterated by four other speakers: "I don't know how we would have got on without her," "It's about time Mrs. NEILL's work was recognised," and "The Council would not be functioning if it had not been for Mrs. NEILL."[49]

Anne Neill was assigned the cover name, "Winston," by the SA office; her case officer, Rod Allanson, was "personally very satisfied that E.J. [Elliott Johnston] or the Party will not demand that Winston's bookings be used by any other person who may be considered 'more suitable' … E.J. is arranging a farewell party for her late in October – another good omen I think." Equally comforting was the fact that Winston was "calm and collected" about the whole operation.[50] In fact, she was happy to speak at a public meeting in Adelaide to promote the Vienna conference. However, the first of many concerns about her cavalier approach to security was aired: she had "so much contempt for the [Communist] Party that she absolutely ignores them and refuses to bother with security precautions." There was also a concern about overconfidence: "Source was not at all worried" and said she had "the whole situation under control."[51] Her case officer felt obliged to remind her of the importance ASIO attached to the trip and the "folly" of risking its compromise so soon before departure. The DG, Colonel Spry, was also advised of these concerns, and he wrote Neill a personal note that impressed upon her the need to take every precaution "at this critical stage."[52] One such precaution was the avoidance of daytime contact meetings. After a subsequent two-hour evening contact in the Adelaide Hills, at which Neill handed over seven reports, her case officer, Allanson, noted that she was "now more conscious regarding security precautions."[53] She was given comprehensive briefing instructions separately (under the rubrics intelligence, operational, financial, precautionary, and general) that detailed ASIO's aims and expectations of Operation Elmtree. These instructions included collecting data for pen portraits and character assessments of the Australian delegates, and the part played by the Russian delegates.[54] Finally, Allanson, who had been running Neill from the outset, visited her: "It was felt that in view of the long period during which Mr. ALLANSON had been handling Source, this would do much to give her confidence before she left."[55] It would appear that Allanson shared at least some of the qualities that characterized the exemplary or "great" case officer.[56]

Neill departed Adelaide on the *Oronsay* on 30 October 1952, bound for Vienna via Marseilles. She posted several letters to her sister in Adelaide concerning her travels and her general well-being. She believed, naively, that incoming letters were censored "but not outgoing."[57] This letter writing greatly alarmed the SA regional director: "Source is taking a grave risk (*contrary to briefing instructions*), in writing all these details in letters." To preserve "Source's protection from compromise," it was recommended that the letters be retained by the SSS controller until Neill returned and was debriefed. Only then would relevant information be released to "consumer sections," as originally intended.[58] Spry was informed of this breach of instructions but believed little remedial action could be taken.[59] What we have here is the conundrum for ASIO of an untrained agent disobeying briefing instructions, undoubtedly unintentionally, when beyond the reach of her case officer. Despite Spry's concern that her cover could be compromised – he referred to the need to "assess any damage done" when she re-entered the "target circles"[60] – she was not suspected, then, by anyone in the CPA or the Peace Council.

The apotheosis of Neill's success as an ASIO agent was her visit to Moscow in December 1952. Photographs of her in Red Square, in the Moscow Underground, and greeting the vice-president of VOKS (the Soviet organization that monitored foreign visitors) accompanied the four articles she wrote for the Adelaide *Sunday Mail* in December 1961. From Moscow she travelled across Siberia and arrived in Peking on 17 January 1953. As in Russia, she met numerous committees, groups, and organizations in China.[61] She also met Ernie Thornton, the aforementioned target of Operation Hunter. Before her departure by boat, in another breach of security, she informed the Australian trade commissioner in Hong Kong that she had been "a secret agent at the Vienna Peace Congress for A.S.I.O."[62] The commissioner was "extremely suspicious" of her "outrageous" (but accurate) claim and requested ASIO investigate.[63] She returned to Sydney on 22 February 1953 and, because of the possibility of compromise, a contingency plan was used. Her case officer rendezvoused with Neill in her cabin aboard the *Anshun*, and she handed over eighty-two pages of notes. Another ASIO officer conducted counter-surveillance. On disembarkation, with the active cooperation of two customs officials, her "large dress basket full of literature etc." was quickly cleared through customs. She was taken to a local hotel, and the bulky literature was forwarded to the Sydney office for transfer to HQ.[64]

In what was to become a regular refrain, Neill's case officer commented that, although fatigued, "subject's morale is very high" and she was very keen "to pursue his [sic] activities as soon as possible."[65] On the other hand, he was clearly perturbed by her "complete disregard for his original briefing" by making detailed notes of her activities on the trip; obtaining autographs; writing letters to her sister; and her indiscretion with the trade commissioner. He believed the first two, in particular, "could only have aroused suspicion" but acknowledged that the possibility of compromise was less than first feared. Neill was briefed on the following: to be on the alert for communists' "traps"; if accused of working for ASIO to deny such accusations "without equivocation"; to desist from talking on the phone to anyone concerning her activities overseas; and to rest completely for three weeks, during which *"no contact"* by the Adelaide office would be made and no activity for the CPA would be undertaken.[66] On 5 March, the DG wrote to Anne Neill. Its positive tone certainly should have boosted her morale:

> I was most happy to learn of your safe return and would like to express my admiration for the way you have carried out a most difficult and trying assignment. I have kept an anxious watch on your progress and hope that the wonderful results you have obtained have not impaired your health.[67]

Neill underwent two lengthy debriefings. The first took place in a safe house in Melbourne in early March and was conducted by the Controller, Special Services Section, and a Miss Fookes (name not redacted), also from the SSS. It lasted a week. A huge volume of information was handed over, and the long processing time required delayed the second debriefing. This occurred in Neill's home in May, lasted three days, and was conducted by ASIO's Miss Fookes, who stayed with her (on the pretext of being a friend). Exacting security precautions under Operation Elmtree were recommended by Spry.[68]

From ASIO's perspective, Neill's various breaches of prearranged security protocol were amply compensated for by the value of her "product." She had returned to Australia with a detailed report on the WPC in Vienna containing evidence of the Soviets' guiding hand, copies of WPC speeches, handwritten notes, photographs, circulars distributed to delegates, and information on various Australian delegates. She was assiduous and prolific. In addition, she gathered communist-authorized documents on the alleged American use of germ warfare in Korea (a "vile accusation," made repeatedly in Vienna, which "nauseated" Neill), on the Korean armistice negotiations, and on the Rudolf Slansky trial in Czechoslovakia. She also collected numerous Soviet and Chinese Communist Party pamphlets. Neill therefore provided ASIO with rare inside intelligence of the "other side," which was highly valued by HQ and the British and American security services. As Spry wrote to his SA regional director, "the information collected from him [sic] has been much appreciated by this organisation and overseas agencies."[69]

Anne Neill's trip behind the iron and bamboo curtains ensured that she was in strong demand as a speaker at CPA meetings throughout 1953. As one party leader remarked, "Comrade Anne is one of the few lucky comrades who has visited the Soviet."[70] Neill told her case officer on 21 July 1953 – and he believed in the veracity of her assessment (she is "rarely wrong") – that "it seems to me that I have gained a new status in the Party."[71] Such status, reportedly, was confirmed by the following. The CPA national president, J.B. Miles, made it "very clear" to a cadres' meeting that Neill was "largely responsible" for the "good work" of the SA Peace Council.[72] The SA state secretary, Eddie Robertson, declared, "You are one of our most important cadres at present."[73] The SA state president, Jim Moss, stated at the Adelaide Section Committee meeting on 9 September 1954 – infiltrated by another ASIO agent, who reported on her, unaware of her double role – that "Anne Neill is a very good mass worker who has done excellent work." Significantly for ASIO, in terms of higher-level penetration, he added, "she could be considered for appointment on the next Branch executive."[74] In short, Neill was proving a highly valuable agent, providing a window into CPA operations of which ASIO had scant knowledge. In mid-July 1953, her case officer reported: "She is working better than ever before. Her enthusiasm and facility for obtaining information from many different people in many different ways has been exemplified by the volume of material she has obtained during the last three weeks."[75]

This trend continued. In September 1953 she travelled to Sydney to attend and report on the Australian Convention on Peace and War. The reports she delivered detailed the communist involvement in the peace convention consistently alleged by the Menzies government.[76] It was in this period, in the spring of 1953, that ASIO agent, Michael Bialoguski was intensifying his efforts to precipitate the defection of Vladimir Petrov, ostensibly third secretary of the Soviet embassy since February 1951 but in fact a colonel in the Ministry of State Security (MGB). And when Petrov did defect, on 3 April 1954, there were profound consequences not only for the Western intelligence community, but also for Anne Neill.

Interrogations, 1954

Because of her Moscow visit, Neill was invited to attend the Soviet National Day celebrations in Canberra on 7 November 1953.[77] At the reception she met Petrov and Nikolai Generalov, the Soviet ambassador to Australia, and Petrov invited her to the Soviet embassy to collect a gift that Generalov had promised her. Presumably, both found her, as John Sendy had, "quite charming." Neill and Petrov talked alone in his office for half an hour. She, in turn, invited him to address a meeting of the Australian–Soviet Friendship Society (which she had helped establish) in Adelaide. She also invited him and his wife, Evdokia, to stay at her Adelaide home. Petrov wrote to her on 4 December and suggested the invitation be deferred for "a month or two."[78] He gave no reason but, as we now know, he was moving closer, and inexorably, towards defection.[79]

When Menzies announced Petrov's defection in the federal Parliament on 13 April 1954, Neill was travelling to Sydney to attend the national meeting of the New Theatre League, on which she provided a "comprehensive" report.[80] On 14 April she met Jean Ferguson (one of Petrov's contacts within the CPA and soon to be a controversial witness in the Royal Commission on Espionage); Ferguson expressed "amazement" over Neill's prior association with Petrov. This was later echoed by a UAW official: "Did you really meet him, and are you sure it was Petrov?"[81] The leadership of the CPA was less awestruck and began two interrogations into her meeting with Petrov. It should be noted that these interrogations may have been influenced by a heightened security consciousness. In 1953, J.D. Blake (CPA Central Committee Secretariat) urged a "tightening up of Party discipline ... on the lines developed by the C.P.S.U. [Communist Party of the Soviet Union]" and to "exercise extreme vigilance to unearth enemies of the Party within the Party."[82] Concern with security was not misplaced. The number of ASIO penetration agents inside the CPA had risen from two in 1950 to forty-three in 1954, with another thirty-five inside front organizations.[83] Anne Neill was penetrating both.

The first interrogation, instructed by the CPA Central Committee, was held on 28 April 1954 in the office of the state secretary, Eddie Robertson, with a "distinctly unfriendly" Elliott Johnston present. ASIO now believed her exposure and expulsion were imminent. The door was locked and barred, she was seated in front of a bright light, and the interview lasted a full two hours. It was *Darkness at Noon* down under. The interrogation was not scheduled, so her case officer was unable to brief her. We are able to discern the content of the discussion because ASIO had planted a listening device and a twelve-page transcript resulted. She was asked about her family, specifically her sister, who lived with her; how and why she joined six front organizations (she was questioned on each); why she went to the Vienna Congress, the Youth Carnival, and the Convention on War and Peace; how and why she became interested in the Communist Party; the purpose of her visit to Melbourne after the Sydney trip in September (when she was actually debriefed by ASIO); and detailed questions about her meeting with Petrov, how she got the invitation to the embassy, her opinion of him, what names were mentioned, and when she first knew of his defection ("You didn't know anything about it before? You didn't know it was going to happen?"). Throughout these questions, sometimes peppered with suspicions – such as "That doesn't tally with something we were told from Sydney" – Neill kept her nerve. Her responses were highly plausible and specific in detail, and recalled earlier conversations she had had with Johnston (who repeated, "Yes, that's right"). She demonstrated a steely resolve and much resilience under considerable pressure.

But she was also asked for financial details: her income, exactly how much she received from her war widow's pension ("That's not much to live on," Robertson commented), and how she could have paid for the Vienna–Moscow–Peking trip herself. On this last point, Neill stumbled. As we have seen, ASIO paid for the trip, and her cover story – an insurance payout after her husband died – was vague: "I can't give you any particulars." When asked to bring in a copy of the letter from either the company or her solicitor confirming the insurance money, she replied, "I might have burnt it."[84] It was ASIO funding that could link her to

ASIO, and her interrogators knew it. And so did ASIO, which feared this information would connect her to Petrov:

> Although it is probable that the C.P. of A. is endeavouring to obtain information to discredit PETROV, it is not improbable that [blank] will be discovered as an A.S.I.O. agent as a result of JOHNSTON's demand for [blank] to produce positive evidence on finance matters. Should this be the case it is possible that [blank] will come under suspicion as the person who induced PETROV to defect.[85]

Source protection became paramount.[86] This was the weak link in the chain, and ASIO acted to remove the danger of compromise. It contacted two people: Neill's solicitor, who was "quite prepared" to state, if questioned, that he had informed his client that insurance money was payable in August 1952; and a cooperative friend (Arthur Owen), who was prepared to state either that he wrote a cheque to pay for Neill's fare overseas or, "as a last resort," provided her with cash. This strategy was both risky and desperate. Unsurprisingly, a marginal note from HQ warned, "Make sure this matter is fully insulated so that there is no possible chance of perjury."[87] Elliott Johnston subsequently raised again the provision of the insurance documents, which Neill attempted to sidestep with the Arthur Owen story ("You can ring Arthur for the cheque number"; Johnston refused), but his insistence on written evidence suggested to ASIO that "he has found a flaw in Source's story." Neill was advised by her case officer to "avoid contact with JOHNSTON" and, if this were not possible or if Johnston persisted, "*Threaten* to resign from the C.P. of A. and frontal organisations, and indicate indignation at the continual questioning."[88] When she did this, and affected righteous indignation and anger that she should be under suspicion, Johnston responded as ASIO predicted with "Now, don't be upset, don't get angry, all I want is that written paper to prove where you got that money from."[89] She played for time, and got it. Her ruse, recommended by her case officer, had, for the moment, worked.

The second interrogation was conducted at the CPA HQ, again with no warning, two days after the first, on 30 April 1954. It was conducted by Jessie Grant, a member of the CPA's Central Control Commission (responsible for internal security, party discipline, and the illegal apparatus) and secretary to Lance Sharkey, CPA general secretary. The interview focused primarily on Petrov and the associated possibility that Neill may be called before a proposed Royal Commission on Espionage (RCE). Her answers, which duplicated those she had given to Robertson and Johnston, apparently satisfied Grant.[90] However, Neill's health was a casualty. Within the space of two days, she had undergone a two-hour grilling, a three-hour briefing with the ASIO group,[91] a long meeting/dinner with Marjorie Johnston that Neill apparently recorded,[92] and the interview with a party apparatchik from Sydney. Not surprisingly, according to her case officer, "Source is showing definite signs of the strain [and] is having disturbed and intermittent sleep."[93]

For much of May 1954, Neill was sick (she contracted a severe, prolonged bout of influenza), her morale was low, and her contact with both the Communist Party and ASIO was minimal. According to CPA state secretary Robertson, with the "indignities" of appearing before both the State Committee and the Control Commission, "she could have told the Party to 'get …'[sic]."[94] She, of course, did not. When she returned to the CPA offices on 25 August, she was confident that she had "passed the test"; however, the regional director was less sanguine, noting that the production of written evidence was "still a moot point with the C.P.A. Executive," referring to the possibility of entrapment and believing her expulsion was still possible.[95] On 27 May her case officer noted that both her health and mental attitude had improved, and that he found it "difficult to restrain [blank] from returning to his [sic] former active role."[96] She began working long hours on the preparation of all the costumes for the New Theatre's June production of Reedy River but by mid-June was "feeling the strain" and developed acute laryngitis.[97] After the production, Johnston complimented her on her hard work, and she was convinced "his former animosity had abated."[98] By early July, it seemed, Neill had come in from the cold: an ASIO memorandum outlined several items of evidence confirming that "Source has been re-instated in the Party Executive's confidence."[99] In September, representing a major achievement for ASIO, she was appointed a delegate to the CPA State Conference. This would yield up-to-date intelligence on personnel and policies, and in the words of the SA regional director, would constitute "a grand finale for Operation 'Swan.'"[100]

Anne Neill had survived this testing interrogation. A combination of her calm steadfastness in the face of interrogation, the careful handling and shrewd advice by her case officer, and the stonewalling of repeated requests to supply documentary proof ensured that her cover was secure. Despite an earlier ASIO assessment that "the effective life of this source must now be drawing to a close,"[101] Neill was not ready to relinquish her full-time life as an undercover agent. She was not interested in any "grand finale" in 1954. Instead, she resumed her intelligence-gathering activities with gusto – more than desired by her case officer – and simultaneously began to write a book on her experiences since she had commenced working for ASIO in June 1950. This was Operation Swan.

Operation Swan, 1954–1955

With Colonel Spry's approval, HQ requested Neill to write this book. Factors influencing this decision were manifold. The principal one was that she "came very close to being exposed" and that her days as an effective source were limited. Other factors included her "outstanding success as a source"; her accurate and well-written reports; her association with a "great number" of prominent communists across Australia; and her trip to Vienna, Moscow, and Peking; as well as the fact that this "white-haired old lady had deluded hard-bitten Communists for five years."[102] Neill (or "Winston," her operational cover name) readily accepted, "like a good soldier."[103] The objectives of Operation Swan were grandiose: to ridicule the party leadership and discredit party members and supporters; expose the methods of the CPA to achieve its far-reaching plans, especially its use of front organizations; highlight the fraudulence of the CPA-controlled peace organization; and emphasize the direction of the CPA from Moscow. A subsidiary aim was "to enable WINSTON to return to a normal life and again take rightful place in the community." In essence, it was to be a "spoiling" operation, designed to "set the Party back for a number of years by throwing it into confusion and forcing it to re-organise completely."[104]

To achieve these significant ends, detailed plans were drawn up: a three-page outline of sixteen events and numerous identified personalities "worthy" of discussion was produced; a "safe house" in Adelaide was secured, where the writing would occur with the assistance of a secretary and typist; her first case officer, now based in Melbourne, was to brief her for two days in Adelaide and discuss the draft plan with her current case officer; Neill would visit ASIO HQ in Melbourne every two months for consultation; and funds were allocated for operational expenses. Knowledge of Swan was to be highly restricted. It was envisaged that Neill would be preoccupied with the book for eight months and resign from the CPA just before publication. She was to avoid expulsion from the party in this period, during which she must take "special security precautions." Each chapter would be sent to HQ for editing, and "all assistance" would be given regarding provision of files and documentary evidence (photographs, names, dates, meetings attended). Publication was to coincide with the conclusion of the RCE "so as to force further troubles onto a seriously worried organisation." To gain the widest circulation, the book would be published in the UK.[105]

Notwithstanding these well-laid plans, Operation Swan failed. It was due not to mishandling by ASIO but to Neill's deficiencies as a writer. After submitting draft chapters for editing, she visited the Melbourne offices (1–5 November). Some criticisms of her writing style were made by the officer in charge,[106] who dictated passages to provide a model to emulate. She took umbrage:

> Your style of writing, as dictated to me, is very good journalism. Mine is simply the ability ... to tell a story. I state that without egotism. I have a First Prize from the Ballarat Literary Competitions to substantiate this claim ... either the whole book must be dictated by you in which case it would not be my book, because, it stands to reason a middle-aged woman does not write like a young man – or I must write it all myself.[107]

She met with her Adelaide case officer, Senior Field Officer (SFO) "Q," who confirmed that she was very "steamed up" and recommended that it was "advisable to handle her feelings more gently." He reported that "she feels that it is well-nigh impossible for a woman of her age to alter her style of writing, or to combine her style with that of Mr. [blank]." According to the SA regional director (RD), the position of SFO "Q" was "an unenviable one," but the RD suggested to HQ that she should continue to "let off steam" to him since this could influence the quality of her future contributions. Lacking any book-writing experience, SFO "Q" was instructed to not participate in any Operation Swan briefings and to act only as a conduit between Neill and HQ; otherwise she may "terminate her confidence" in him.[108] "Mac" from ASIO HQ wrote to "Winston" on 15 November. The tone was "gentle" and conciliatory – "We are all rather 'green' at book-writing and I think we must expect to encounter growing pains" – and a plan of action granting Neill greater ownership over the writing style was proposed. It concluded, "Please do not worry yourself too much about these early problems. We have every confidence in you."[109]

However, these "early problems" persisted. By early February 1955, Colonel Spry, who was closely monitoring Operation Swan, had read the near-complete manuscript, made numerous deletions, and considered it unsuitable for publication in its present form. He recommended that Michael Thwaites, when available, should rewrite it "to bring it up to the required standard." "Winston" was not to be informed of this.[110] Thwaites, a former lecturer in English at the University of Melbourne and now director of B2 (counter-espionage), was at this time "wrestling" with writing the Petrovs' story. He had to work "long and patiently" because they had "no idea whatsoever of arranging the [diverse] elements into a coherent whole."[111] He completed his "ghost-ing" in the winter of 1955, and the book was published in London in 1956 as *Empire of Fear*.[112] So Spry knew that "an experienced writer of Mr. Thwaites' calibre" could transform Neill's book.[113] The SSS control-ler agreed. Neill, he wrote, was "incapable" of holding the interest of the reader. In a damning comment, he stated, "Her style is something like that of Ethel M. Dell."[114] His final point signalled the death knell: "If a ghost writer cannot be provided a pretext will be decided upon to advise [blank] to abandon the operation."[115]

Whether or not Thwaites refused this commission – which he had when requested to write a refutation of Bialoguski's book[116] – is un-clear, but on 25 May 1955, Spry recommended that the operation "be postponed for an indefinite period, probably forever." In addition to the quality of the book, another more recent consideration was the threat of libel action by persons mentioned in the book, and "in order to write the book names must be mentioned."[117] The manuscript of *Empire of Fear* was then being subjected to intense legal scrutiny, and an entire chapter concerning Petrov's work in Australia was deleted to circum-vent potential libel suits.[118]

These legal difficulties were personally explained to Neill by the re-gional director on 1 June 1955. He also emphasized the associated stress and embarrassment to her if libel action were brought, and the personal desire of the DG to minimize her anxiety,[119] which was not without ba-sis: her case officer was concerned about her "very poor state of health" and noted that she was "under definite Doctor's orders to refrain from any anxiety." He conveyed the "pleasure" of HQ at her advancement in the Communist Party to the level of the State Committee and wished her to continue this operational progress, albeit with "added security precautions." The RD reported that Neill accepted this "without argu-ment or discontent." Indeed, she realized the many possibilities of her new role within the CPA and "began to reel off a number of lines of action to be followed."[120] The RD remarked on her "strong sense of loyalty ... to this Organisation and Australia." He anticipated that Neill would "apply the same energy" to her new role within the CPA as she had in her past one.[121] Her acceptance of the closure of Operation Swan was helped by a personal letter dated 6 June (to "Dear Mrs. Winston") from Spry that the RD delivered (and retained, as was customary, for security reasons); a "courtesy I appreciate to the full," she wrote back.[122] But six months later, Colonel Spry's assessment had changed. Although he proposed giving her a Christmas gift (up to £5) because of her "ster-ling and loyal efforts over a very long period," he considered her value as an agent to be diminishing: "A replacement for her is obviously an urgent necessity."[123] At the same time, her case officer discerned that Neill was "harbouring a definite hurt" by the decision to close down Operation Swan; she told him, "I can't understand Mr. O'LEARY'S suggestion that Headquarters feared I might be involved in a libel case."[124] She was deliberately kept ignorant of the legal issues that swirled around the Petrovs' book and of the critical assessment of her first draft.

Neill's case officer's comments during this period are especially pertinent to understanding ASIO tradecraft and the difficulties and complexities of handling undercover agents. Psychological insight, empathy, and an ability to foretell and, if required, modify future behaviour are some of the necessary attributes. The assessment is worth quoting at length:

> The life of this Source is obviously drawing to a close in more ways than one, and the urgency of obtaining a "stand in" to cover the multitude of Frontal Organisations etc. is made very apparent by her present attitude. Her disappointment at the cessation of her literary effort and the almost "countless hours of unproductive time" spent on this project, have no doubt contributed in a greater degree to her "browned off" attitude than any other factor.
>
> Repeated briefings to restrict activities to certain important factors are to no avail and as long as this Source is operating she will continue to work at full speed and with complete disregard for personal comfort and senility. It is this Case Officer's opinion that [blank] will, at the end of the month's rest [from 16 December 1955] come up again full of enthusiasm and the will to carry on. The question is which will happen first, her death; her possible compromise through tiredness; or the eventual possibility … of her souring and resigning too suddenly from C.P. of A. activities, because of frustration following inability to clear her name through her book and return to L.C.L. circles – an obviously underlying ambition.

A handwritten postscript was added: "A woman of her age and with such a strong personality could react strongly if this feeling of frustration plays on her mind."[125]

Post-Swan, 1956–1957

Despite Spry's order to find a replacement, Anne Neill was not replaced. There was no "souring," and her "will to carry on" was revived. She continued, indefatigably, as an undercover penetration agent for another two and a half years. A regular stream of reports was handed to her third case officer throughout 1956 recording meetings and personnel of the CPA and its front organizations. These included reports on John Sendy (nineteen pages of notes), the Australian Assembly for Peace in Sydney (on which she wrote 18,600 words), and the SA Peace Conference (for which she produced an "excellent coverage" of seventy-five pages).[126] There were also reports on matters as diverse as the *Tribune* fair, Professor Marcus Oliphant, CPA "plans" for the Olympic Games, and CPA reactions to the Hungarian Uprising.

By late 1956, Neill was again feeling the strain of her heavy, self-imposed workload. She told her case officer, "It has been suggested to me many times that I must give up some of the work I am doing, but in Communist organisations it is *not* possible to do so."[127] She was unable to take a holiday, she said, because of the large number of meetings she had to attend.[128] Once again her case officer urged her to ease up, although he also told her that she *"was* indispensable" and her worth was "well known" by HQ.[129] The difficulties in transitioning to a new case officer emerged in November. Neill rang the wife of her second case officer (the handover to the third occurred on 14 July 1956), with whom a "bond of friendship" had developed over the years. She told the wife that she "could not understand why I [the case officer] had not rung her" and "now feels completely lost." He sought direction from the controller, SSS, regarding the attitude his wife should adopt and how he should best avoid "undermining the control of the present Case Officer."[130]

By the beginning of 1957, this former case officer was based at the Melbourne HQ. His communication with Neill, after consulting with the new RD SA (D.A. McDermott), was a model of careful and sensitive case handling. He telephoned her on 25 April 1957 and apologized for failing to meet her on Christmas 1956, "when I was busy packing up my furniture etc. preparatory to my move to Melbourne." He tried to convince her that her belief that he had "given her away" was unfounded and that it was poor policy for former case officers to interfere with sources once handed over to a new case officer. She replied, "If they would let me see Mr. [Allanson] why could I not see you!" She also told him that their close understanding built up over the past four years "would never be replaced." It was then time to assuage her sense of loss. He conveyed a personal message from Colonel Spry, which expressed his "sincere appreciation for her continued and vigorous efforts on ASIO's behalf" and to which she "voiced her pleasure." The former case officer reassured her that over time, a close bond with her current case officer would "eventually exist" and added that he "would always look back on my association with her as an absolute honour and an inspiration to me."[131]

Reinvigorated by Spry's letter, Anne Neill immersed herself in a wide range of CPA activities. One was a cadres' meeting on 21 August, for which she was instructed to "act strictly in accordance with briefing."[132] She was also keen to be more active in a B2 sphere "directly associated with Russia"[133] – she still wished to expose Russian espionage in Australia – and was convinced, after being asked to become secretary of the Australian-Soviet Friendship Society, that "this is not time for me to walk out of the Party."[134] Her new case officer made sure he generously acknowledged her productivity:

> When not attending meetings, Source has spent most of the past week writing out her report on the Nat. Peace Conf. This totals 80 handwritten pages. Case Officer spent approx. 3 hours reading through this in torch light and questioning Source for additional details etc., not forgetting to congratulate her in suitable terms on one more excellent effort.[135]

His final contact with Neill in 1957 followed the CPA State Conference; Neill attended every session over the three days. Because of heightened CPA security precautions, she refrained from taking any notes: "This was impressed on Source at several contacts prior to the Conf. and by phone every day during it." Despite this impediment, she provided a voluminous amount of "most valuable" information, especially on CPA identities. This constituted intelligence, according to the case officer, "not yet achieved by any other Source" and was "due entirely to her unique perceptive ability and shrewd observations." Her "fine effort" was again congratulated.[136] The assessment by the Russian imperial security service in 1911 of Anna Serebryakova, a model agent for the Moscow Okhrana, could easily have applied to Anne Neill: "As a secret penetration agent she had connections with the leaders of many subversive organizations ... Her motivation for hard work came from her strong personal convictions ... having little interest in monetary remuneration ... Despite the emotional and spiritual conflicts she had to suppress unshared with anyone, her devotion to duty never failed."[137]

1958: Exfiltration from the Communist Party

Within two days in late May 1958, two very different reports were submitted to the SA RD. One, from Neill's case officer, was by now very familiar: it itemized the "intelligence production" (twelve items) and commented that "Source has been working almost day and night for a fortnight." The other, by a "Q" agent training officer, was highly disturbing and ultimately put an end to Neill's continuing role. It reported a conversation between an unidentified agent, probably a woman, and Annie Sendy, mother of John, on 29 May. It is rare for an agent to participate in such a confidential conversation. Deep suspicions about Neill's links to ASIO were voiced, even far more troubling than the questions four years earlier. The issue of her financial status was once again revived. Sendy told the double agent that Neill was

> in everything ... [She] goes about getting information from people and she is so charming and so nice about it ... She gets paid to do it. Actually, I hate mentioning the word, but it is Security ... She was put on to me by Security. She must know that I spoke to John about it ... John said, "Look, Mum, there is nothing we can do at present ... [but] we will hold her back from getting in too far" ... We know she only gets a widow's pension, yet she can have a trip abroad ... I couldn't do it. How does she do it? She is always ready to pay her payments to the Party. She will give anything to the Party. You or I couldn't do it ... We are watching her closely now. John has suspected her for some time, but it is only recently that he told me that he was now fairly certain about it.[138]

This conversation was assessed by ASIO as "a most important one" – indeed, one that should be brought to the DG's "personal attention."[139]

Accordingly, on 9 July Spry sent a memorandum headed "SOURCE CONTROL" to all eight regional directors across Australia. It summarized the basis for CPA suspicion of "a Source who has been active for many years": overzealousness in courting information; paying dues and levies promptly, donating large amounts of money frequently, and travelling extensively, all considered to be inconsistent with financial circumstances; and calling upon other party members without invitations or logical excuses. Spry emphasized that, while these points had invariably been stressed by case officers, "this case is a reminder to ensure that all Sources are properly briefed and continually warned of actions which are likely to isolate them and endanger their roles." He also added that this case "forces home" the CPA's "ever-increasing security consciousness."[140]

The result of this conversation – and Neill remained blissfully unaware of the CPA's suspicions – was the decision taken by both the SA RD and HQ to withdraw her from operational activities. "This is obviously the end of the road and a long road it was too," commented an (unnamed) ASIO officer.[141] The DG similarly stated that the "overall situation" demanded that "Source should make a clean break from *all* activity."[142] Accordingly, her case officer briefed her on 23 June 1958 to "taper off" her involvement on the grounds of ill health. This diplomatic approach was helped, he believed, by the fortuitous fact that she had recently spent three days ill in bed.[143] But extricating this committed agent was not easy. At his next contact, the case officer reported in detail ("in view of the importance of this matter and in case lessons can be learned for the future") Neill's misgivings:

> Re this matter of my easing out. I don't know who was responsible for the plan, but I feel that Comrades do not leave the Party on account of illness. That's so unreal ... Even if you are sick, you still take your "Trib" and you still pay your dues. (Here, Source became somewhat emotional, but did not shed tears.) ... Not this illness business; it just won't work.[144]

Over the next three weeks in a succession of memoranda, a range of options were considered regarding the timing of and reasons for withdrawal. Several meetings, including one that lasted three hours, were held with Neill to canvass these options.[145] The complicated details need not concern us, but the eventual outcome was that she was briefed to inform party officials that the primary ground for dissociating herself from the CPA was the revival of her religious beliefs. This was not altogether disingenuous. Increasingly, she had been attending her revivalist church (the Commonwealth Revival Crusade) with her brother and sister; "frequently discussed" with her patient case officer the long-coming retribution to be visited on Russia, quoting freely from Ezekiel 39; and later spoke "at length and in detail" about the "miracles of faith healing" she had witnessed weekly in Adelaide.[146]

On 20 August 1958, Anne Neill formally notified the Adelaide branch of the CPA of her resignation. She had desired a phasing-out over a period of six months, with which her case officer had concurred. From a penetration operations angle, he argued, this plan would make her withdrawal "easier and comparatively unnoticed" while a replacement, under Operation Sparrow, was recruited. Thus, the exact date of her termination should be "flexible."[147] Spry would have none of this. Money was tight at ASIO HQ. On 8 July he wrote to the RD SA that because of "our close budget which promises to be a vital factor in this fiscal year," Neill was budgeted for only until 1 September and that her withdrawal should be finalized before then.[148] It wasn't, so the DG became blunter: "The brutal fact is that our finances are so acute that we cannot afford to pay a Source who is under Party suspicion and only in a position of restricted access to the target." He directed the RD to exfiltrate her according to the plan previously outlined.[149] He also attached a handwritten, signed letter of commendation, which the case officer was to show her, acknowledging and appreciating her "great personal sacrifice" and conveying his "sincere thanks for all the wonderful work ... since 1950."[150] This was followed by a formal letter from Spry, equally effusive, which Neill retained and later published:

> Over the years I have watched closely all the moves you have made and I must say the value of the information you have supplied to my Organisation can never be adequately assessed ... Your personal experience has been so great that we would like to benefit from it – and obtain your appreciation of certain matters ... Please accept my good wishes and appreciation for all you have done.[151]

This represented the conclusion of Neill's formal association with ASIO. She received her final payment on 28 August 1958 and was subsequently presented with an expensive cutlery set as a farewell gift – "a lasting token of our appreciation for her loyalty and long-devoted service."[152]

This chapter has found Hindersmann's judgment that the intelligence service was "willing to sacrifice the agent like a pawn in a chess game"[153] to be – at least in this instance – incorrect. ASIO closely observed, and gauged, Neill's physical and psychological well-being throughout the eight years she was its agent. It had not, as Hindersmann argued, "lost contact with feeling and humanity," nor had it yet become "an anonymous bureaucracy" ignorant of or unconcerned with the repercussions of its briefings and handling on her morale. She was reassured and acknowledged by the director general, who regularly assessed her progress, gave direction, and provided operational support. She gained his respect and he gained her loyalty. Well before the professionalization and expansion of ASIO, the officers' handling of her in the first decade of the organization's existence was characterized by shrewdness, wisdom, and sensitivity. They provided a bulwark against the isolation of agent work. Careful to praise her efforts and her sacrifice, they were rewarded with comprehensive reports, devotion to duty, and longevity of service. Operation Elmtree yielded rich intelligence, even if Hunter was thwarted and Swan was dropped. Neill joined a long tradition of spying on organizations deemed a threat to national security. Wherever targets are identified, and whenever willing recruits are found, agent penetration will always be a priority of security service intelligence work. As John le Carré, a former MI5 and MI6 case officer, wrote in 2017, "The practice of infiltrating spies into supposedly subversive organizations is as ancient as the hills."[154] And, thus, this practice continues today.

NOTES

1　*Report of Enquiry by Sir Norman Brook into the Secret Intelligence and Security Services,* 1951, TNA, CAB 301/17, National Archives (UK). The chapter title alludes to the greeting given by an ASIO officer to Anne Neill upon returning from Russia: "Our No. 1 Spy Has Come Home." *Herald* (Melbourne), 16 December 1961, 23.

2　See, for example, Angela Calomiris, *Red Masquerade: Undercover for the FBI* (Philadelphia: Lippincott, 1950); Herbert A. Philbrick, *I Led 3 Lives: Citizen, "Communist," Counterspy* (New York: McGraw-Hill, 1952); Harvey Matusow, *False Witness* (New York: Cameron & Kahn, 1955).

3　These include Amy J. Martin, "America's Evolution of Women and Their Roles in the Intelligence Community," *Journal of Strategic Security* 8, no. 5 (2015): 99–109; Martha Denny Peterson, *The Widow Spy: My CIA Journey from the Jungles of Laos to Prison in Moscow* (Wilmington, NC: Red Canary Press, 2012); Kathryn S. Olmstead, "Blond Queens, Red Spiders, and Neurotic Old Maids: Gender and Espionage in the Early Cold War," *Intelligence and National Security* 19, no. 1 (2004): 78–94; Sandra C. Taylor, "Long-Haired Women, Short-Haired Spies: Gender, Espionage, and America's War in Vietnam," *Intelligence and National Security* 13, no. 2 (1998): 61–70.

4　David McKnight, *Australia's Spies and Their Secrets* (Sydney: Allen & Unwin, 1994), 191–3; David Horner, *The Spy Catchers: The Official History of ASIO 1949–1963,* vol. 1 (Sydney: Allen & Unwin, 2014), 211–13, 406–9. The internal history of ASIO mentioned fleetingly her overseas trip: A6122, 2037, folio (f.) 56, National Archives of Australia (NAA).

5　Phillip Deery, "ASIO and the Communist Party: New Light on an Old Tradition," in *Labour Traditions: Proceedings of the 10th National Labour History Conference,* ed. Julie Kimber, Peter Love, and Phillip Deery (Melbourne: Australian Society for the Study of Labour History, 2007), 67–74; Phillip Deery "Double Agent Down Under: Australian Security and the Infiltration of the Left," *Intelligence and National Security* 22, no. 3 (2007): 346–66.

6　See, for example, Horner, *The Spy Catchers,* chapters 3, 6.

7　Jost Hindersmann, "'The Right Side Lost but the Wrong Side Won': John le Carré's Spy Novels before and after the End of the Cold War," *Clues: A Journal of Detection* 23, no. 4 (2005): 26.

8　As she wrote to her first case officer, "As I told you, I grew up in an atmosphere of orthodox Liberalism, and Christianity, and for years I conformed rigidly to the tenets of both of these philosophies." Letter, 19 May 1951, A6119, 4286, f. 11, NAA.

9　*Adelaide News,* 19 April 1945, 8.

10　*Chronicle* (Adelaide), 17 March 1949, 34.

11 This paragraph is primarily drawn from chapters 1–2 of her 268-page unpublished memoir, "The Universal Embrace," a copy of which was retained by ASIO; see A6119, 4289, NAA. It was first drafted in 1955, redrafted in 1964, and redrafted again in 1966.

12 Horner, *Spy Catchers*, 211–12.

13 See "The World Peace Council and the Australian Peace Council," M1505/1, 87, NAA; "History and Aims of the Soviet Peace Offensive," part 1, A1838/1/69/1/1/16/1, NAA; "The Peace Movement," part 5, A1838/1, 69/1/1/16/1, NAA; "Soviet Foreign Policy and the Peace Movement," A4311/5, 43/1, NAA; "The World Peace Council: Its History, Structure and Activities, 1947–54," part 1, A1838/2, 563/5, NAA; "The World Congress of Partisans for Peace," FO1110/271, NA [UK]; "The Soviet Peace Campaign," FO1110/349, NA; "Peace and Soviet Policy," FO975/50, NA; "The Record of the World Peace Council," FO975/54, NA.

14 *Commonwealth Parliamentary Debates*, 27 April 1950, 1995. See also David Lee, "The National Security Planning and Defence Preparations of the Menzies Government, 1950–53," *War and Society* 10, no. 2 (1992), 119–38.

15 "History of ASIO by Bob Swan, 47/2/170 Volume 1," A6122/49, 2022, f. 113, NAA.

16 Horner, *Spy Catchers*, 38–40, 45–51; [ASIO], "Chronological Note on the Establishment of the Australian Security Intelligence Organisation," August 1975, A12386, A/1, ff. 63–70, NAA; Chris Northcott, "The Role, Organization, and Methods of MI5," *International Journal of Intelligence and Counter-Intelligence* 20, no. 3 (2007), 453–79.

17 Colonel Longfield Lloyd, Director, CIS, to Secretary, Attorney-General's Department, "Transfer of Files to A.S.I.O.," 24 May 1950, A800, S8679, f. 93, NAA.

18 "History of ASIO, Volume 1."

19 Press release, Prime Minister's office, 15 August 1949; "Australian Security System 'Chaotic Farce,'" *Sydney Morning Herald*, 12 March 1950; "Intelligence Service Purge Begins," *Sydney Morning Herald*, 11 June 1950, in A432, 1955/4410 [nf], NAA. There were also overlap and duplication between the New South Wales Special Branch (specifically the Subversive Organisation and Intelligence Bureau) and ASIO; see "Overlapping Investigations," Detective Inspector A.A. Wilks to Deputy Director, CIS, Sydney, 26 July 1950, in CIS file marked M.S. 238 Vol. 3 (original copy of still-classified file, stamped Secret, covering March 1950 to February 1951, in author's possession).

20 "Operational Particulars," A6119, 4286, f. 12, NAA. The regional director, South Australia, added "hatred of Communism": TS. S.Pol.F.30/3, A6119, 4286, f. 7, NAA.

21 Johnston, who joined the CPA in 1941, was elected to the State Committee and Central Committee of the CPA in 1954. He became a Queen's Counsel in 1970, a Supreme Court judge in 1983 (the first communist ever on the bench), and a Royal Commissioner into Deaths in Custody in 1987. See Penelope Debelle, "Judge Red: The Communist on the Bench," *Adelaide Advertiser*, 24 February 2011.

22 Contact Sheet No. 1266, 17 July 1952, A6119, 4286, f. 45, NAA. Some of the fruits of her labours can be discerned, notwithstanding extensive redactions, in Johnston's ASIO files: A6119, 463, 464, 465, NAA.

23 "Universal Embrace," 258, in A6119, 4289, NAA.

24 Ibid., 28.

25 John Sendy, *Comrades Come Rally! Recollections of an Australian Communist* (Melbourne: Nelson, 1978), 116.

26 Penelope Debelle, *Red Silk: The Life of Elliott Johnston QC* (Adelaide: Wakefield Press, 2011), 56.

27 In a highly secret party directive, Sendy "went away" to a training school in Communist China: he was one of four trusted CPA cadres intended to be the nucleus of a new "leadership in exile" in the event that, in conditions of imminent illegality, the existing party leadership was incarcerated. Eric Aarons, *What's Left? Memoirs of an Australian Communist* (Ringwood [Victoria]: Penguin, 1993), 75; John Sendy, "Remembering China," *Eureka Street*, July/August 1999, 20–2.

28 Ibid., 33–4 (emphasis in original); "Brief Report on Conversation with E. Johnston, 27/7/51," A6119, 926, f. 28, NAA.

29 See [CPA], *Menzies' Secret Police—Threat to Democracy* (Newtown: R.S. Thompson, n.d.).

30 NAA: A6119, 5599; https://www.smh.com.au/national/a-spy-like-horrie-20131013-2vgbd.html.

31 *Adelaide Advertiser*, 14 February 1950, 10.

32 Letter to the Editor, "A Political Pamphlet," *Adelaide Advertiser*, 29 November 1949, 2.

33 Sendy, *Comrades Come Rally*, 116. One newspaper later described her as "a white-haired widow with a kind face. She could be the woman from the house across the corner." *Herald* (Melbourne), 14 December 1962, A6119, 932, f. 33, NAA. Much later, he referred (in an intercepted telephone call) to Neill as an "old bitch – she was so nice all the time." Intercept report, VIC W.469/59, AW 15, item 5, 2 August 1967, A6119, 4288, f. 136, NAA.

34 (T.S.) S.Pol. F/30/2, memorandum to Q. Section, 14 July 1952, A6119, 926, ff. 61–12, NAA. For a discussion of the carnival, see Phillip Deery, "Community Carnival or Cold War Strategy? The 1952 Youth Carnival for Peace and Friendship," in *Labour and Community: Historical Essays*, ed. Ray Markey (Wollongong: University of Wollongong Press, 2001), 313–45.

35 The preliminary conference was held in Peking in June; see Provisional Sponsoring Committee for the Asian and Pacific Peace Conference, *We Talked Peace with Asia* ([n.p.]: Sydney [1952]); J.P. Forrester, *Fifteen Years of Peace Fronts* ([n.p.]: Sydney, 1964), 23. *in the Pacific!* in ibid., f. 71; RD SA to HQ, 28 July 1952, ibid., f. 75.

36 DG memo, "Persons at A.S.I.O. HQ Conscious of Operation Hunter," 8 July 1952, A6119, 4286, f. 161, NAA. Spry was DG from July 1950 to January 1970.

37 See Phillip Deery and Craig McLean, "'Behind Enemy Lines': Menzies, Evatt and Passports for Peking," *The Round Table: The Commonwealth Journal of International Affairs* 92, no. 370 (2003): 407–22, especially 415–17.

38 Contact Sheet No. 1280, 21 July 1952, A6119, 4286, f. 43, NAA; Contact Sheet No. 1429, 26 September 1952, A6119, 4286, f. 56, NAA.

39 "Briefing by A.S.I.O. of Subject, 2nd July 1952," A6119, 4286, f. 14, NAA.

40 See, for example, his *The Communist Party and You* (Sydney: Current Book Distributors, 1958), highly praised by the CPA: *Tribune*, 18 February 1959, 5.

41 DG to M.O.9, 9 July 1952, A6119, 4286, f. 18, NAA.

42 "Briefing by A.S.I.O. of Subject, 2nd July 1952."

43 "Notes for Contacting Officers," (c) (ii) Subject: HUNTER, A6119, 4286, f. 15, NAA.

44 DG to M.O.9, 9 July 1952.

45 *Commonwealth Parliamentary Debates*, vol. 218, 10 September 1952, 1187; Deery and McLean, 'Behind Enemy Lines," 412–13.

46 R.H. Rodger to Spry, 19 September 1952, A6119, 4286, f. 51, NAA.

47 Barbara Stelzl-Marx, "Death to Spies! Austrian Informants for Western Intelligence Services and Soviet Capital Punishment during the Occupation of Austria," *Journal of Cold War Studies* 14, no. 4 (2012): 167–96.

48 A6119, 4287, ff. 1,4, 6, NAA.

49 Memorandum, Controller, 10 October, 2, SSS, A6119, 4287, f. 10, NAA. The controller was Ernest Wiggins.

50 Telegram, "Rod" [Allanson] to "Bob" [Rodger], "Personal + Secret," 7 October 1952, A6119, 4287, f. 3, NAA.

51 Contact Sheet, 30 October 1952, A6119, 4287, f. 21, NAA.

52 Contact Sheet No. 1517, 22 October 1952, A6119, 4287, f. 14, NAA.

53 Contact Sheet No. 1518, 24 October 1952, A6119, 4287, f. 13, NAA.

54 "Briefing Given to South Australian Source – Operation 'Elmtree,'" attached to Top Secret Minute, Controller, SSS to Director, B1, 30 October 1952, ff. 18–20. She had requested all briefing instructions earlier, since the "excitement" and CPA send-off celebrations "will make assimilation of such instructions difficult" if given too late. DG to HQ, 15 October 1952, A6119, 4287, f. 120, NAA.

55 Contact Sheet, No. [illegible], 30 October 1952, A6119, 4287, f. 21, NAA.

56 Joseph W. Wippl, "The Qualities That Make a Great Case Officer," *International Journal of Intelligence and CounterIntelligence* 25, no. 3 (2012): 595–603.

57 Letter, 29 November 1952, A6119, 4287, f. 23, NAA. Miss Parsons was aware of her sister's double life. During Anne's absence, her case officer from 6 November 1952 through 13 February 1953 phoned an anxious Parsons twice weekly (using a cover name) and, later, personally visited her weekly to "ease her mind." RD SA to HQ ASIO, 12 December 1952, f. 125; Contact Sheet, 6 March 1953, A6119, 4287, ff. 77–9, NAA.

58 RD SA to HQ, 18 December 1952, A6119, 4287, f. 24, NAA. Emphasis in original.

59 DG to RD, [n.d.] January 1953, A6119, 4287, f. 25, NAA.

60 DG to Controller, SSS, 12 January 1953, A6119, 4287, f. 30, NAA.

61 Her excessively detailed descriptions of her experiences in Vienna, Moscow, Peking, and Nanking can be found in chapters 9–15 of her "Universal Embrace."

62 RD to Controller, SSS, 10 February 1952, f. 46; Security Liaison Officer to DG, 12 February 1952, A6119, 4287, f. 47, NAA.

63 Spry to RD SA, 6 May 1953, A6119, 4287, f. 92, NAA.

64 SFO "Q" (Adelaide) to Controller, SSS [n.d.], Appendix A "Method Used in Carrying Out Operation," A6119, 4287, f. 52, NAA.

65 "His" was used for source protection.

66 SFO "Q" to Controller, SSS, A6119, 4287, f. 53, NAA. Emphasis in original.

67 Spry to Neill, 5 March 1953, A6119, 4287, f. 95, NAA.

68 DG to RD SA, 30 March 1953, A6119, 4287, f. 89, NAA.

69 DG to RD SA, May 1953, A6119, 932, f. 91, NAA.

70 Report No. 2835, 7 July 1954, A6119, 932, f. 13, NAA.

71 Contact Sheet No. 6, 24 July 1953, A6119, 927, f. 2, NAA.

72 Contact Sheet No. 6, 24 July 1953.

73 Contact Sheet No. 5, 15 July 1953, A6119, 927, f. 4, NAA. However, with the benefit of hindsight, Robertson later commented, "Her political level was not high and her contributions in discussion were never of a high level." Acting RD SA to HQ, 4 September 1958, A6119, 928, f. 205, NAA.

74 Report No. 3426, 26 October 1954, A6119, 927, f. 106, NAA.

75 Contact Sheet No. 5, 15 July 1953. At this contact, on the evening of 13 July, she delivered intelligence for no fewer than sixteen reports, numbered 2097–2113.

76 For a contrary view, see Phillip Deery, "War on Peace: Menzies, the Cold War and the 1953 Convention on Peace and War," *Australian Historical Studies* 122 (2003): 248–69.

77 The source of Neill's invitation to the Soviet embassy remains a mystery. Neither Neill nor anyone inside the CPA could explain it. It is possible,

therefore, that ASIO may have orchestrated the invitation to get its source close to Petrov as a contingency measure when its relations with Bialoguski became fractious. Eddie Robertson requested and retained the invitation card Neill was sent. Minute, Controller, SSS, to Director, B2, 7 May 1954, A6119, 927, f. 59, NAA.

78 "Operation Cabin 12 A," 5 May 1954, A6119, 927, f. 56, NAA.

79 Robert Manne, *The Petrov Affair: Politics and Espionage* (Sydney: Pergamon, 1987), 37–42.

80 A6119, 927, f. 22, NAA.

81 Acting RD SA to Controller, SSS, 27 May 1954, A6119, 927, f. 71, NAA.

82 "History of ASIO by Bob Swan, Volume 6," A6122, 2037, f. 55, NAA.

83 "History of ASIO by Bob Swan, Volume 1," A6122, 2022, f. 123, NAA.

84 It later transpired that her bank account had been investigated by CPA officials. Acting RD to HQ, 4 September 1958, A6119, 928, f. 205, NAA.

85 Controller, SSS, to Director, B2, 5 May 1954, 2, A6119, 927, f. 55, NAA.

86 Within ASIO, an alternate symbol to designate Neill was introduced, "if only to mislead those A.S.I.O. officers who … have become too familiar with the [existing] symbol." Acting RD SA, to Controller, SSS, 29 March 1954, A6119, 927, f. 13, NAA.

87 Acting RD SA, to Controller, SSS, 27 May 1954, A6119, 927, f. 71, NAA. The handwritten comment is dated 31 May 1954. See also f. 85, which refers to "perjury implications," and Telephone Message, 21 May 1954, f. 66.

88 A6119, 927, 12 July 1954, f. 98, NAA. Emphasis in original. Spry also emphasized the word "threaten," since if the bluff were called and resignation resulted, "future plans" could be jeopardized if her withdrawal from the CPA was "too sudden." DG to RD SA, 12 July 1954, A6119, 927, f. 97, NAA.

89 DG to RD SA, 8 July 1954, A6119, 927, ff. 95–96, NAA. When she next saw Johnston on 25 August, neither brought up the insurance money, and they parted "on good terms." RD SA to Controller, SSS, 9 September 1954, A6119, 927, f. 101, NAA.

90 Attached report to memorandum, Acting RD SA to Controller, SSS, 3 May 1954, A6119, 927, folios 33–37, NAA.

91 This shrewd briefing covered ten main points, and Neill agreed to follow all points; see SSS, HQ ASIO to DG, 4 May 1954, A6119, 927, ff. 38–40, NAA. ASIO's tradecraft most likely saved her from exposure.

92 See A6119, 927, ff. 29–32, NAA.

93 A6119, 927, ff. 29–32.

94 Acting RD SA to HQ, 4 September 1958, A6119, 928, f. 204, NAA.

95 RD SA to HQ, 9 September 1954, A6119, 927, f. 100, NAA. Much later, an SFO commented that "it must be (and has been) accepted that [blank] has been under a degree of suspicion ever since her investigation by the Central Committee." SFO "Q" to RD SA, 3 June 1958, A6119, 928, f. 158, NAA.

96 RD SA to Controller, SSS, 27 May 1954, A6119, 927, f. 70, NAA.

97 A6119, 927, f. 90, NAA.

98 A6119, 927, f. 91, NAA.

99 Acting RD SA to Controller, SSS, 7 July 1954, A6119, 927, f. 94, NAA.

100 A6119, 927, f. 100, NAA.

101 Acting RD SA to Controller, SSS, 29 March 1954, A6119, 927, f. 13, NAA.

102 Controller, SSS, to DG, 14 February 1955, A6119, 4285, f. 39, NAA.

103 DG to RD SA, 3 August 1954, A6119, 4285, ff. 6, 9, NAA.

104 "Objects of Operation Swan," A6119, 4285, f. 5, NAA.

105 A6119, 4285, ff. 4, 5, 9, NAA. The report of the RCE was released on 14 September 1955.

106 For example: the manuscript was "inundated with a sea of names, and the reader would be very hard pressed to keep up with them and maintain interest." RD to HQ, 28 October 1954, A6119, 4285, f. 16, NAA.

107 Letter, Neill to Mr. [blank], nd [7 November 1954], A6119, 4285, f. 25, NAA. Emphasis in original.

108 RD SA to HQ, 9 November 1954, A6119, 4285, ff. 26–7, NAA.

109 Mac to Neill, 15 November 1954, A6119, 4285, f. 29, NAA.

110 DG to RD SA, 7 February 1954, A6119, 4285, f. 41, NAA.

111 Michael Thwaites, *Truth Will Out: ASIO and the Petrovs* (Sydney: Collins, 1980), 139, 141.

112 Vladimir and Evdokia Petrov, *Empire of Fear* (London: Andre Deutsch, 1956).

113 DG to RD SA, 7 February 1954, A6119, 4285, f. 41, NAA.

114 Ethel Dell was a prolific British writer of popular romance novels, mainly in the interwar period; they were panned by the critics.

115 Controller, SSS, to DG, 14 February 1954, A6119, 4285, f. 39, NAA.

116 Manne, *The Petrov Affair*, 257. Michael Bialoguski's *The Petrov Story* (Melbourne and London: Heinemann, 1955) was published while the RCE was still sitting and had thereby "scooped" *Empire of Fear*.

117 DG to RD SA, 25 May 1954, A6119, 4285, f. 53, NAA.

118 Thwaites, *Truth Will Out*, 142.

119 RD SA to HQ, 19 May 1955, A6119, 4285, f. 48, NAA. ASIO paid her doctor's bills (for a "nervous disorder") in March 1955.

120 She previously spoke about getting "very close" to John Sendy, who had returned from China and (more fancifully) who may offer her "an Espionage task" enabling her to unravel CPA "Espionage activities." RD SA to HQ, 23 May 1955, A6119, 4285, f. 48, NAA. Her case officer gave her a copy of E.H. Cookridge's *Soviet Spy Net* (London: Frederick Muller, 1955), which she "thoroughly appreciated" and intended to use as a future reference. Contact Report Sheet No. 34, 12 June 1956, A6119, 928, f. 47, NAA.

121 RD SA to HQ, 3 June 1955, A6119, 4285, f. 54, NAA. In fact, despite the book, Neill was still active in CPA circles. For example, at a cadres'

meeting addressed by Laurie Aarons, she and Aarons had a "long conversation" and Aarons was "most friendly." RD SA to HQ, 6 June 1955, A6119, 927, f. 142, NAA. She also attended her first one-week party education school in June; her case officer shrewdly briefed her to "indulge in liberal self-criticism in front of the class and the tutor [Gloria Garton]," which was "very favourably" received by Garton. He also briefed her to repeat her self-criticism to the state secretary. RD, SS to HQ, 21 June 1955, A6119, 927, f. 150, NAA. On 17 July she was a delegate to the CPA Annual State Conference, sat next to John Sendy throughout the conference, and provided "excellent coverage." Contact Sheet No. 1, 19 July 1955, A6119, 927, f. 152, NAA.

122   Letters, 6 and 8 June 1955, A6119, 927, ff. 143–34, NAA. Spry wrote that he had been following "your work with considerable interest" and was "amazed and delighted" with the intelligence she had provided since 1950.

123   DG to RD SA, 8 December 1955, A6119, 4285, f. 142, f. 57, NAA. She was thrilled with the gift and wrote a personal note of appreciation to the DG. RD SA to HQ, 26 January 1956, A6119, 928, f.7, NAA.

124   ASIO Contact Record Sheet, Contact No. 12, 21 November 1955, A6119, 927, f. 208, NAA. Citing the absence of libel suits against the books by Michael Bialoguski, Herbert Philbrick, and Douglas Hyde, she asked, "So why should there be in regard to mine?"

125   Contact Report Sheet No. 12, 18 November 1956, A6119, 927, f. 207, NAA.

126   Contact Report Sheet No. 34, 12 June 1956, A6119, 928, f. 47, NAA. In October 1956 she flew to Melbourne to attend the National Conference of the WILPF and a debriefing at ASIO HQ.

127   Report No. 5547A (SA Peace Committee), 19 March 1957, A6119, 931, f. 32, NAA. Emphasis in original.

128   Contact Report Sheet No. 37, 23 July 1956, A6119, 928, f. 53, NAA.

129   Contact Report Sheet No. 30, 30 April 1956, A6119, 928, f. 20, NAA. Emphasis in original.

130   Minute Paper, Top Secret, 9 November 1956, A6119, 928, f. 62, NAA. He was at pains to emphasize his security consciousness, having trained in "G" ops. Advance LHG during the Second World War. In a handwritten response, the controller commented that "this is quite a normal thing"; that "Mrs C does not 'dry up'"; and that the RD SA be informed. Minute Paper, Top Secret, 9 November 1956. Not only did Mrs. C not "dry up," she took Neill to a Christmas dinner, which Neill considered a "fitting conclusion" to their almost daily conversations during the course of Neill's operations. Memorandum, Top Secret, to Controller, SSS, 29 April 1957, A6119, 928, f. 87, NAA.

131   Memorandum, Top Secret, to Controller, SSS, 29 April 1957, A6119, 928, f. 87, NAA.

132   Case Officer's Report No. 66, 21 August 1957, A6119, 928, f. 109, NAA.

133   RD SA to HQ, 21 August1957, A6119, 928, f. 110, NAA.

134   RD SA to HQ, 20 September 1957, A6119, 928, f. 114, NAA.

135   Contact Report Sheet No. 70, 22 October 1957, A6119, 928, f. 122, NA.

136   Contact Report Sheet No. 71, 28 October 1957, A6119, 928, f. 126, NA.

137   "The Okhrana's Female Agents, Part I: Russian Women," Center for the Study of Intelligence, *Studies Archive Indexes* 9, no. 2 (1993): 1.

138   Minute, SFO "Q" to RD SA, 30 May 1958, A6119, 928, ff. 156–7, NAA. Annie Sendy later said to the same agent on 13 August that "we have tried all ways to trap her but we couldn't" and that Neill's house was watched for fourteen days and nights, "but she wasn't seen." Field Officer to Acting RD SA, 4 September 1958, A6119, 928, f. 202, NAA.

139   RA SA to HQ, 3 June 1958, A6119, 928, f. 161, NAA.

140   DG to Regional Directors,.9 July 1958, A6119, 928, ff. 170–1, NAA.

141   RA SA to HQ, 3 June 1958, A6119, 928, f. 161, NAA.

142   DG to RD SA, July 1958, A6119, 928, f. 177, NAA. Emphasis in original.

143   Contact Record Sheet No. 80, 23 June 1958, A6119, 928, f. 164, NAA.

144   Contact Record Sheet No. 81, 3 July 1958, A6119, 928, ff. 175–76, NAA.

145   Her reluctance was evidenced by "Why so suddenly? It will lead to all sorts of speculations. They won't have to ask questions if it's gradual because they will have observed it." Contact Record Sheet No. 82, 13 July 1958, A6119, 928, f. 180, NAA.

146   Contact Record Sheet No. 81, 3 July 1958, A6119, 928, f. 174, NAA; Contact Record Sheet No. 87, 4 November 1948, A6119, 928, f. 219, NAA. In 1959 she became more active in her church and rejoined the LCL.

147   Contact Record Sheet No. 82, 13 July 1958, A6119, 928, ff. 178–79, NAA. An earlier recommendation favoured a "very gradual" phasing-out of certain commitments only over a period "of NOT less than12 months" and that she continue her membership of the CPA, UAW, and ASFS "for several years." SFO "Q" to RD SA, 3 June 1958, A6119, 928, f. 158, NA. Emphasis in original.

148   DG to RD SA, 8 July 1958, A6119, 928, f. 168, NAA.

149   DG to RD SA, 31 July 1958, A6119, 928, f. 184, NAA. No mention was made to Neill of the financial issue.

150   DG to RD SA, 31 July 1958, A6119, 928, f. 185.

151   Department of Defence [n.d.], "Communism. Secret Service Housewife," A5954, 1117/6, NAA.

152   Contact Record Sheet No. 109, 15 March 1959, A6119, 928, f. 267, NAA.

153   Hindersmann, "The Right Side Lost but the Wrong Side Won," 26.

154   John le Carré, *The Pigeon Tunnel: Stories from My Life* (Penguin Random House, 2017), 225.

5 Operation Profunc: The Cold War Plan to Intern Canadian Communists

FRANCES REILLY

In 2010, the Canadian public became aware of a Cold War plan called "Operation Profunc," a surveillance program that monitored "Prominent Functionaries of the Communist/Labor Progressive Party."[1] The targets were key members of communist organizations whom the police surveilled for fear of an uprising, sabotage of vital industries in wartime, and, most concerning, communist subversion of Canadian society. Running from 1948 to 1983, Operation Profunc provided a blueprint for government, military, and police action in the case of a communist conspiracy.[2] It was a disaster plan through which planners tried to imagine a future war. Should Cold War proxy conflicts, such as the Korean War, extend to Canada, the Royal Canadian Mounted Police (RCMP) and army, working under the War Measures Act, would round up and intern Canadian communists in camps similar to those for "enemy aliens" during the First and Second World Wars. Operation Profunc anticipated foreign attack by international communist powers and from within by Canadian communists. Although Operation Profunc wavered little in its anti-communist focus for nearly forty years, the manner in which the plan would be enacted evolved with the changing Cold War climate and fluctuated with the ever-intensifying threat of destruction in the nuclear age.

Operation Profunc was a top-secret program, and thanks to its recent declassification it is an important addition to the study of police surveillance and disaster planning in Canada.[3] The surviving documents of the massive surveillance and internment plan indicate that initially the RCMP, Department of National Defence, and Ministry of Justice jointly managed Operation Profunc. Because confidentiality was paramount to the program's function and its operation was on a "need to know" basis, departmental awareness of this top-secret plan oscillated over the decades. In 1983, Solicitor General Robert Kaplan, newly aware of Operation Profunc (unlike his predecessors, who were part of the planning process), cancelled the program, declaring it out of date. Following this termination, the newly formed civilian-led spy agency CSIS (Canadian Security Intelligence Service) archived the remaining Profunc documents. The 2010 transfer of the documents from CSIS to Library and Archives Canada revealed to the public a surprising history of Cold War preparedness. By and large, Canadians were astonished and horrified to learn the extent to which the RCMP surveilled civilians over the decades, one of the most famous targets being architect of Medicare and New Democratic Party leader Tommy Douglas.[4] For some other Canadians, however, this news confirmed what they had suspected for years: they or family members were watched for political activities and membership in certain associations.[5] For those who were aware of, or suspected, police surveillance, what was surprising was *how* this information was used and on what scale. The declassified records reveal material on tens of thousands of Canadian men and women, including their associations and political activity, their children, their homes, and their employment and workplaces.

What remains of Operation Profunc are thousands of pages of records, some of which are significantly redacted. Issues of access (Steve Hewitt, chapter 6) and document secrecy (Dennis Molinaro, chapter 7) are central to this period of Canadian Cold War history and policing. The available Operation Profunc documents cover plans for arrests, detainments, and the location and construction of internment camps. Evident in these memos, letters, and reports is an overall sense of uncertainty – those running Operation Profunc (particularly in the RCMP) were ultimately unsure about what type of national threat or emergency they were to anticipate. A future war was difficult to imagine in the early atomic era – would it be by "traditional" military means or a thermonuclear attack? Would it be an invasion from overseas or insurgence from within? Operation Profunc records did not specify the type of conflict, only that Canada should be prepared for an impending emergency. This insecurity clashed with the plan's prevailing optimism. In spite of the increasing difficulties of maintaining the plan for mobilization, Operation Profunc was elaborate, expansive, and long-lasting.

Over the last thirty years, historians like Reg Whitaker, Gregory Kealey, and Steve Hewitt have explored the extent of anti-communism and police surveillance. My work on Operation Profunc considers where police surveillance might have led in a future war. Operation Profunc is extraordinary because it provides historians with evidence of a systematic and purposeful use of surveillance data: to confine a select group of civilians. Operation Profunc was also unusual for its length of time and broad reach. Moreover, it provides a window through which historians can see the government's inability to understand how to cope with the Soviet threat. In this way, Operation Profunc exhibits the uncertain world of counter-intelligence.

In March 1948, Assistant Commissioner Leonard Nicholson presented the specific purpose and importance of a top-secret surveillance and internment plan to RCMP Commissioner Stuart Wood:

> I submit it is reasonable to suspect that there are Soviet Agents in this country and a sizeable group of undercover party members. In the event of war we should be able to move *immediately* to thwart enemy espionage by:
> (a) breakup of existing espionage rings (the timing is just as important as the action itself)
> (b) arrest of under cover [sic] party members.[6]

Remarking that Canadian communist groups were not outwardly subversive in their actions, Nicholson surmised that it was the undercover members who were "surely the most dangerous 5th Column source."[7] As he stated to Wood, preparedness and timing were paramount in the face of this elusive enemy and the "deteriorating" international situation.[8]

During the Cold War, and Operation Profunc's lifespan, the Canadian surveillance system gradually turned from a police-based operation, the RCMP Security Service, to a civilian-based agency, CSIS (see Hewitt's chapter in this volume). The case of Operation Profunc exemplified the dangers of having intelligence in the hands of law enforcement, as it was prior to 1984. This chapter looks at the full lifespan of Operation Profunc (1948–83) in two parts. The first section examines the optimism of the early plan, which was challenged by significant changes in international relations and military technology in the late 1950s. The second part discusses planners' renewed focus, which took into consideration the reality of limited resources and time in the early 1960s. Because of the concentrated focus on communism through the decades, the program shrank in size and significance by the 1970s. It was finished before its cancellation in 1983.

In retrospect, it is easy to dismiss preparations for a disaster that never occurred, but to ignore Operation Profunc is to overlook how Canada remained in a perpetual state of emergency planning for decades. Much like civil defence plans of the same era, Operation Profunc was a disaster plan that revealed how authorities struggled to imagine an unprecedented emergency. The Profunc records display planners' efforts to achieve a smooth and cohesive operation that would prevent chaos in wartime. Because Operation Profunc was never enacted, historians can make the mistake of seeing it as merely hypothetical. Such a disaster plan, regardless of whether or not it was realized, shows how a threat was perceived, an emergency anticipated, and a future war imagined.

Part One: Postwar Optimism (1948–1956)

In early 1950, two years after the official inception of Operation Profunc, RCMP divisions across the country began surveys for internment sites. These provincial and territorial divisions were responsible for gathering information on prominent functionaries along with possible sites for internment camps, and amalgamating this data to be sent to Ottawa for review.[9] Over time the program's focus broadened to encompass leftist Canadians in general, but at the beginning it was limited to "Prominent Functionaries" of the Canadian Communist Party and related organizations. Civilians with leftist affiliations, or more importantly a Communist Party of Canada or related background, were monitored for a "criminal mindset," tendency to violent action, leadership potential, and an ability to go underground in an emergency.[10]

Cold War internment would follow the patterns set by the previous World Wars. The War Measures Act and the Defence of Canada Regulations (DOCR) were spawned in 1914 and enabled the suspension of civil liberties in the name of national security. They allowed for the internment of some Ukrainian Canadians during the First World War and twenty-two thousand Japanese Canadians during the Second World War, along with a number of other civilians, such as German and Italian nationals and Canadian leftists. Operation Profunc was the result of several decades of police surveillance of leftists and was fostered in a well-established climate of anti-communism. The Canadian Cold War communist "witch-hunts" were not without American senator Joseph McCarthy's influence, but they grew from separate roots. Compared with histrionic McCarthyism, Operation Profunc and RCMP surveillance was subtle but consistent.[11] Operation Profunc stemmed from a long-cultivated history of fear and suspicion of communism, socialism, and collectivist activity that was then placed in the context of the Cold War.[12] Following the First World War, Bolshevism became the primary focus of national security, which was evident in the violent reaction of the city of Winnipeg, the RCMP, and the Canadian Army to the 1919 Winnipeg General Strike.[13] Throughout the Great Depression, relief camps, located in remote areas, acted as internment sites for unemployed working-class men. The men's isolation and containment, ironically, helped foster leftist ideology and led to the 1935 On-to-Ottawa Trek, an iconic national protest that culminated in violent police intervention in Regina. The vetting of leftist ideology became more pronounced during the Second World War when, under the War Measures Act of 1939, the RCMP focused on pacifists and war resisters, targeting groups such as Jehovah's Witnesses, Quebec anti-conscriptionists, communists, and the radical Left.[14] The Second World War internment of leftists reflected the strong sentiments within the Canadian government and RCMP that communists were fundamentally different. Charles Rivett-Carnac (head of RCMP intelligence) declared communists to be worse that Nazis, noting that fascism was more or less a "modified form of capitalism."[15] Even though fascism was Canada's enemy, communism was worse.

The "Gouzenko affair" of September 1945, when Russian cipher clerk Igor Gouzenko uncovered a Soviet spy ring in Ottawa, marked a turning point in both Canadian anti-communist sentiment and North American awareness and fear of Soviet espionage. While the arrests and interrogations of the suspects were understandable given the breach of security, the extreme view that socialism was an inherent menace to Canadian society went beyond Gouzenko's findings and was fed by deep-seated anti-communist sentiment. The Gouzenko revelations marked a turning point in Canada's concept of subversion.[16]

Commissioner Wood articulated the growing sentiment that communism was a particularly devious menace when he stated in 1950 that the threat posed by the Soviet Union could not be compared with anything from the two World Wars.[17] A future attack, as he saw it, would be one of organized sabotage and infiltration that could not be anticipated nor dealt with in the same manner that Canada had previously managed wartime threats. Canada had to be ready and better equipped than it was during the Second World War when, as Wood noted, "the Force put up with inferior personnel and material and conditions which were far from satisfactory. Similar circumstances could not be tolerated in a future conflict; especially so should the Soviet Union be the enemy."[18] To properly prepare for a future attack or infiltration, prominent functionaries were to be kept under constant review. While membership in leftist organizations was not outlawed in Canada for any significant period of time, the RCMP kept surveillance on labour organizations, peace groups, and ethnic associations with political undertones or links, however weak, to larger communist parties. A list of suspect organizations was compiled by 1950, and Operation Profunc categorized them into three groups: Recognized Communist Organizations, Ethnic or Mass Language Organizations, and Front Organizations.[19] According to the "Profunc Manual," a handbook reprinted, and to some extent revised, over the course of the Cold War, a communist organization was deemed "recognized" at RCMP headquarters following approval from the Profunc Advisory Committee on Internment, established in 1950.[20] Through this process, the manual states, the governor-in-council was then enabled "at the outset of a national emergency to declare all said organizations illegal and thus empower this Force to close down and search in the name of the Custodian all property belonging to any illegal organization."[21] In addition to labour and communist organizations, many other groups profiled in Operation Profunc were of non-Anglo-Saxon origin, pointing to the RCMP's discrimination and belief that these groups were more susceptible to the spreading force of international communism.

On the surface Operation Profunc's internment plan mirrored those in previous wars, but the police, army, and government had more time to anticipate a future war, unlike when Canada was thrown into action in 1914 and 1939. This time allowed for Profunc planners to consider several eventualities, work through possible shortcomings, and avoid panicked blunders when an emergency finally arrived. Planners also had time to consider not just the efficiency of pick-ups, arrests, and internments, but also the ethics behind these plans. One of these ethical problems was how to intern women and children. A Cold War emergency would not have been the first time families were interned in wartime, but the large number of Canadians slated for internment across the country pushed the planners to reconsider how they envisioned security at the planned camps. Early reports anticipated that once surveillance teams had approved the country's prominent functionaries, Canada would intern over ten thousand civilians in an emergency.[22] Women made up a significant portion of these future internees. The pertinent question of who would guard the women prisoners lingered uncomfortably in the memos sent between the army, police, and penitentiary services, as both the army and RCMP had no legislation in place to recruit women for this operation, nor did they plan to do so, and penitentiaries did not typically use women guards in women's prisons.[23] The question of how women were to be guarded at the internment sites persisted over the next few decades, but the documents provided few viable solutions.

More worrying for planners was how the internment of women would lead to the internment of children. Indeed the Canadian government interned Japanese Canadian children during the Second World War and separated Indigenous children from their families for decades, but Profunc planners likely did not consider these cases as blueprints for what to do with white children. Planners weighed the different options of placing children with fathers, friends, and neighbours, making them wards of the state, or interning them with their parents in camps.[24] Out of the three options, passing children to friends and relatives was the most attractive.[25] Planners, however, anticipated friends and relatives might be unavailable at the time of arrest or be communist themselves. The second option of placing children in the care of the state was modelled after the internment of Jehovah's Witnesses during the Second World War. In the case of a mass internment of communists and sympathizers, however, the state would not be able to manage a massive influx of children without significant warning to the services in question. As a top-secret organization, Operation Profunc could not prepare child welfare services for an arrival of several thousand children without compromising the plan's security.[26] The course of action to which most planners agreed was to intern the children with their parents as "protected persons" under the Geneva Convention.[27] Despite this general consensus, planners remained uncomfortable with the internment of children, a fact made clear by the continued discussion of the matter over the years.[28]

The camps would be organized by region and gender. In 1951 planners drew up the first internment sites based on early numbers provided by the divisions (see figure 5.1).

The map listed a total of eight camp locations, to hold over 2,800 Canadians. Two camps were suggested for British Columbia (Kelowna and Kamloops), one for Alberta (Lethbridge), four in Ontario (Neys, Burwash, the Niagara Peninsula, and Parry Sound), and one for Quebec (Rawden). Women from the western provinces would be interned at Kelowna, while those east of Manitoba would be interned at the Niagara facility. Men from the west were broken into two categories: the Prairies (to be interned at Lethbridge) and British Columbia (to be interned at Kamloops). Men from Ontario would be interned at Neys and Burwash, while men from Quebec and the Atlantic provinces would be interned at Rawden. The camp at Parry Sound would contain "protected persons," a yet-undefined number of people in 1951 that largely comprised families with young children. These locations were re-evaluated, and this map was soon considered, as the note scribbled at the bottom states, "out of date." An almost-regular process of planning and revising followed over the years as a result of constant concerns about the remoteness, accessibility, and security of internment centres. As with plans for accommodating children, the multiple revisions of internment locations demonstrate the preoccupation with a future war and the difficulty imagining it.

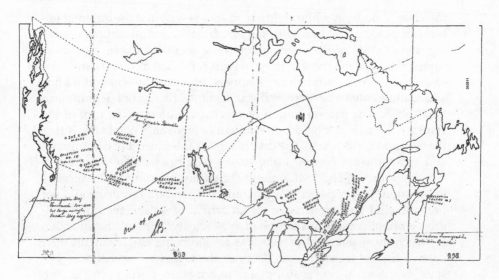

5.1 Map of possible internment sites, circa 1951. Reference no. 2011-00179-09-54-13, LAC.

Notable in these early plans was the focus on reusing prisoner of war (POW) and internment camps from the Second World War as a simple and cost-saving measure. Multiple surveys and evaluations of old sites confirmed that neither would be suitable. Neys in particular exemplified the planners' attention to historical precedence of war-time sites. Appearing as a possibility throughout the 1950s until the mid-1960s, Neys, and the plans to refurbish it, demonstrated the problems involved in planning for disaster, safely containing a large group of home-grown dissidents, and the changing accessibility to the Canadian wilderness in the postwar era.

Located on the north shore of Lake Superior, far from cities and large communities, Neys was a prime candidate for an internment site. It was remote but was accessible by road and rail. Between 1941 and 1946, it was one of twenty-six camps across Canada that held German POWs and was a work camp for Japanese Canadian men.[29] During the Second World War, German POW camps were categorized into two groups: greys, for German soldiers, and blacks, for Nazis. Neys, also known as "Camp 100," was one of nine "black" camps in Canada. These were maximum-security facilities for a prison population deemed high risk for violence and escape. The Neys site was enclosed by three separate barbed-wire fences three metres in height with guard towers at each corner.[30] Following the war, Neys became a work camp for a local jail that the Ontario government closed in October 1952. Until the mid-1960s Operation Profunc continued its discussions and plans for how to convert the old camp, and now-abandoned jail, into a place of internment. By this point, the POW camp of twenty years earlier had all but disappeared, and so too had the plan's initial enthusiasm; to convert the remnants would be costly and impractical. In addition to the cost of renovations, there was the issue of the site's accessibility. The Canadian Pacific Railway (CPR) ran past the camp, which proved useful in one of a number of POW camp escapes during the 1940s, oddly a point not addressed in the Profunc survey reports. The most dramatic wartime POW escape in this region took place in 1941 from the camp at nearby Angler. This escape involved a forty-five-metre tunnel, eighty prisoners (out of a camp of 559), and the escape of twenty-eight men. In the process five escapees were shot – two of whom died from their wounds soon after. Those who successfully escaped acquired civilian dress and boarded boxcars on the CPR. Two of these men got as far as Alberta before they were arrested.[31]

In 1962, another main transportation route opened through this previously remote location: the Trans-Canada Highway. With this highway Canadians and international tourists could access the north shore of Lake Superior more easily than ever before. Accessibility brought the possibility of escape and posed a problem for the secrecy of the plan as it unfolded. If the internment camps and the preparation for sites to imprison Canadian communists were an open secret the whole operation would be compromised.

Operation Profunc's success in a future war depended on the element of surprise. Prominent functionaries, whose homes and workplaces were closely monitored over the decades, would be arrested in the early hours of the morning by a small team of RCMP officers. A 1949 memo to the RCMP commissioner suggested simultaneous arrests be conducted across the country "to avoid Communist residents in different time zones receiving prior warning" and going underground.[32] This memo specified, "The greatest measures of success would undoubtedly be achieved if all Divisions could commence their raids at a time not earlier than 3:00 am."[33] Canada's multiple time zones made simultaneous arrests at this optimal time impossible. According to the 1949 memo, in order to maintain synchronized arrests that would occur at night, "when the persons to be apprehended will be home in bed," the arrests would then begin at 5:00 a.m. Atlantic Time, 3:00 a.m. Central Time, and 1:00 a.m. Pacific Time.[34] The energy spent on planning for the details of the arrest time points to the desire to be prepared in the face of unprecedented disaster *and* secure ultimate effectiveness in containing the perceived threat.

RCMP "raiding teams" sent to arrest prominent functionaries also had to be efficient. These teams would be made up of three men, one Security Service officer and two uniformed police officers, in addition to a matron when women and children were involved.[35] While one officer made the arrest, the others would perform a search of the premises and the individual's place of work and automobile for compromising material. Seditious material could include communist literature, personal papers, writing paraphernalia (such as telephone writing pads, typewriters, and mimeographing machines), photographs, and anything that could indicate a connection with questionable organizations or individuals.[36] After conducting extensive searches of homes, offices, and places of work for evidence, the police would bring the arrestees to a local reception centre, usually a public building such as a school or immigration hall, where they would be processed and held for a few weeks before being transferred to an internment camp.[37] The RCMP and army would ready the facilities of the internment camps while civilians were held at reception centres across the country. Early plans called for roughly one reception centre per division, but over the years this number grew to nearly one reception centre per city.[38]

The camps themselves were another matter that posed challenges to maintaining secrecy. In 1950 a reviewing committee identified that Operation Profunc's main hurdle was building camps clandestinely: "How to arrange for some advance action on the building of internment camps and at the same time have that action suitably camouflaged so it would not attract public attention."[39] The RCMP suggested that the army could solve this problem; they had the finances to construct internment camps. A total of two camps could be built in peacetime, and supplies could be made readily available to build more in the case of an emergency. Eight camps would be required to house a total of three thousand people across the country. The interment structures would be prefabricated huts, those typically used by hydro workers and the army stationed in remote areas, because they allowed for quick construction and easy stockpiling of material for future building. They were spartan in design, often without proper insulation, and the extent of their lifespan was questionable, but they could be constructed surreptitiously, effectively satisfying the desire to keep the plan top secret (see figures 5.2 and 5.3).

There is an element of optimism in these early plans – namely that there would be enough time following an emergency to build huts across the country to hold thousands of potential dissidents. There was also faith that the army would be available to construct huts, transport internees, and then act as guards during an unfolding communist

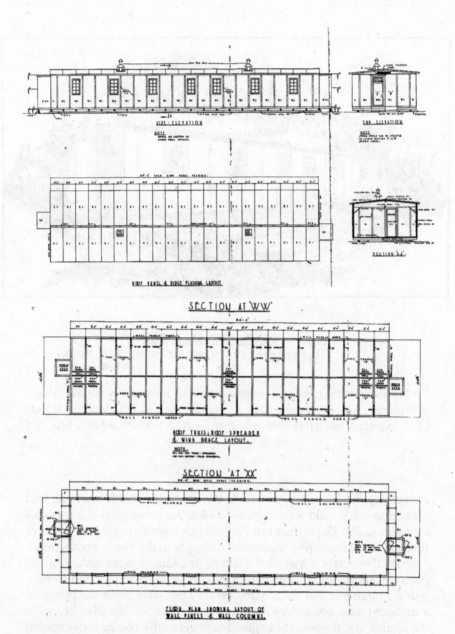

5.2 Blueprints of prefabricated army huts, each measuring eighty-four by twenty feet. Source: "Use of Prefab Huts for Internment Camps," package from W.W.K. McConnell and J.R.B. Jones to Cook, 3 July 1950, reference no. A 2011-00179-09-51-14, LAC.

(0)   COMPLETE ASSEMBLY.
Perspective view of complete unit.
001969

5.3 Hut exterior. Each hut was capable of holding forty adults. Source: "Use of Prefab Huts for Internment Camps," package from W.W.K. McConnell and J.R.B. Jones to Cook, 3 July 1950, reference no. A 2011-00179-09-51-14, LAC.

conspiracy.[40] While the army made it clear to the RCMP early on that arrangements should remain loose to allow for potential military duties in wartime, the Department of National Defence carried the weight of financial and labour responsibilities throughout the plan's early years.[41]

From the outset, Operation Profunc organizers were aware of the potential shortcomings and complications of rounding up and imprisoning a large number of civilians. Still, in the early 1950s the plan had a distinct focus: prominent functionaries. Although the plan began in the atomic era, the war it imagined was generally one of conventional means without the complicating factors of thermonuclear attack and radioactive fallout. By the end of the decade, the military climate had changed, as had surveillance methods. In 1957, Operation Profunc's focus became more refined with the creation of the Crash Plan, a system built to keep the program on track. Because the numbers of listed subversives increased annually, effectively inundating the RCMP, Profunc planners created a separate list of high-profile leftists to arrest immediately following an emergency before the mass arrests began in the days that followed.[42] The Crash Plan epitomized the need to maintain an effective surveillance program in the nuclear age that required a "fresh approach" to the problem of internal security measures.[43] As the 1950s drew to a close, planners changed their visions for internment to better fit the anticipated future war of the nuclear era.

Part Two: The Sharp Peak and Steady Decline (1957–1983)

Nuclear war made few appearances in Operation Profunc's early records, but as the threat increased so too did concerns for the viability of detention and internment in the wake of a nuclear attack. Planners reconsidered the use of reception centres located in areas now identified as target cities.[44] Civil defence evacuation plans of the late 1950s, which were public in nature, began to impede the top-secret pickup and internment plans of Operation Profunc.[45] The expectation of potential conflict changed with each ground-shaking advance in nuclear weaponry and technology. In the wake of the development of larger bombs and intercontinental ballistic missiles (ICBMs), the imagined World War Three stalked closer to North America and the stakes rose higher than ever.

In 1959, Ottawa directed the RCMP divisions to revisit their earlier choices for internment sites and, in their next line of surveys, to pay attention to prospective target areas of nuclear attack and potential fallout zones. Although the divisions had previously made recommendations for specific internment sites in 1951, no firm decisions were reached, and discussions about the location of internment centres faded, even as concerns about Soviet espionage, domestic communism, and nuclear war heightened through the 1950s. By the 1960s, Ottawa was demanding that the divisions pay significant attention to the anticipated fallout of a possible Soviet attack on Canada. The future became shorter; Operation Profunc's long-term plan for six to nine months after an attack became a detailed one-month plan following an emergency.[46] Then, in October 1962, Operation Profunc planners were shaken from any lethargy about the impending possibility of nuclear war. Referred to in the RCMP documents as "the recent crisis," the near miss of the Cuban Missile Crisis pressed Operation Profunc planners to settle the issue of unconfirmed internment sites and reception centres.[47] With this near disaster in mind, planners focused their attention on protection from nuclear attack and radioactive fallout.[48]

Radioactive fallout was not the only aspect of a nuclear war that worried Profunc planners – there was a growing anxiety about how a "new war" would affect civilians psychologically.[49] One RCMP officer, whose name was redacted on declassification, wrote to an inspector in 1956 stating that in the nuclear era "all defence plans are largely speculative."[50] Operation Profunc as a disaster plan, he noted, needed to adapt to the new military developments of ICBMs and the hydrogen bomb. "The direct effect of such warfare," he wrote, "coupled with its by-products of homeless, hungry, dispirited, maimed and grieving people thronging everywhere, would seem to preclude any appreciable action on the part of our Special Branch."[51] Uncertainty coupled with chaos were by-products of nuclear war. The officer drew particular attention to civilian panic, contemplating how it would be the inevitable result of nuclear attack and likely aid the spread of communism, as defences would be low and people vulnerable.[52] Drawing from his own military experience in France during the Second World War, the officer speculated how much more terrible the resulting panic and chaos would be in a nuclear war. A weakened people in a broken country would become open to subversive ideology. The psychological effect of war, as he saw it, was particularly worrisome and difficult to predict – communism could prey on the weakness of a population in a period of compromised security.

The future war became harder to anticipate, making the question of how to manage the threat of communist invasion or infiltration more pressing. How to easily contain a group of dissidents also became more difficult to plan when compounded with the issue of manpower and funding. To save money on facilities and guards, planners turned to the country's already-existing incarceration facilities. Canada had recently undergone a series of prison reforms, and in the 1960s the federal and provincial governments financed the construction of several new prisons across the country. RCMP divisions had surveyed facilities such as schools and government buildings throughout the 1950s, but never with the concentrated focus of the following decade. In late May 1962, Ottawa requested that divisions submit lists of all facilities, including provincial and municipal jails, prisons, lock-ups, reform schools, and farm camps.[53] The responses from the divisions varied and ultimately illustrated the regions' overall commitment to the plan. There is an element of familiarity to the correspondence between the divisions and Ottawa that brings to mind students responding to a vaguely designed class assignment. What Ottawa requested was interpreted freely by the divisions, and the responses indicate the different levels of interest, anxiety, and financial resources across the country.

Southern Ontario ("O" Division) and the Montreal-area division ("C" Division) were two of the most active divisions in planning for Operation Profunc because they had the largest populations in the country. Both responded in a timely fashion with extensive lists to Ottawa's request to provide information about existing incarceration facilities. "O" Division had a total of eighty-nine institutions listed, which included fifty-three county jails, two city jails, three municipal institutions, and eighteen provincial reform institutions, along with a collection of reform schools and diagnostic centres for youth.[54] "C" Division had a list of twenty-eight institutions, which included one penitentiary, two city jails, two "female jails," and twenty county jails, along with some smaller facilities.[55] The divisions provided little in the way of description of the facilities or plans for them. By contrast, British Columbia ("E" Division), while sending its list a month later, was keener in its response. Ottawa was treated to a small but comprehensive list of seven locations, complete with a report that detailed the capacity and level of security of each institution listed, a projected timeline for activating these institutions in an emergency, and comments about the proximity of sites to estimated fallout zones or target cities.[56] Outside of "O" and "C" Division, "E" Division consistently had one of the highest lists of prominent functionaries in the country and was regularly up to date in its reports to Ottawa, showing an eagerness to be prepared in the case of an emergency.[57] Newfoundland, "B" Division, was British Columbia's opposite in terms of preparation and enthusiasm. This province presented Ottawa with an unprocessed file of correspondence that was in some cases sent directly from the province's subdivisions. Many of "B" Division's facilities were little more than police lock-ups and were, as their officers noted, incapable of holding prisoners for longer than an overnight visit.[58] "G" Division (the Territories and Hudson Bay region) also did not have many internment resources and was even less involved with Operation Profunc. To Ottawa's request Yukon and the Northwest Territories were polite but curt in their statement that they had no facilities other than the small RCMP guard rooms, noting that it was against regulations to use these facilities for long-term imprisonment. Most of the northern facilities, with few exceptions, were little more than single-capacity cells and, as "G" Division noted, what facilities existed were "decidedly inadequate in recent years and are at the most times greatly overcrowded."[59] While "E" Division was ready to pick up its carefully monitored prominent functionaries at the outset of war, "G" Division was dealing with its own issues in peacetime.

Plans to adapt existing incarceration facilities, all of which were currently in operation, satisfied earlier problems finding secure and easily readied sites for internment. But the decision to use jails brought about new worries, namely, could these facilities be made available in a future war? And how were they to go about releasing inmates to free space for wartime internees?[60]

In 1962 planners narrowed the sites provided in the division reports into three regions: British Columbia, the Prairie region, and Ontario. In these areas they settled on a total of five facilities: Agassiz (British Columbia), Saskatchewan Farm Camp (Prince Albert, Saskatchewan), Stony Mountain (Manitoba), and Joyceville Institution and Farm Camp and Collins Bay (Ontario).[61] Of these, Agassiz was newly constructed in 1962 and Joyceville in 1963, and Stony Mountain, an old facility from 1877, added a new medium-security facility in 1962. Discussions continued as the questions of how to prepare these sites at a time of emergency or nuclear attack lingered. The Agassiz institution was eventually dropped because of its proximity to Vancouver, less than one hundred kilometres away, which was a target city for Soviet attack. All of the institutions, even the newly built facilities, required additional protective measures such as fences and flood lighting, which would take time, labour, and money.[62]

In autumn 1963, the RCMP agreed to undertake another survey of all federal penal institutions to ascertain their suitability. Surveying concluded in December 1964, and findings were forwarded to the commissioner of penitentiaries. No further progress was made, however, until June 1967. At this point the list was updated again – this time to include some of the country's newest incarceration facilities: British Columbia's Matsqui Institution (1966), Alberta's Drumheller Institution (1967), Ontario's Joyceville Institution (1963) and Warkworth Institution (1967), Quebec's Cowansville Institution (1966), and Nova Scotia's Springhill Institution (1967).[63] These facilities had up-to-date security, such as electric doors, and plans noted it would be "advantageous" if key and experienced penitentiary personnel could be retained to supervise the operation of the modern equipment.[64] All of these institutions were deemed attractive for their modernity, capacity, and proximity to transportation – all were reasonably accessible by rail, road, and air, allowing for smooth movement of prisoners in wartime. By the end of the 1960s, what was initially a list of a dozen facilities spanning across the country in the early 1950s had been reduced to three facilities: Drumheller (for men west of Ontario), Warkworth (for eastern men), and Joyceville (for all women).[65]

An initially massive plan was suddenly small, and it shrank further still. The declining importance of the program was especially evident in the rapidly decreasing membership of the organizations that had remained under surveillance since 1950. For thirty-five years the RCMP had kept annual reports of Profunc numbers. In the early 1950s, prior to the creation of the Crash Plan, these numbers were unstable and reports were compiled every few months. For the year 1951, for instance, the estimated total of prominent functionaries ranged from 6,149 in June to 7,138 in December, with the number of prominent functionaries approved for pickup ranging from 668 to 1,641.[66] The numbers peaked in the mid-1950s: over the course of 1955 the total ranged from 10,623 in January to 11,210 in September (2,734 to 2,845 approved).[67] This variance (and these numbers) indicated a lack of focus and perhaps an effort to present the program as relevant and worthy of funding. These figures were also indicative that the RCMP was ill equipped to manage such an extensive surveillance program.

The numbers plateaued in the late 1950s, and the reports steadied, becoming annual and showing numbers that gradually climbed and fell rather than jumping wildly. The total numbers hovered between five and six thousand in these years, indicating a direct and stable focus of the surveillance program, which came from the more organized method of the Crash Plan that was introduced in 1957. The Crash Plan's focus on key members became more useful when it became clear in the early 1960s that Operation Profunc had extended its focus to leftists in general.[68]

Between 1960 and 1969 the number dropped from a total of 5,300 (2,640 of which were approved, with an additional 135 listed under the Crash Plan)[69] to a total of 1,016 (800 approved and 103 under the Crash Plan) in 1969.[70] This was effectively a drop of 4,284 total cases (1,840 approved) in just nine years, while the Crash Plan dropped by 32 cases. The numbers decreased even more through the 1970s. In 1970, the total was 996 (730 approved and 98 under the Crash Plan).[71] By 1979 the total number was 56, with 46 approved and 23 listed under the Crash Plan.[72] In nine years the total number dropped by 940, the approved number by 684, and the Crash Plan by 75.

Although the RCMP continued to maintain surveillance records through this last decade, the importance of the program itself faded. Beginning in the 1960s, planners worked to keep the surveillance program and arrest plan current by regularly updating the Profunc lists. Names were added and dropped as civilians under surveillance moved, joined and left organizations, grew old, and died. In the late 1960s these updates more commonly involved the removal of names than the creation of files on new subjects. Officers made adjustments to existing files with comments indicating, for instance, that it had "been reliably reported" that two subjects had recently died.[73] Others evaluated the likelihood of subjects actually posing a threat to national security – one noted that because of a subject's "age and mental condition" it seemed "highly unlikely that he would be able to carry out an act of sabotage."[74] One memo from 1972 recommended that two subjects be removed from the Crash Plan list on account of "the advanced age and withering influence of [name redacted] and the fact that [name redacted] does not hold a position at the national level."[75] Other updates pointed to a general lack of interest of group members towards political activity or a general decline of activity among members.[76] These groups, many of which came out of the Great Depression and the Second World War, did not fit the politics of the late Cold War. Even though the groups listed as targets in the early 1950s remained under police surveillance for the duration of the program,[77] the RCMP recognized that these targets were "revolutionaries of a bygone era, peripheral to events."[78]

In the 1970s, as discussed in chapter 6, the RCMP Security Service encountered more grave threats to national security in the form of Quebec separatism and international terrorism. Operation Profunc's limitations did not go unnoticed by the RCMP in the wake of the 1970 October Crisis in Quebec. In 1973 M.R. Dare (director general of the Security Service) expressed his concern for the datedness of Operation Profunc. He stated, "Considering that these plans were formulated in 1948 it is not surprising that time and technology have combined to render them unworkable, proof of which was reflected in the 1970 F.L.Q. crisis when they were virtually ignored."[79] Times were changing. A 1980 memo from the director of Protective Policing to the Security Service stated, "The problem with this system [Operation Profunc] is that it was developed when the USSR and its satellites were considered to be Canada's sole adversaries."[80] The memo went on to state that under the system of Operation Profunc, terrorism, which was of "considerable concern to security forces today," did not fall within Profunc's scope.[81] By the time Operation Profunc was cancelled in 1983, it had already begun its slow death as an outdated disaster plan.

Conclusion

What remains extraordinary about Operation Profunc was its extent and its intent. Over the years, historians have speculated about plans for communist internment in Canada. Operation Profunc's records give evidence that for thirty-five years there *was* an active plan to intern Canadian leftists in camps across the country. Similar to the wiretapping discussed by Molinaro in chapter 7, this was a serious endeavour lasting decades and many governments. Confirmation of these suspicions is only one aspect that makes the Operation Profunc documents valuable to historians and the larger history of Cold War counter-intelligence in Canada. These plans vividly show how the RCMP, army, and Canadian government tried to imagine a future war. Plans were regularly rerouted and locations reconsidered over the years to fit the Cold War climate, the shifts in military technology, and changes to the country itself. Plans for internment in 1950 differed from those in the late 1960s because of this attention.

It is also telling what aspects of the plan did *not* change over the decades, namely the continued concentration on a communist conspiracy. This single-mindedness soon dated the plan, rending it unworkable and archaic in the late Cold War. The continued focus on communists betrayed the deep-seated prejudice of the RCMP and Canadian government towards leftism and collectivist politics, and the shortcomings of having law enforcement responsible for the delicate matter of counter-espionage and disaster preparation.

Finally, the thirty-five-year operation strategizing a smooth and secure disaster plan exemplified the desire for order in a period of disorder. The decades of resources spent on blueprints (both literal and figurative), and the labour and funding invested in the multiple surveys of sites, institutions, and prisons, demonstrated the need for a cohesive and workable plan in a period of anxiety and uncertainty. A nuclear attack on Canada or a home-grown insurgence against the government would be chaotic and unprecedented. For this, Operation Profunc offered a solution through a logical course of action and a concrete and viable strategy for dealing with disaster. Whether or not it would have been a successful operation is a less important question than why and how it was maintained, secretly, for nearly four decades.

NOTES

1 Over the twentieth century, the official Canadian Communist Party changed names from the "Communist Party of Canada" (CPC) to the "Labor Progressive Party" (LPP) and back again. In Canada, "labour" was spelled with a "u" only in the late twentieth century, and this chapter uses the spelling contemporary to the Cold War documents.
2 Emergency internment plans existed throughout the Five Eyes. The United States attorney general, for instance, also instituted an emergency detention program in 1948, which involved Security Index cards for communists and "dangerous individuals." Elizabeth Grace and Colin Leys, "The Concept of Subversion and Its Implications," in *Dissent and the State*, ed. C.E.S. Franks (Toronto: Oxford University Press, 1989), 68.

3 This chapter is the result of research conducted for my PhD dissertation, which – because of recently declassified files – was the first comprehensive study of the program, "Controlling Contagion: Policing and Prescribing Sexual and Political Normalcy in Cold War Canada" (University of Saskatchewan, 2016).

4 Joan Bryden, "Tommy Douglas's Intelligence File Not about History: Feds," *Canadian Press*, 4 February 2013 [updated 6 April 2013], http://www .ctvnews.ca/politics/fight-over-tommy-douglas-intelligence-file-not-about -history-feds-1.1142668.

5 Individuals who believe that they or their relatives were under surveillance between the 1940s and 1980s can submit requests for personal records from Library and Archives Canada.

6 "Re: Special Branch Organizations," memo from L.H. Nicholson to Commissioner, 27 March 1948, reference no. A 2011-00179-11-37-03, unprocessed collection, Library and Archives Canada (LAC). Emphasis in original.

7 "Re: Special Branch Organizations," memo from L.H. Nicholson to Commissioner, 27 March 1948.

8 "Re: Special Branch Organizations," 27 March 1948.

9 The RCMP divisions were the following: "A" (Eastern Ontario and parts of Quebec), "B" (Newfoundland), "C" (Montreal), "D" (Manitoba and Northern Ontario), "E" (British Columbia), "F" (Saskatchewan), "G" (Hudson Bay region, which included Yukon and Northwest Territories), "H" (Nova Scotia), "J" (New Brunswick), "K" (Alberta), "L" (Prince Edward Island), and "O" (Southern Ontario).

10 "Re: Profunc," memo from Inspector J.L. Forest ("A" Division) to RCMP Commissioner, 5 June 1964, reference no. A 2011-00179-11-29-01, LAC.

11 In *Cold War Canada: The Making of a National Insecurity State, 1945–1957* (Toronto: University of Toronto Press, 1994), Reg Whitaker and Gary Marcuse challenge the idea that Canada avoided having its own "witch-hunts," providing a history of Canada's own culture of Cold War anti-communism. Whitaker has disputed many of the popular ideas concerning the American influence on Canadian politics, stressing the anti-communism inherent in Canadian politics and society following the First World War. Reg Whitaker, "Official Repression of Communism during World War II," *Labour/Le Travail* 17 (Spring 1986): 135–66.

12 Steve Hewitt traced the longevity of Canadian Cold War anti-communism to the Great War in *Spying 101: The RCMP's Secret Activities at Canadian Universities, 1917–1997* (Toronto: University of Toronto Press, 2002). Greg Kealey argues that the classification of immigrants, labour, and the Left as threats to national security reaches back to the fundamental years leading up to Confederation in *Spying on Canadians: The Royal Canadian Mounted*

Police Security Service and the Origins of the Long Cold War (Toronto: University of Toronto Press, 2017).

13 Ian Angus, *Canadian Bolshevism: The Early Years of the Communist Party of Canada* (Montreal: Vanguard Publications, 1981), 55–6.

14 Whitaker, "Official Repression of Communism During World War II," 136.

15 Quoted in ibid., 137.

16 Grace and Leys, "The Concept of Subversion and Its Implications," 70.

17 "Joint Committee on Internment Operations Security Guard Forces of Vital Points (RCMP-Army)," Meeting Minutes, 29 March 1950, reference no. A 2011-00179-09-49-40, LAC.

18 "Joint Committee on Internment Operations," Meeting Minutes, 29 March 1950.

19 Confirmed subversive associations as of 1952 included the following: Labor-Progressive Party, National Federation of Labour [sic] Youth, Association of United Ukrainian Canadians, United Jewish Peoples' Order, Finnish Organization of Canada, Federation of Russian Canadians, Polish Democratic Association, Council of Canadian South Slavs (which later changed its name to Federation of Yugoslav Canadians), Lithuanian Literacy Society, Hungarian Literacy Association, Independent Mutual Benefit Federation, Bulgarian Canadian Peoples' League, Macedonian Canadian Peoples' League, Canadian Peace Congress, and Canadian Slav Committee. Under consideration were the following: Canadian Soviet Friendship Society, German Canadian Federation, Workers Benevolent Association, Canadian Lithuanian Benefit Society, Carpatho Russian Society, Congress of Canadian Women, and League for Democratic Rights. "Re: Subversive Organizations, Canada Generally," memorandum from G.H. Ashley to George B. McClellan, 27 May 1952, reference no. A 2011-00179-11-40-13, LAC.

20 "Top Secret: Directorate of Security and Intelligence: Profunc Manual," 26 January 1971, 3, reference no. A 2011-00179-11-38-32, LAC.

21 Ibid.

22 "Joint Committee on Internment Operations," Meeting Minutes, 19 March 1950. These minutes note that the RCMP and army were anticipating the internment of fifteen thousand communists in Canada.

23 "Re: Emergency Planning," memorandum from S.T. Wood to R.B. Gibson, 9 May 1950, and "Re: Emergency Planning," memorandum from R.B. Gibson to S.T. Wood, 23 May 1950, reference no. 2011-00179-09-49-40, LAC.

24 Memo from George B. McClellan to Officers Commanding of "A," "C," "D," "E," "F," "H," "K," and "O" Divisions, 23 January 1950, reference no. A 2011-00179-09-51-14, LAC.

25 "'A' Division Apprehension of Persons under the Internal Security Regulations, 'A' Division SIB Operation Order," Order to Commissioner RCMP, April 1964, 4, reference no. A 2011-00179-11-30-32, LAC.

26 "Re: Civilian Internment Operations – General," Letter from Inspector K.N. Lockwood to Officer in Charge of 'D' Division, 13 March 1951, reference no. A 2011-00179-09-41-00, LAC.

27 "Re: Civilian Internment Operations – General," memo from George McClellan to Officers in Charge of Provincial Divisions, 23 January 1951, reference no. A 2011-00179-09-50-21, LAC. Babies, young children, and girls under eighteen would be interned with their mothers and boys between twelve and eighteen with their fathers. Children of single parents posed additional problems to these plans. "Royal Canadian Mounted Police: 'A' Div. SIB Operation Orders," Report to RCMP Commissioner, circa April 1964, 3, reference no. A 2011-00179-11-30-32, LAC.

28 Despite this apparent discomfort, children were still part of the internment plan and the RCMP "carded" children "either because they or their parents were deemed to be involved in subversive activities." Steve Hewitt, "Sunday Morning Subversion: The Canadian Security State and Organized Religion in the Cold War," *Love, Hate, and Fear in Canada's Cold War* (Toronto: University of Toronto Press, 2004), 60.

29 Barbara Chisholm, Andrea Gutsche, and Russell Floren, *Superior: Under the Shadow of the Gods* (Toronto: Lynx Images, 2001), 161.

30 Ibid., 166.

31 Ibid., 161–4.

32 "Re: Apprehension of Persons under the Defence of Canada Regulations in the Event of War (Plans 'E' Division)," memorandum from J. Healey to RCMP Commissioner Ottawa, 3 February 1949, 2, reference no. A 2011-00179-11-33-00, LAC.

33 Ibid.

34 Ibid.

35 "'A' Division: Apprehension of Persons under Internal Security Regulations," Operation Orders, May 1971, reference no. A 2011-00179-11-30-32, LAC.

36 "'E' Division Apprehension Plan," Booklet, March 1965, 9, reference no. A 2011-00179-11-34-43, LAC.

37 "Plan for Employment of the Army in Support of the RCM Police in Internment Operations," 16 June 1950, 4–5, and "RCMP-Canadian Army Plan for Internment Operations," signed by Charles Foulkes Lt. Gen, Chief of General Staff, and S.T. Wood, 3 August 1950, reference no. A 2011-00179-09-49-40, LAC.

38 In 1950, plans listed eight centres (Halifax, Montreal, Toronto, Winnipeg, Regina, Edmonton, Calgary, and Vancouver) for 2,363 men and 616 women. "Appendix 'A,'" 16 June 1950, reference no. A 2011-00179-09-49-40, LAC. In 1968 there were sixty-two reception centres listed for fifty-six communities across the country. "Division Reception Centres," memo from DSI to Officer in Charge of Emergency Planning Branch, 15 August 1968, reference no. A 2011-00179-09-50-53, LAC.

39 "Re: RCMP-Canadian Army Committee on Vital Points and International Operations," memo from L.H. Nicholson to RCMP Commissioner, 21 April 1950, reference no. A 2011-00179-09-49-40, LAC.

40 Ibid.

41 "Internment Operations," memo from Cook to Nicholson, 4 July 1950, reference no. A 2011-00179-09-49-40, LAC.

42 Prior to the Crash Plan, the RCMP had by 1953 21,000 active files on individuals and 2,300 on organizations. Carl Betke and S.W. Horrall, *Canada's Security Service: An Historical Outline, 1864–1966* (Ottawa: RCMP Historical Section, 1978), 665.

43 "Re: Apprehension of Persons under the D.O.C.R. in the Event of War – Crash Plan," Brief from J. Brunet to Officers Commanding "C," "E," and "O" Divisions, 2 May 1957, reference no. 2011-00179-11-37-20, LAC.

44 "Re: Internment Operations – General, Reception Centres," memo from G.W. Mudge to Director of Military Operations and Plans (Department of National Defence), 15 November 1955, reference no. A 2011-00179-09-51-14, LAC.

45 "Re: Internment Operations – General – Reception Centres," memo from Inspector L.J.G. Watson ("K" Division) to RCMP Commissioner, 14 January 1957, reference no. A 2011-00179-09-50-21, LAC.

46 "Re: Internment Operations, General," memo from G.W. Mudge to Major D. Owen, 12 January 1960, reference no. A 2011-00179-09-50-21, LAC.

47 "Re: Emergency Planning Organization, Function and Procedure," memo from Superintendent C.B. Macdonell ("E" Division) to RCMP Commissioner, circa 26 October 1962, reference no. A 2011-00179-09-50-21, LAC.

48 "Re: Federal Buildings – Protection Factor," memo from R.P. Stone to the Director General of Canadian Emergency Measures Organization [name redacted], 19 October 1967 and 30 October 1967, reference no. A 2011-00179-09-50-53, LAC.

49 The medical concern for the physical and psychological effects of a future nuclear war on civilians grew in the wake of the Cuban Missile Crisis, as was evident with the collection of papers edited for Physicians for Social Responsibility by Saul Aronow, Frank R. Ervin, and Victor W. Sidel, *The Fallen Sky: Medical Consequences of Thermonuclear War* (New York: Hill and Wang, 1963).

50 "Re: Crash Action," memo to N.O. Jones from Sgt. [redacted], 7 May 1956, reference no. A 2011-00179-11-37- 20, LAC.

51 Ibid.

52 Ibid.

53 Memo from A.W. Parsons to All Divisions, 30 May 1962, reference no. A 2011-00179-09-50-21, LAC.

54 "Re: Internment Operations – General," report from Inspector K.B.M. Fraser to RCMP Commissioner, 18 June 1962, reference no. A 2011-00179-09-50-11, LAC.

55 "Re: Internment Operations – General 'C' Division," report from Inspector M.J. Nadon to RCMP Commissioner, 10 July 1962, reference no. A 2011-00179-09-50-11, LAC.

56 "Re: Internment Operations – General," report from Superintendent F.S. Spalding to RCMP Commissioner, 6 July 1962, reference no. A 2011-00179-09-50-11, LAC.

57 In 1950 "E" Division anticipated 586 prominent functionaries for internment, the second-highest number in the country ("O" Division had 1,132 listed and "K" Division had the third-highest number at 346). "Appendix 'A,'" 16 June 1950. In the late 1960s, "E" Division had the highest number of reception centres planned: twenty-five. By contrast, "O" Division had the second-highest number at ten. "Division Reception Centres," 15 August 1968.

58 Between 12 and 14 July 1962, "B" Division sent a number of reports to the RCMP commissioner in Ottawa directly from detachments in Grand Bank, Habour Grace, and Goose Bay, Newfoundland.

59 "Internment Operations – General," report from Superintendent J.T. Parsons to RCMP Commissioner, 7 June 1962, reference no. A 2011-00179-09-50-11, LAC.

60 Letter from R.P. Stone (Emergency Planning Branch) to G. Suprenant (Commissioner of Penitentiaries), 1 November 1967, reference no. A 2011-00179-09-50-53, LAC.

61 "Internment Camps – Canada General," memo from [name redacted] Senior NCO (Emergency Planning Branch) to Officer in Charge (Emergency Planning Branch), 30 May 1967, reference no. A 2011-00179-09-50-53, LAC.

62 "Internment Camps – Canada General," 30 May 1967.

63 Letter from Stone to Suprenant, 1 November 1967.

64 Ibid.

65 Letter from [name redacted] (Emergency Government Operations) to Superintendent C.A. Lougheed, 26 April 1968, reference no. A 2011-00179-09-50-53, LAC. This document indicates that there was fallout protection available for Drumheller, Warkworth, and Matsqui. It also indicates that the protection factor of each facility was calculated, but unfortunately the attached appendix that detailed this information remains redacted.

66 "Profunc Recapitulation," Tables, 15 June 1951 and 31 December 1951, reference no. A 2011-00179-09-54-13, LAC.

67 "Profunc Recapitulation," Tables, 17 January 1955 and 26 September 1955, reference no. A 2011-00179-09-54-13, LAC.

68 Memo from Sergeant [name redacted] (Statistical Office) to Inspector Parent, 20 March 1963, reference no. A 2011-00179-11-29-34, LAC.

69 "Profunc Recapitulation," Table, 23 February 1960, reference no. A 2011-00179-09-54-13, LAC.

70 "Profunc Recapitulation," Table, 9 December 1969, reference no. A 2011-00179-11-37-20, LAC.

71 "Profunc Recapitulation," Table, 1 April 1970, reference no. A 2011-00179-11-39-34, LAC.

72 "Profunc Recapitulation," Table, 6 June 1979, reference no. A 2011-00179-09-52-06, LAC.

73 "Re: Profunc," memo from Inspector G.J. Douglas ("D" Division) to RCMP Commissioner, 6 January 1965, reference no. A 2011-00179-11-29-01, LAC.

74 "Re: Profunc," memo from Inspector R. McKernan ("D" Division), 16 December 1968, reference no. A 2011-00179-11-29-01, LAC.

75 "Re: Profunc," memo from T.E. Linning ("D" Division) to RCMP Commissioner, 31 May 1972, reference no. A 2011-00179-11-29-34, LAC.

76 "Re: Profunc," memo from Sergeant [redacted] (Thunder Bay Security Service) to Officer in Charge of "D" Division, 26 April 1972, reference no. A 2011-00179-11-29-01, LAC.

77 "Profunc Manual," booklet, 1980, 3, reference no. A 2011-00179-11-37-48.

78 "Re: Advisory Committee on Internment," memorandum sent by M.R. Dare to Robin Bourne, April 1974, reference no. A 2011-00179-11-42-35, LAC.

79 Letter from M.R. Dare to Robin Bourne (Ministry of Solicitor General), July 1973, 1, reference no. A 2011-00179-11-37-20, LAC.

80 "RCMP Department War Book," memo from J.B. Giroux (Security Service) to Director Protective Policing, 31 October 1980, 1, reference no. A 2011-00179-1128-08, LAC.

81 "RCMP Department War Book," 31 October 1980, 2.

6 "A Threat against What …?" Transnational Threat Construction and the Destabilization/Stabilization of the Canadian Domestic Security Environment in the 1970s

STEVE HEWITT

In a 1974 speech, Michael Dare, then director general of the Royal Canadian Mounted Police (RCMP) Security Service,[1] observed that "international terrorism like aggression or subversion, is not a precise concept which lends itself to definition … [there are] no internationally-accepted definitions of international terrorism."[2] In making the connection between terrorism and subversion, Dare was unknowingly connecting the past of Canadian domestic security with its future, including the counterterrorism world of the post-9/11 period. Specifically, the two perceived threats, and the state security responses to them, intersected; the Mounted Police had been "policing" subversion as far back as the First World War and would continue to do so until 1984, when the Canadian Security Intelligence Service (CSIS) replaced it. In turn, the RCMP's first proper counterterrorism unit emerged in September 1972 within the counter-subversion branch of the Security Service.

On the basis of thousands of pages of security records obtained from Library and Archives Canada through forty Access to Information requests, this chapter argues that the 1970s do not represent the beginning of a transition from the Cold War domestic security environment of previous decades to a counterterrorism world that would eventually emerge as dominant after 11 September 2001.[3] Rather, that decade was the start of a fusion between the Cold War security milieu and the modern counterterrorism that would come to be the main priority in the post–Cold War period at least until the 2020 pandemic. In other words, when it comes to domestic security, the Cold War remains in the twenty-first century a fundamental part of the so-called "war on terror." Intelligence collection methods, such as informants, tactics deployed against targets, including disruption efforts, and the significance of allies, particularly the United States, remain as relevant in the twenty-first century as they did during the Cold War.[4] The security environment did begin to destabilize in the 1970s as the movement away from security targets based on the Cold War towards those that would dominate in the post–Cold War period began. Nonetheless, continuity remained via the aforementioned methods and in the tendency to blame domestic security problems on foreign elements, as had occurred in Canada since at least the First World War.[5] Similarly, the counterterrorism of the 1970s would concentrate on "foreign" threats to Canada, in contrast to earlier efforts against the Front de libération du Québec (FLQ), which the Canadian state viewed as a domestic threat despite its transnational nature. Both counter-subversion and counterterrorism "othered" those deemed a threat. The security state would frame many of them as, in the words of political scientists Rita Dhamoon and Yasmeen Abu-Laban, echoing Donald Avery's work on an earlier era, "internal dangerous foreigners."[6]

Historicizing modern Canadian counterterrorism by exploring its birth in the 1970s is important for offering a new take on Canadian security and intelligence in keeping with the groundbreaking research on the Five Eyes nations included in this collection. This chapter provides much-needed historical context to practices and approaches in the current war on terror while at the same time offering a fuller portrait of domestic security approaches in the Cold War, such as the plans to intern communists in the event of a Third World War as documented in the chapter by Frances Reilly. Such an emphasis also challenges in a fundamental fashion the notion, which became popular after 9/11, particularly in American circles, that intelligence agencies created in the Cold War were unprepared for the emergence of a "new" threat posed by terrorism.[7] A prime example of this idea within the academic literature is Amy Zegart's *Spying Blind: The CIA, the FBI, and the Origins of 9/11*.[8] Although Zegart acknowledges that the Federal Bureau of Investigation (FBI) performed more than just a crime-fighting role during the Cold War, she speeds over its lengthy role not only in counter-intelligence but especially in counter-subversion. She also does not reflect on the FBI's counterterrorism role, which began in earnest in the 1970s. Instead, counterterrorism for the FBI in the post–Cold War period represented doing "a different job entirely."[9] According to Zegart,

> this law enforcement orientation served the bureau well. The problem came when the Cold War ended and counterterrorism required a radically different approach. Suddenly, agents who had devoted careers to investigating past tragedies were supposed to prevent them. Officials were expected to work across cases rather than within them. An organization geared to guarding information was now supposed to share it. And the most highly prized result was no longer a conviction, but a non-result: the absence of terrorist attack.[10]

Similarly, Gregory F. Treverton's *Intelligence for an Age of Terror* creates the impression that terrorism and counterterrorism really began only with the end of the Cold War. The book additionally does not acknowledge fully the extent of Cold War domestic surveillance against targets beyond foreign intelligence agents such as the FBI's targeting of Carl Marzani, as documented in Marcella Bencivenni's contribution to this collection.[11]

The assumptions in these secondary sources miss the importance of the Cold War to modern domestic counterterrorism. Indeed, that decades-long conflict is crucial to the story, as the instruments at hand for the state to engage with the rise of new threats from terrorism in the 1970s were Cold War constructs developed through the securitization of communism. Although this process included counter-espionage in Canada, a major focus of the RCMP's intelligence branch was counter-subversion.[12] It was within the counter-subversion branch of the Mounted Police, that the Security Service's first unit dedicated to countering international terrorism would arise.[13] The trigger was the attack by Palestinian terrorists on the Israeli athletic team at the Munich Olympics in 1972, extreme violence that generated unprecedented global media coverage, much of it live, a unique aspect to this point in the history of terrorism.[14]

One word from RCMP Security Service Director General Michael Dare's 1974 reflection on the difficulty in defining terrorism that opened this chapter is highly significant in relation to what follows and in connection with the evolution of Canadian counterterrorism in the 1970s and 1980s. He listed "subversion" as a concept lacking a precise definition. The comparison between terrorism and subversion was not chosen at random. Rather, subversion, or, more precisely, counter-subversion, represented a key Mounted Police intelligence function from the force's effective beginning during the First World War through to the 1980s. Although the emphasis at the end of the Cold War was on counter-espionage as the defining characteristic of domestic state security during the previous decades, in fact countering subversion was the central activity – hence the creation of a massive paper trail connected to Canadians and non-Canadians and to their groups and organizations. According to the McDonald Commission, which investigated misconduct by the RCMP, the force's intelligence branch opened files on over eight hundred thousand individuals and organizations between 1919 and 1979. This number was a cumulative total. To provide a snapshot from a particular year, the RCMP Security Service held active files in 1967 on forty-eight thousand individuals and six thousand organizations; its description of what constituted a subversive included "CP of C [Communist Party of Canada] member, suspected Trotskyist, self-admitted

Marxist, black nationalist, student agitator, anarchist, red power advocate, or an associate of communists."[15]

The nebulous nature of subversion, combined with the shifting face of the security landscape by the 1970s, caused confusion even in the ranks of those carrying out investigations. At a 1971 conference in Ottawa, Mounted Police Security Service personnel gathered to reflect on the nature of their work including targeting. What, for instance, constituted a security threat? For one member present, that query led to more fundamental questions about the RCMP Security Service's role:

> A threat against what or, paraphrased, what or whom are we protecting – the public at large? the constitution? the Government? the present Administration? the Liberal Party while it is in power? or are we defending our capitalist or neo-capitalist socio/economic/political order? Are we to be ultra-reactionary, arch defenders of the status quo standing in the path of any and all change? If change is to be permitted in society then how much change, what are the limits of change? At what point is change no longer evolutionary but revolutionary?[16]

Despite the self-reflection by Canada's domestic spies, the pursuit of subversion continued. That task served as a gateway into the new world of counterterrorism, not only in Canada but elsewhere too. In his influential *Low Intensity Operations: Subversion, Insurgency, and Peacekeeping*, British general Frank Kitson, who served in Kenya during the Mau Mau conflict and in Northern Ireland during "The Troubles," broadly defines subversion as

> all measures short of the use of armed force taken by one section of the people of a country to overthrow those governing the country at the time, or to force them to do things which they do not want to do. It can involve the use of political and economic pressure, strikes, protest marches, and propaganda, and can also include the use of small-scale violence for the purpose of coercing recalcitrant members of the population into giving support.[17]

Security agencies would perceive an intersection between subversion, communism, insurgency, and terrorism in an era when definitions of the latter were contested and fluid not only among academics but among states as well.[18] Thus, subversion could be a tactic of communists or terrorists or insurgents, and, indeed, in the early 1980s, the administration of President Ronald Reagan, influenced by Claire Sterling's book *The Terror Network*, viewed almost all transnational terrorism as being under the control of the Soviet Union and international communism.[19]

The 1972 terrorist attack at the Munich Olympics had brought counterterrorism squarely onto the RCMP's plate, especially since by then the International Olympic Committee had already selected Montreal to host the 1976 games.[20] The new counterterrorism priority in part led the Liberal government of Prime Minister Pierre Trudeau in 1975 to provide the first ever clearly defined mandate for the RCMP Security Service. It named counterterrorism as a core function and charged the agency with performing "a preventive and support/advisory function":

(a) The preventive function involves the timely use of intelligence to anticipate and prevent acts of violence by Terrorists.
(b) In the event of terrorists planning or committing an act of violence within Canada, the RCMP security service provides a support/advisory function to Law Enforcement Departments. This includes a rapid exchange of intelligence to deal with the situation at hand.[21]

How did the Security Service understand terrorism and the threat from terrorism in this period, and what did it do about it? In his aforementioned 1974 speech, the then head of the Security Service explicitly suggested that some terrorism had legitimate motivations, a common view at the time.[22] "There is an element of truth ... in the assertion that political violence is the product of 'just grievances,' of social deprivations and intolerable oppression," Dare observed, although he added that these grievances did not justify resorting to violence. He went on to outline six implications or threats to Canada from international terrorism, several of which played into the foreignness narrative:

1 The general danger to Canada and Canadian interest by Canada's support for a party involved in a conflict;
2 The specific threat to Canadians related to a conflict by reason of ethnic background;
3 The threat to foreign officials and premises in Canada and to Canadian officials abroad;
4 The participation of Canadians in terrorist attacks and/or support for such attacks;
5 The possibility of relations within Canada to terrorist activity;
6 Concern over the possible use of Canada as a base or place of convenience for subversive, espionage or terrorist activity directed against other countries.[23]

In Dare's speech and in the nature of both RCMP counter-subversion and counterterrorism at the time, perceived subversion remained intertwined with "extremism," another popular security buzzword of the post-9/11 period, and the threat of terrorism.[24] This response partially reflected the changing security landscape that began in the 1960s and continued into the 1970s. The 1960s saw the rise of a variety of new entities, including the Black Power and Red Power movements, shattering the unipolar security environment of decades previous in which state security agencies perceived only communism as a major threat.[25] However, this shift also stretched into violence associated with various ethnic conflicts around the world and with the left-wing terrorism that played a prominent role in extreme violence by non-state actors in the 1970s. Dare warned in his 1974 speech of the possibility of "racially-motivated violence-oriented elements," specifically referencing "Serb, Croat, African and Caribbean groups" because of a

> capacity for violence and social disruptions, and their solidarity with international extremist movements and national liberation groups. This is particularly true of a small group of black extremists in Canada which has assumed a strong support role for Black revolutionaries in Africa and the Caribbean.

He added Chilean and Irish groups in Canada as being of "specific concern." In terminology that reflected the intersection of counter-subversion and counterterrorism, he advised that the solution was to have proper police intelligence "to keep track of possible subversive activity and combat it effectively." There was a crucial need, he added, to "know your enemy."[26]

Analysis created by the Department of the Solicitor General in 1974 to reflect on the rise of international terrorism and its implications for Canada mirrored Dare's rhetoric. Its content emphasized the transnational nature of the terrorism of the early 1970s, which, it argued, again reflecting the conceptual fluidity of the period, came "under various names, i.e. dissident groups, terrorists, urban guerrillas," but with – in Cold War terms that also mirrored the left-wing nature of some terrorism in the 1970s – "the same goal and that is to destroy the social and economic values of our 'capitalistic' system."[27] Canada, argued the report, could become a "staging ground" for attacks elsewhere, undoubtedly against the country's only neighbour, the United States.[28]

In a 1974 RCMP report examining the potential threats of violence to the 1976 Montreal Olympics, a similar pattern of emphasizing the foreign aspect of terrorism appeared with mentions of the Israeli–Palestinian conflict, the British and the Irish in relation to Northern Ireland, "liberation movements," and "Black extremism."[29] A report the following year regarding the Olympics' threat situation that circulated at the highest levels of the Trudeau government viewed Canada's diversity as a key component in the terrorism threat: "The multi-national composition of Canadian society is indeed the very basis of our concern *as certain residents are members of and others could become involved with or [a] target of the various terrorist organizations.*"[30] The stress on the foreignness in terrorism percolated through the Canadian state and eventually led the Trudeau government to update previous Cold War–dominated criteria around excluding immigrants or visitors to Canada. The Cabinet agreed to new rules in 1975 in the Temporary Immigration Security Act, which it explicitly introduced because of the perceived terrorist threat to the Olympics in Montreal.[31] The changes authorized the solicitor general (through intelligence supplied by the RCMP) and the Department of External Affairs in conjunction to draw up lists of individuals who could be excluded from Canada based on their membership in certain organizations, including those deemed to be terrorist groups.[32] Many of these "temporary" measures became permanent in the Immigration Act of 1976, a piece of legislation that political scientist Reg Whitaker has described as a law in which "national security overrode civil liberties and individual rights to a remarkable extent, actually providing a tougher basis for enforcing security than had existed in the earlier legislation." Mounted Police concern over terrorism and subversion drove the legislation, as security worries centred, in Whitaker's words, "around points of entry – in an age when the technology of air travel, as well as instant electronic communication, had already raised the problem of controlling border flows to entirely new levels of complexity."[33] As part of security preparations for the Olympics, "terrorist lookout" lists were established at border points. At major airports, this included from November 1975 a system known as the Computerized Olympics Immigration Lookout System (COILS) into which the RCMP Security Service contributed names, frequently derived from non-Canadian sources, of potential terrorists.[34]

Beyond the wider legislative, bureaucratic, and policy levels, there existed the everyday practical counterterrorism as carried out by the RCMP Security Service. The Mounted Police restructured frequently in the 1970s in an effort to address the threat of terrorism within the existing counter-subversion branch. In September 1972, because of the Munich terrorist attack, there was a specific "desk" within the counter-terrorism unit to concentrate on Middle Eastern-related terrorism. An organizational chart dating from 1974 to 1975 shows several additional groupings related to terrorism. An Irish Republican Army section existed on its own. Then there was "C-1 International Terrorist/Guerrilla Section" with categories such as "Arabs" in Canada as diplomats, "International Terrorism," "Hijackings and Letterbombs [*sic*]," and

"Special projects." A second section, "C-2 National Extremists and V.I.P. Security Section," covered the security of diplomats and visiting dignitaries, far-right terrorism, "Ethnic Extremists (Yugoslavs etc.)," "Greek and Hungarian Extremists," and research.[35] In March 1976, the Security Service, reflecting the significance of far-left terrorism at the time, established sections related to Japanese, Latin American, and Western European terrorism. Three years later, it moved to "Regional Desks" to focus on the transnational dimensions of a particular terrorist threat along geographical as opposed to ideological lines. Some confusion plainly emerged because of the frequent restructuring and personnel changes, and the RCMP organized a conference to address key issues such as source recruitment and handling, "technical source applications," and liaising with federal government agencies and foreign allies. The number of key personnel dedicated directly to international terrorism remained small, with thirty (eighteen from the field and twelve from headquarters in Ottawa) invited to attend the gathering in Ottawa.[36]

Practical obstacles existed for the Security Service when it came to investigating terrorism. The main issue was a lack of experience around terrorism, excluding the FLQ, in a Cold War agency that had for decades concentrated solely on a perceived threat involving subversion or espionage from the far left. Also contributing to the confusion, undoubtedly, was the overall lack of clarity around terrorism definitions in the 1970s. Headquarters in Ottawa instituted annual work plans out of a belief that divisions "still do not fully understand or appreciate the requirements and ultimate objectives of investigation into terrorism." As a result, personnel were encouraged to discuss "trends, priorities and procedures prior to … ensur[ing] a co-ordinated national program outlining national priorities and objectives and a unified co-ordination thrust in dealing with terrorism in Canada."[37]

A more fundamental issue in the way the RCMP perceived the threat of international terrorism was in the makeup of the police itself. Staffed predominantly by Euro-Canadian males, the force had historically lacked diversity. This began to change with the admittance of women in 1974, but the force did not, nor does it in the twenty-first century, reflect the diverse nature of many Canadian urban centres.[38] With the RCMP constructing the threat of terrorism as something "foreign," it turned its attention to immigrant and ethnic minority communities. Because the monocultural Mounted Police found it difficult to collect intelligence about such groups, it meant the police had to take a blanket approach, viewing entire communities with suspicion and thus rendering them, to use Paddy Hillyard's concept, "suspect communities." This passage from 1978 demonstrates the difficulties the Security

Service encountered in attempting to obtain intelligence on elements within communities that it had no connections to or roots within:

> Montreal have conducted extensive investigation into the [deleted under the Access to Information and the Privacy Act (ATIP)] communities within Montreal. Due to the difficulties in penetrating these ethnic communities, there have been problems in identifying key individuals. However, Montreal have identified [deleted under ATIP] as a key figure [deleted under ATIP] with numerous links in Montreal and Toronto.[39]

In locations such as Montreal, the Security Service would have had little choice but to rely on informants to supply information from within these communities, including what the Mounties referred to in 1979 as "casual sources in various ethnic areas."[40] This is an approach in Canada that began as early as the First World War, when the state constructed some minority ethnic communities as threats because of Bolshevism;[41] it is a pattern equally evident elsewhere such as in the United Kingdom in relation to the campaign against the Provisional Irish Republican Army and in the United States since the attacks of 11 September 2001 as the FBI and the New York Police Department have relied heavily on informants blanketing entire Muslim communities as part of counterterrorism investigations.[42] When it came to counterterrorism informants, headquarters emphasized a sense of urgency with Mounties in the field encouraged to cultivate "casual sources before anything serious occurs – i.e. don't wait until something drastic takes place before you try to develop sources."[43] Although the reference was to "casual sources," the Security Service did emphasize the need to discover "individuals who have the capability or will to participate in or support a terrorist act" instead of taking a blanket approach to "a suspect ethnic group."[44] Nevertheless, reports at Security Service conferences offered brief ethnic profiling of communities across Canada, a sort of forerunner to a much more sophisticated effort by the FBI after 9/11 to use census data to map targeted communities in an attempt to turn up signs of acts of terrorism being planned.[45] Here is a taste of this in 1978 from the Security Service office in the province of Nova Scotia:

> Investigations into the [deleted under ATIP] ethnic community has [sic] progressed well during the past year. Out of [deleted under ATIP] in Nova Scotia, [deleted under ATIP] reside in the Halifax area. New immigration [deleted under ATIP] appear to centre in Halifax and, due to their strong cultural ties, many do not speak English. For the most part, acculturation has been slow [deleted under ATIP].[46]

A similar pattern occurred in various western Canadian cities. As these excerpts demonstrate, commentaries were still heavily infused with Cold War priorities and rhetoric:

Winnipeg Security Service has concentrated on monitoring the [deleted under ATIP] community within Winnipeg and the influence being exerted by local leftist groups to draw upon [deleted under ATIP] support to enhance their own position. However, it appears the reverse has occurred with [deleted under ATIP] using the C.P. of C. [Communist Party of Canada] to propagate their own campaign of condemning the [deleted under ATIP] government ...

Edmonton have good cover of [deleted under ATIP] and have been concentrating more resources on [deleted] groups in Edmonton. Efforts in this regard are progressing well and they are being provided with information on [deleted under ATIP] organization. To date, from all indications, [deleted under ATIP] has not displayed any violence tendencies since moderates have firm control over the direction of the group's activities. Calgary are also concentrating the majority of their effort towards [deleted under ATIP] and are monitoring individuals associated with [deleted under ATIP]. Again, there is no evidence that these groups will resort to violence in an attempt to achieve more recognition for their cause ... Vancouver has concentrated on four major areas:

Activities within [deleted under ATIP] have [deleted under ATIP] considerably receded since 1976. This has been attributed to the constant in-fighting which has factionalized the community with no cohesive group capable of taking control and directing the activities of [deleted under ATIP] For the most part, the community is very conservative, which has also detracted from the development of a more militant line [deleted under ATIP] continue to hold cultural meetings, however, these activities are strictly social affairs [deleted under ATIP].

The possibility of [deleted under ATIP] links within Vancouver came to light after [deleted under ATIP] however investigations to date have failed to provide any information of interest.

Information came to our attention in 1977 that [deleted under ATIP] spent last summer in British Columbia. It is significant to note that [deleted under ATIP] would use Canada as a safe haven which reinforces our suspicions that Canada performs a role for a number of international terrorist groups.[47]

At various points through the 1970s, the police discussed proactive tools for dealing with targeted individuals from ethnic communities that have resonance with a post-9/11 environment. One example was the use of Canada's Immigration Act to remove those deemed security threats. Under the legislation at the time, specifically Section 39 of the Immigration Act, individuals labelled as a security threat to Canada could be deported without an opportunity to appeal and without any evidence being given at a hearing simply if two federal Cabinet ministers signed an authorization to do so.[48] The Canadian government deported six "individuals of interest" from Quebec in the late 1970s using Section 39 warrants, although the Solicitor General stressed that this approach should be used only as a last resort.[49] Additionally, the Security Service enjoyed a strong relationship with the Department of Immigration when it came to accessing records.[50]

The profiling of entire communities became more systematic in the early 1980s, culminating in the 1982 creation of a file entitled "General Conditions and Subversive Activities – Census Re: Immigration Statistics." It began after the director general of the Security Service, J.B. Giroux, inquired at a briefing about the "population of the various Arab nationalities in Canada" by asking, in the words of the note taker, "What are the numbers and where are they located?"[51] The Security Service soon assembled statistics covering 1971, the year of a previous Canadian census, to 1980 for the numbers of immigrants from twenty-two countries; all were located in the Middle East or North Africa: Egypt, Saudi Arabia, Turkey, Iran, Iraq, Libya, Israel, Lebanon, Syria, Oman, Kuwait, Jordan, Morocco, Algeria, Tunisia, Sudan, United Arab Emirates, Qatar, People's Democratic Republic of Yemen, Arab Republic of Yemen, Bahrain, and Cyprus. The police broke the numbers down further for all twenty-two countries by specific Canadian provinces and cities.[52]

It is not clear what specific use was made of the census material, although such information about certain ethnic communities would remain of interest to CSIS when it replaced the RCMP Security Service in 1984. A 1985 CSIS document on terrorism "threat assessments" noted that in part these threats would be based on a "support structure in Canada or abroad" that would include "ethnic concentrations and their political activism, and pro and anti-community, or national sentiment in Canada."[53]

In the end, the RCMP's blanket approach to ethnic minority and immigrant communities failed to counter the threat that did exist. The issue of Armenia, including its historic treatment at the hands of the Turks and its lack of an independent state, would lead to the assassination of a Turkish military attaché in Ottawa in August 1982 in a crime that remains unsolved to this day.[54] Most significantly of all,

in June 1985 elements within the Sikh community in British Columbia planted bombs on two different airplanes; one killed two baggage
handlers in Tokyo, and the other was responsible for the deaths of 329
people, including 268 Canadians, the worst act of mass murder in Canadian history.[55] Links to violence in majority communities in Canada
also existed, except these communities never faced being generalized
and targeted as a "suspect community" by state security agencies.[56]
For instance, in October 1982, Direct Action, an anarchist group, with
members from the broader white community, carried out a bombing at
a Toronto factory that was involved in manufacturing components for
American cruise missiles.[57]

With terrorist attacks within Canada and against Canadians in the
1980s, counterterrorism would finally surpass counter-subversion
within Canadian domestic security priorities. In particular, the 1982
killing of the Turkish diplomat sparked a sense of urgency from the
highest levels of the Trudeau government. The prime minister himself
requested in the autumn of 1982 that a detailed briefing paper on the
threat posed by terrorism and efforts to combat it be prepared.[58] The
RCMP was among the eleven different contributors (External Affairs,
Solicitor General, RCMP, Privy Council Office, Defence, Immigration,
Customs, Transport, Atomic Energy, Control Board, and Communications) tasked with assembling the paper, which went through a series
of drafts over a two-year period.

In its contribution, the RCMP complained about a lack of resources,
which required them to "prioritize the targets which will receive the
major thrust of Security Service attention relegating lower priorities to
a passive collation or monitoring mode." The main obstacle for counterterrorism from the perspective of the police again concerned the perceived foreignness of the threat: "In a liberal democratic society where
legitimate dissent is recognized in law and practice, one must recognize the sensitivity of investigating ethnic or other interest groups on
the premise that there could be, within these groups, elements sympathetic to a terrorist cause, whatever it may be." In turn, this impediment
made it difficult to discover "the identity of the small core of Canadians
and neo-Canadians who are violence prone and would render active
support to foreign terrorists intent on perpetrating a terrorist act in
Canada."[59]

Additionally, the RCMP produced an aide-memoire detailing
what it called the "limitations on the capability of Security Service
Counter-Terrorism operations."[60] The first six points demonstrated the
complex nature of counterterrorism investigations, particularly within

liberal-democratic states, but they could equally have been applied to decades of counter-subversion operations during the Cold War:

(i)   limited manpower resources, which necessitates the prioritiza-
         tion of targeting efforts;
(ii)   the sensitivity of investigation ethnic and issue-orientated
         groups;
(iii)   the difficulty in determining the line that distinguishes legitimate
         dissent from terrorist sympathy and support;
(iv)   the problem of balancing the rights of the individual with the se-
         curity requirements of the State;
(v)   the lack of coordinated analytical resources within the Security
         and Intelligence community;
(vi)   the different interpretation and definitions that various
         States apply to the field of terrorism which makes it diffi-
         cult for the Security Service to verify information and threat
         assessments;
(vii)   problems of a legal nature in the conduct of some types of
         Counter-Terrorism investigations, these have been identified by
         the McDonald Commission [Royal Commission of Inquiry into
         Certain Activities of the RCMP].[61]

At the time this list was written, counterterrorism had already become the Security Service's top priority as a result of the killing of the
Turkish diplomat, with 199 "person-years" allocated, which, despite
complaints about limited resources, was listed as adequate.[62] Even
with its new prioritization, counterterrorism remained part of the
counter-subversion branch.[63]

Countering subversion as a security function finally ended in the
late 1980s, although it remains part CSIS' mandate to this day.[64] By
then, the Cold War had reached its conclusion. In the 1990s, with the
perception of an increasing threat from terrorism, the notion would
arise that intelligence agencies, as Cold War constructs, lacked the
competency and experience to deal with a radically different threat
from that of the past. However, while the dominant form of terrorism arguably differed from its past form, terrorism itself, including
the transnational version, was not new. Indeed, domestic intelligence agencies in Canada, the UK, and the United States had begun
their efforts against terrorism while the Cold War was still on, de-
ploying methods used against communists and other perceived radicals. The Cold War may have ended with the 1980s, but it lived on in
counterterrorism.

NOTES

1 The RCMP's intelligence branch went by a number of names over the years, including informally as the security service and formally from the mid-1970s on as the Security Service. For the sake of consistency, I will refer to it as the "Security Service" throughout this chapter.

2 Mike Dare, "International Terrorism – The Canadian Viewpoint," 5 December 1974, RG 146, Records of the Canadian Security Intelligence Service, Library and Archives Canada (LAC), access request A201100060_2011-10-17_11-02-31.

3 For more on the complexities and complications around using Access to Information and on security records obtained through access requests, see Christabelle Sethna and Steve Hewitt, *Just Watch Us: RCMP Surveillance of the Women's Liberation Movement in Cold War Canada* (Montreal and Kingston: McGill-Queen's University Press, 2018), 170–99.

4 Steve Hewitt, *Snitch: A History of the Modern Intelligence Informer* (London and New York: Continuum, 2010), 121–46.

5 Donald Avery, *"Dangerous Foreigners": European Immigrant Workers and Labour Radicalism in Canada, 1896–1932* (Toronto: McClelland and Stewart, 1979).

6 Rita Dhamoon and Yasmeen Abu-Laban, "Dangerous (Internal) Foreigners and Nation-Building: The Case of Canada," *International Political Science Review* 30, no. 2 (2009): 163; Avery, *"Dangerous Foreigners"*; For more on the "framing" of such security threats, see David Cunningham and Barb Browning, "The Emergence of Worthy Targets: Official Frames and Deviance Narratives within the FBI," *Sociological Forum* 19, no. 3 (2004): 347–69.

7 Paul R. Pillar, "Intelligent Design?" *Foreign Affairs* 87, no. 2 (2008): 138.

8 Amy B. Zegart, *Spying Blind: The CIA, the FBI, and the Origins of 9/11* (Princeton, NJ: Princeton University Press, 2007).

9 Ibid., 120.

10 Ibid., 125.

11 Gregory F. Treverton, *Intelligence in an Age of Terror* (Cambridge: Cambridge University Press, 2009), 1–7. Historians have challenged these notions in an American context, most notably Athan G. Theoharis and Daniel Chard. See Athan G. Theoharis, *Abuse of Power: How Cold War Surveillance and Secrecy Policy Shaped the Response to 9/11* (Philadelphia: Temple University Press, 2011); Daniel Chard, "Nixon's War on Terrorism: The FBI, Leftist Guerrillas, and the Origins of Watergate" (PhD dissertation, University of Massachusetts-Amherst, 2016).

12 Reg Whitaker, Gregory Kealey, and Andrew Parnaby, *Secret Service: Political Policing in Canada from the Fenians to Fortress America* (Toronto: University of Toronto Press, 2012). For more on the concept of securitization, see

Rita Taureck, "Securitisation Theory and Securitisation Studies," *Journal of International Relations and Development* 9 (2006): 53–61.

13 In the United Kingdom, the Security Service (MI5) during the same period established its unit dedicated to countering international terrorism also within its counter-subversion branch. Christopher Andrew, *The Defence of the Realm: The Authorized History of MI5* (London: Penguin Books, 2009), Kindle, loc. 13328–33; Stella Rimington, *Open Secret: The Autobiography of the Former Director-General of MI5* (London: Random House, 2011), Kindle, loc. 1825–33.

14 Timothy Naftali, *Blind Spot: The Secret History of American Counter-Terrorism* (New York: Basic Books, 2006), 54–77; Charles Townshend, *Terrorism: A Very Short Introduction* (Oxford: Oxford University Press, 2011), Kindle, loc. 1411; Richard English, *Does Terrorism Work? A History* (Oxford: Oxford University Press, 2016), 152.

15 Memorandum of Supt. Draper for D.S.I., 7 November 1967, Canadian Security Intelligence Service (CSIS), Key Sectors–Canada, access request 88-A-18.

16 Directing NCO, Key Sectors Section, to [deleted under Access to Information and Privacy Act (ATIP): name of Mountie], 15 December 1971, CSIS, access request 117-98-71.

17 Frank Kitson, *Low Intensity Operations: Subversion, Insurgency, and Peacekeeping* (London: Faber and Faber, 1971), 3.

18 Lisa Stampnitzky, *Disciplining Terror: How Experts Invented "Terrorism"* (Cambridge: Cambridge University Press, 2014); Naftali, *Blind Spot*, 25–33.

19 Claire Sterling, *The Terror Network* (New York: Henry Holt, 1981); Bob Woodward, *Veil: The Secret Wars of the CIA, 1981–1987* (New York: Simon and Schuster, 1987), loc. 1532, 2116, 2123, 2147.

20 Dominique Clément, "The Transformation of Security Planning for the Olympics: The 1976 Montreal Games," *Terrorism and Political Violence* 27, no. 2 (2015): 1–25.

21 Briefing Note on International Terrorism Prepared for RCMP Commissioner Speaking to Canadian Bar Association, 26 August 1980, RG 146, LAC, access request A201100060_2011-10-17_10-5-1.

22 Stampnitzky, *Disciplining Terror*, loc. 129–40, 211–18.

23 Dare, "International Terrorism – The Canadian Viewpoint."

24 For more on the concept of extremism, see J.M. Berger, *Extremism* (Cambridge, MA: MIT Press, 2018).

25 For some discussion of these elements in a Canadian context, see Bryan Palmer, *Canada's 1960s: The Ironies of Identity in a Rebellious Era* (Toronto: University of Toronto Press, 2009), loc. 7115–8020; David Austin, *Fear of a Black Nation: Race, Sex, and Security in Sixties Montreal* (Montreal: Between the Lines Press, 2013).

26 Dare, "International Terrorism – The Canadian Viewpoint."

27 Report on International Terrorism, 1974, 1, R1184, Records of the Solicitor General, vol. 903, file 11-98, "C," pt. 1, LAC; David C. Rapoport, "The Four Waves of Modern Terrorism," in *Attacking Terrorism: Elements of a Grand Strategy*, ed. Audrey Kurth Cronin and James M. Ludes (Washington, DC: Georgetown University Press, 2004), 46–73. For more on the lack of a rigid application of the terrorist label in this period see Naftali, *Blind Spot*, 25–33.

28 Report on International Terrorism, 1974, 8.

29 Security Threat Estimates–Olympics 76, RCMP Report, 7 January 1974, 000006-000009, RG 146, A2009-00020, LAC.

30 "Olympics in Montreal, Que, Cabinet Committee on Security and Planning, Threat Assessment," 1975, 000841, RG 146, A2009-00020, LAC. Emphasis in the original.

31 "Memorandum to the Cabinet – Subject: Revised Criteria for the Exclusion of Immigrants and Non-Immigrants on Security Grounds," 19 March 1975, 000864-9, RG 146, LAC; Reg Whitaker, *Double Standard: The Secret History of Canadian Immigration* (Toronto: Lester and Orpen Dennys, 1987), 241. For more on the RCMP and the security of the Olympics, see Clément, "The Transformation of Security Planning for the Olympics."

32 "Memorandum to the Cabinet ...," 000870.

33 Whitaker, *Double Standard*, 239.

34 Clément, "The Transformation of Security Planning for the Olympics," 41; Department of Immigration to RCMP Commissioner, 8 May 1975, 000235, RG 76, Records of the Department of Immigration, file 256-Q-3, part 2, LAC, access request A0037545.

35 Organizational Charts – "D" Ops, "Organizational Chart Depicting Span of Control and Chain of Command," no date [1974–75], 000097-98, RG 146, LAC, access request A-2015-00291.

36 Security Service Operational Conference, Memorandum, 12 December 1979, 000180, RG 146, LAC, access request A2011-00054.

37 Security Service Operational Conference, 12 December 1979, 000052; Security Service Operational Conference, RCMP Memorandum, 21 March 1977, 000075, RG 146, LAC, access request A2011-00054.

38 In 2012, 8.1 per cent of regular members of the RCMP were members of visible minorities, compared with 20.6 per cent of Canada's population in 2011. "Results and Respect in the RCMP Workplace," Royal Canadian Mounted Police, 14 April 2016, http://www.rcmp-grc.gc.ca/en/results -and-respect-the-rcmp-workplace; "Immigration and Ethnocultural Diversity in Canada," Statistics Canada, 15 September 2016, https://www12 .statcan.gc.ca/nhs-enm/2011/as-sa/99-010-x/99-010-x2011001-eng .cfm. See also "Police Diversity Fails to Keep Pace with Canadian Populations," CBC News, 14 July 2016, http://www.cbc.ca/news/canada /police-diversity-canada-1.3677952.

39 Security Service Operational Conference "D" Operations, Letter, 26 July 1978, 000004-000008, RG 146, LAC, access request A2011-00054; Paddy Hillyard, *Suspect Community: People's Experience of the Prevention of Terrorism Acts in Britain* (London: Pluto Press, 1993).

40 Security Service "D" Ops – Conference on International Terrorism, RCMP Memorandum, 12 March 1979, 000088, RG 146, LAC, access request A2011-00054.

41 Gregory S. Kealey, "State Repression of Labour and the Left in Canada, 1914–20: The Impact of the First World War," *Canadian Historical Review* 73, no. 3 (1992): 281–314.

42 Hewitt, *Snitch*; Adam Goldman and Matt Apuzzo, "With Cameras, Informants, NYPD Eyed Mosques," *San Diego Union-Tribune*, 23 February 2012, https://www.sandiegouniontribune.com/sdut-with-cameras-informants-nypd-eyed-mosques-2012feb23-story.html.

43 Security Service Operational Conference "D" Operations, Memorandum of Understanding, 000095, RG 146, LAC, access request A2011-00054.

44 Cpl. [name deleted under ATIP] to Officer i/c "D" Ops, 9 February 1978, 000147, RG 146, LAC, access request A2011-00054.

45 Trevor Aaronson, *The Terror Factory: Inside the FBI's Manufactured War on Terrorism* (Brooklyn, NY: IG Publishing, 2013), 48–9.

46 Security Service "D" Ops – Conference on International Terrorism, Cpl. [deleted] to S/Sgt. [deleted], 26 July 1978, 000004-000008, RG 146, LAC, access request A2011-00054.

47 Ibid.

48 Security Service Operational Conference "D" Operations, 7 March 1979, 000096, RG 146, LAC, access request A2011-00054.

49 Security Service Operational Conference "D" Operations, 7 March 1979, 000089; Whitaker, *Double Standard*.

50 RCMP Memorandum, 5 March 1980, 000165, RG 146, LAC, access request A2011-00054.

51 "General Conditions and Subversive Activities – Census Re: Immigration Statistics," 22 September 1982, 000032, RG 146, LAC, access request A2016-00189.

52 General Conditions and Subversive Activities," 22 September 1982, 000033-000052.

53 CSIS, "Threat Assessments: Proposed Threat Levels and Assessment Format," 15 July 1985, 000028, RG 146, LAC.

54 "Ottawa Unveils Monument to Slain Turkish Diplomat," *Globe and Mail*, 20 September 2012, http://www.theglobeandmail.com/news/politics/ottawa-unveils-monument-to-slain-turkish-diplomat/article4557798/. For more on Armenian terrorism, see Michael M. Gunter, "Armenian Terrorism: A Reappraisal," *Journal of Conflict Studies* 27, no. 2 (November 2007):

109–28, and David A. Charters, "The (Un)Peaceable Kingdom? Terrorism and Canada before 9/11," *IRPP Policy Matters* 9, no. 4 (2008): 19.

55 Ian Mulgrew, *Unholy Terror: The Sikhs and International Terrorism* (Toronto: Key Porter Books, 1988); Kim Bolan, *Loss of Faith: How the Air-India Bombers Got Away with Murder* (Toronto: McClelland and Stewart, 2005).

56 For more on the concept of the "suspect community," see Hillyard, *Suspect Community*.

57 Ann Hansen, *Direct Action: The Memoirs of an Urban Guerrilla* (Toronto: AK Press, 2002).

58 "Terrorism and Its Implications for Canada," 28 October 1982, 000058, RG 146, LAC, access request A2012-00613; Hansen, *Direct Action*; Robert Fowler, Privy Council Office, to De Motigny Marchand, 24 September 1982, 000186, RG 146, LAC, access request A2012-00613.

59 Federal Cabinet Briefing on Terrorism, 22 November 1982, 000013, 000014, 000016, RG 146, LAC, access request A2012-00613.

60 Cabinet Paper on Terrorism and Its Implications for Canada, C/Supt J.A. Venner, Officer i/c "D" Operations, to A/Commr F.J. Bosse D.D.G. (Ops), no date, 000040, RG 146, LAC, access request A2012- 00615; Aide-Memoire, 17 May 1983, 000044-5, RG 146, LAC, access request A2012-00615.

61 Aide-Memoire, 17 May 1983, 000044-5, RG 146, LAC, access request A2012-00615.

62 Aide-Memoire, 17 May 1983, 000040, RG 146, LAC, access request A2012-00615; Aide-Memoire, 17 May 1983, 000044-5, RG 146, LAC, access request A2012-00615; Organizational Charts – "D" Ops, "'D' Operations," 4 October 1982, 000019, RG 146, LAC, access request A2015-00291.

63 Cabinet Paper on Terrorism and Its Implications for Canada; Aide-Memoire, 17 May 1983, 000040; ibid., 000044.

64 Whitaker, Kealey, and Parnaby, *Secret Service*, 394–6.

7 Hunting "the Canadians": Wiretapping, Counter-Intelligence, and the Search for Legal Authority

DENNIS G. MOLINARO

The history of the Official Secrets Act and wiretapping in Canada is largely unknown. Until recently, the secrecy behind the topic prevented researchers from having any sources with which to explore it. The period of the Cold War for the RCMP has been overshadowed by the McDonald Commission, charged with investigating RCMP tactics in the surveillance of Quebec separatists in the 1970s. This commission capped the existence of the service and established the Canadian Security and Intelligence Service (CSIS) but also left the public with the perception that the RCMP Security Service was a law unto itself during the Cold War and was engaging in all sorts of illegal activities unbeknown to government.[1] Understandings about Canada's early wiretapping ventures, which were run by its security services through the RCMP, were largely framed in the absence of primary source material and/or sources from the pre–Cold War period. What was known, to a degree, was that RCMP wiretapping in counter-intelligence operations was done in an ad hoc fashion, with bugging and surreptitious entries being conducted on suspected subversives.[2] New primary sources that never entered Canada's national archives have complicated and begun to change this history. These sources have revealed that Canada's Official Secrets Act, the act that criminalized the leaking of classified information, was also covertly being used by the RCMP as the legal authority to engage in wiretapping. What's more, it was Canada's federal government that instructed the RCMP to use the Official Secrets Act in this manner, quietly supporting its activities for decades.[3] This wiretapping began in 1951 and continued secretly until 1973, when the Protection of Privacy Act amended the Official Secrets Act, providing the RCMP with publicly established parameters for wiretapping in national security operations. But the legislation did not come about due to the government's attempt to control an RCMP gone rogue in its wiretapping activities – far from it. New declassified sources reveal that it was the RCMP that struggled to carry out the government's wishes in keeping its wiretapping activities secret – that is, to conduct wiretapping covertly and also legally – and it was the RCMP that sought legal clarity from the government, even proposing a National Security Act in the late 1960s that would publicly detail what the RCMP could and could not do. But that legal authority did not come until the Protection of Privacy Act in 1973. In this chapter I argue that far from going rogue and wiretapping Canadians indiscriminately, the RCMP did its best to remain within the parameters of the secret legal authority the federal government had created. Even when the targets of surveillance shifted over time from potential foreign subversives to terrorists, the service took care to ensure its actions were approved by the government and were legal. All of this concern and care for remaining within the boundaries of the law was at odds with the illegal activity conducted in Quebec in the 1970s that was presented at the McDonald Commission. I detail the creation of the program and the state of wiretapping law in the 1950s before revealing how the RCMP tried to secretly implement wiretapping in the 1960s before finally getting the public law it had sought in the 1970s.[4]

The Secret Order

The world was at the height of the Cold War in the early 1950s. The Korean crisis raised tensions even further. With Japan's defeat in the Second World War, the northern half of Korea fell under the control of the Soviet Union, with the United States occupying the southern half of the peninsula. Failures to unify the country led to the establishment of two separate governments, one in the North and one in the South. The country became divided along ideological lines. On 25 June 1950 North Korean forces invaded the South, triggering the Korean crisis and what would become the Korean War, the first hot war of the Cold War. The North's invasion was almost successful, but it was beaten back after the United Nations agreed to support South Korea. Led by the United States, the UN forces, which included Canada, beat back the Northern forces and continued their advance into North Korean before intervention by China. Chinese support pushed the UN forces back in 1951. In March 1951 the Canadian government, led by the Liberals under Prime Minister Louis St. Laurent, enacted the Emergency Powers Act, a form of emergency legislation that permitted the creation of orders-in-council in a similar vein as the War Measures Act. The government believed that this legislation would allow the government to enable emergency regulations as needed without worrying the population by enacting the

War Measures Act. One of those regulations was P.C. 3486. This order enabled the RCMP, with the cooperation of phone companies such as Bell Canada, to wiretap the phone lines of individuals, organizations, and foreign embassies, or essentially anyone officials suspected of disloyalty. The order was never made public (it was withheld from Library and Archives Canada) and remained in the Privy Council Office (PCO) until 2017, when an Access to Information request led to its publication. While the emergency powers were in effect, the government sought ways of preserving the RCMP's ability to wiretap phone lines after the Emergency Powers Act was set to end in 1954. The government wanted the RCMP to have this power without the knowledge of the public or the country's courts, and the Official Secrets Act seemed like the ideal existing law to use for wiretapping. It already contained sections devoted to punishing the leaking of classified information, and in section 7(1) it provided for the minister to have the right to order the production of copies or receive the originals of telegrams sent out of Canada.

Various schemes were entertained by PCO staff as to how the government could legally enable the RCMP to wiretap phone lines. They included making many amendments to the Official Secrets Act all at once to distract Parliament from the government's desire to amend the act to allow for interception of telephone communications, and using an order-in-council under the authority of section 382 of the Railway Act, which permitted the seizure of telephone and telegraph lines. In June of 1954 the government ultimately decided to use section 11 of the Official Secrets Act, the search warrant section. Deputy Minister of Justice F.P. Varcoe provided the legal justification for this course of action, suggesting that electronic communications could also be considered evidence that could be seized. Government officials in the PCO, and in Cabinet, such as Justice Minister Stuart Garson and the prime minister, along with Bell Canada's president, were satisfied with Varcoe's justification. The RCMP commissioner, or the deputy in his absence, would write the warrants, and they would be stored in the PCO and in Bell's vice-president's office. The RCMP also had to pay rent on the surveillance network.

The wiretapping of those suspected of disloyalty occurred during a period of heightened paranoia and fear of communist subversion. Other well-known surveillance operations occurred in this period, as other authors in this book point out, such as Frances Reilly in her chapter on Operation Profunc and Lomas and Murphy in their chapter on security screenings in the UK of LGBTQ+ government officials. As Kealey and Taylor demonstrate in their chapter, Canadian surveillance policy in the realm of counter-intelligence was in line with the operations and policies of other Five Eyes members.[5] Indeed, Prime Minster

St. Laurent also stated in the House of Commons in regard to questions about the secret wiretapping order P.C. 3486 that "all the NATO countries are doing it [wiretapping]." He was careful to avoid providing details in the House. This wiretapping occurred not only in an era of heightened paranoia and fear, but also during a period when the legalities of wiretapping were not well established and Soviet spies were living in Canada as "illegals."

The Canadians?

The critically acclaimed FX drama *The Americans* dramatizes the lives of a KGB couple secretly living as "Americans" in the 1980s, complete with American-born children. The show's creator, former CIA officer Joseph Weisberg, based the show partly on the notes of Vasili Mitrokhin, the famed KGB defector, as well as the 2010 arrest of deep-cover Russian spies, or "illegals" as they are known. While the series exaggerates much in terms of sex and violence, many aspects of spy tradecraft in the show are accurate, including the role Canada could play in an illegal's life.[6] Illegals assumed fake identities and sought to build lives that appeared real, and Canada played an important role for spies heading to America. To identify these Soviet officers under deep cover, the RCMP established what became known as the Watcher Service. The service fell under the RCMP's counter-intelligence division, known at the time to RCMP members as the B Ops Branch. In its early years it was easily outmatched by the more experienced KGB, as Donald Mahar notes. The small surveillance team was dedicated to monitoring and keeping close watch over illegals.[7] Wiretapping formed part of this surveillance. In June 1972 the RCMP put out a report documenting the situation in Canada when it came to illegals. It prefaced its report by stating that it was not all encompassing and that there were likely operations that had escaped detection. The report identified seventy-one individuals, with approximately fourteen names redacted. Canada was an attractive option for KGB deep-cover operations. It had a good reputation abroad, making it a good place to backstop an agent's identity. Sometimes it was used as a stopping point on the way to a third country, sometimes it was used as an emergency escape route (most illegals were required to have one), and other times it was itself the target of illegals, even though the United States was most often the target. Illegals who entered Canada would meet with specific Soviet embassy staff who were part of the Soviet Intelligence Service (RIS) and trained by the KGB's or GRU's (Russian military intelligence) Illegals Directorate. They would help coordinate agent activities. The most desirable illegals were born in North America or raised there from a young age and so had acquired English-language skills and knowledge of the culture. Officers were required to build their "legends," that is, their artificial Canadian identities, over time. Sometimes this was done by travelling to locations in Canada to familiarize oneself with places that were supposed to be a part of a fictitious childhood. These "Canadians" often assumed Canadian identities abroad, using forged Canadian passports, which were a particular problem in this period. In one instance two married GRU illegals travelled to numerous countries together, including Japan, eventually forming a successful electronics firm there, and using the identities of real Canadians. They convinced many that they were just a Canadian couple living in Japan. Sometimes illegals could be turned to help Canadians. Eugene Vladimirovich Breek was an illegal who came to reside in Toronto. His parents were Soviet citizens who had lived in New York in the late 1920s, giving him the opportunity to learn North American culture and English. He made connections with RIS staff in New York and Ottawa and worked on his "legend" in Toronto and while travelling to Western Canada. He was given the name of three known Canadian communists to make contact with who would backstop his legend. While in Winnipeg he became romantically involved with a woman and he defected. Once he had made himself known to the RCMP and made them aware of his spying for the Soviets, Breek agreed to work for Canada. He came under Canadian control, agreeing to work as a double agent, and still received instructions from the "Centre" (Moscow), which included setting up a small photo studio in Montreal with a radio link. In 1955 he was recalled to the Soviet Union for a presumed leave, but he unfortunately never came back. His cover had actually been blown in 1954. The RCMP surmised he was a bad recruitment option for the RIS because of his lack of strong loyalty and allegiance to the Soviet Union. While the RCMP security services certainly participated in overzealous security screening and surveillance, particularly of the LGBTQ+ community, there were illegals at work for the Soviets in Canadian society. Wiretapping was one method of not only identifying but also keeping watch over them.[8]

Warning ... Your Telephone Is Not Secure

Once the RCMP received the authority from the government to covertly use the Official Secrets Act for wiretapping in June 1954, logistics and ground rules for the operation were set, but also changed as circumstances did. T.M. Guernsey, inspector of the RCMP Special Branch (the security services), wrote to "E" Division in Victoria on 22 June 1954 informing them of the new arrangement. He instructed the office that when submitting warrants to the phone companies, a copy of Deputy Minister of Justice Varcoe's legal rationale should be included. He noted that the branch was hesitant to go along with the plan given that it may invite all sorts of warrants being served from other police services. Transitioning from a system of secret ministerial orders for wiretapping during an emergency period to one where the RCMP had to make regular requests for wiretapping in non-emergency periods required the creation of policies and regulations that would be standardized across all divisions and regions. The process included holding copies of warrants in the operations room, with the commanding officer of a division signing off on copies sent to headquarters. Under section 12(2) of the RCMP Act, these officers were considered justices of the peace and were able to sign the wiretapping warrants. Guernsey told regional divisions that the security services wanted strict control kept over the warrants that were out and distributed a revocation order sample for offices to fill out should a warrant be revoked; new filing systems also had to be created.[9] As the program entered the 1960s, headquarters was also quick to jump on regional offices if they thought they were taking too many liberties with the wiretapping technology at their disposal. In one exchange, Inspector C.J. Sweeny wrote to the Vancouver division stating that "it would be appreciated if you would impress upon your staff the need to carefully assess each target ... our records reveal a tendency on the part of those who have this source [wiretapping] at their disposal to utilize the source as a means of opening investigative leads." Sweeny noted that the short duration of warrants and frequent requirement changes from HQ seemed to confirm this but accepted that address changes also accounted for it. Sweeny quoted from a field manual to reinforce his point (the manual has been redacted). But his comments to the division also reveal the tensions that existed between Ottawa and regional offices that were tasked with intelligence collection. He told them, "Please do not interpret this as a criticism of your operation," noting that some of the changes in wiretapping orders were to satisfy headquarters, but that "we are concerned about the possibility of compromise and do feel that our source [redacted] is too delicate and easily compromised should it be used to open investigative leads." Of critical concern for RCMP headquarters in Ottawa (HQ) was officers' use of wiretaps as a means of determining whether to open investigations rather than seeking them after investigations had determined they were necessary. HQ believed that the latter was important to preserving the security services' methods of intelligence collection, which would be compromised if officers were given too free a hand with the technology.[10] Preserving intelligence collection methods required strict levels of control in the use of the technology. Respecting the revocation of wiretapping orders was also important to preserving these methods. In 1964 HQ notified "C" and "O" Divisions (Quebec and Ontario) that when an Order of Revocation was sent out cancelling a warrant, "we have no legal right to continue." Even if new leads emerged, they had to be followed and new warrants issued. HQ wanted to ensure a minimum of change in operations to ensure security and to also, as W.L. Higgett stated, "not disturb our good relations with [redacted]," presumably the phone company, in this case likely Bell.[11]

HQ also reminded divisions in a separate letter that no "product," that is, the content from wiretaps, was to be received until a warrant was served.[12] The notice seemed to indicate that officers may have begun wiretapping once an order went out but before it had been approved by HQ. It was a practice the top brass wanted stopped. The process, though, of applying for new warrants and revoking old ones proved to be cumbersome and difficult, especially when targets of the orders moved frequently. Money and costs also played a role in how things evolved. By 1970 the services had introduced a new method of surveillance that was first tested by "O" Division, specifically in Toronto and mainly as a cost-saving method. The system was known as "selective switching." It entailed compiling a list of primary and secondary targets of surveillance. Secondary targets were usually already assigned to transcribers/translators and reviewers. The idea was to obtain maximum coverage of a high-value target and have these staff listening during "off-peak" hours to secondary targets. The cost savings were in the thousands per division, as coverage of high-value targets was increased and time and worker hours were not wasted on targets that were not active, though HQ noted that this increased coverage would put an extra workload on workers, so people should not be "overburdened."[13] The RCMP also had to regularly update the solicitor general on warrants, and HQ was keen to point out to divisions that because it was in contact with the minister "so often," it did not want to overload him with new targets in one sitting.[14] While section 11 of the Official Secrets Act (OFA) made no mention of requiring ministerial approval for warrants, it appears that the RCMP still brought their wiretapping warrants to the minister for final approval. It's not clear whether the government or the RCMP asked for this, but regardless, it meant that the federal ministers who oversaw the security services were always fully aware of warrants that were being served and who the targets were. It may have been the government that requested that it be kept fully up to date on wiretaps. Indeed in 1970, internal service memos detail how Justice Minister Guy Favreau stated that commissioner requests for wiretapping warrants under section 11 of the OFA had to be made in writing and to sufficiently detail the target, addresses, and phone numbers and provider information, as well as "facts and other grounds."[15]

In 1970 the RCMP underwent a reorganization, and the Special Branch became the Security Service, headed by a civilian who reported to the commissioner and the solicitor general. This reorganization was in response to the 1969 Report of the Royal Commission on Security, also known as the Mackenzie Commission. Part of the commission's mandate was to investigate issues of national security, and it concluded that the intelligence function of the RCMP should be civilianized because the service lacked expertise beyond that of its officers in the realm of analysis. There were also incompatibility issues between law enforcement and intelligence. The reorganization was the government's response to the commission, as it rejected complete civilianization of the intelligence portion of the service. But the commission also weighed in on the Official Secrets Act. It recommended revisions to it, as it was too broad in its application of what "official" or "secrets" meant. The report also noted that wiretapping for national security purposes should be separate and handled differently than Criminal Code cases. The commission stated, "We think it important that any such legislation should contain a clause or clauses exempting interception operations for security purposes from the provisions of the statue," and that "control should be ministerial rather than judicial."[16]

A similar conclusion was reached by the British Birkett Committee, which studied the issue in 1957, and indeed the Mackenzie Commission report concluded that the committee agreed with the commission. The United States had also had wiretapping legislation put in place in 1968.[17] The RCMP was willing, perhaps even eager, for the act to be revised or scrapped altogether. It had been using the legislation clandestinely at the behest of the government and took this opportunity to push for the creation of a National Security Act. John Starnes, the director general of the Security Service, made this suggestion to both the solicitor general, Warren Allmand, and Commissioner Higgitt. The legislation proposed by the RCMP was sweeping. It included much of the Official Secrets Act but also the Code sections on treason and sedition, as well as the unlawful organization section once contained in the infamous section 98 of the Criminal Code, which was repealed in 1936. It also included a specific section on wiretapping, authorizing the solicitor general to approve intercepts if satisfied under oath on their merit. A warrant was to indicate the type of communication to be intercepted, the length of time of the warrant, and who would be intercepting. There were problems with the act in its broad application and reporting requirements. Reasons for intercepts included preventing espionage and sabotage but also "any other subversive activity" aimed at Canada. The commissioner would also be tasked with reporting to the minister "from time to time" on the status of the warrants. As much as the act needed revisions in these areas because of its broad application and vagueness, it was still an attempt to have the RCMP's wiretapping activities come out of the shadows and be on firm and public legal footing.[18]

For unknown reasons, the National Security Act drafted by the Security Service's lawyers was rejected by the government. Instead, the Official Secrets Act was amended when the government passed the wiretapping law, called, as Martin Friedland put it best, "named, or, arguably, misnamed" Protection of Privacy Act in 1974, which added section 16 to the Official Secrets Act. The act clarified the illegality of using wiretaps while simultaneously amending the Official Secrets Act to stipulate that certain kinds of wiretapping were permitted if done for national security. Section 16 authorized the solicitor general to issue a warrant permitting the interception of communications if satisfied by evidence presented under oath that it would aid in preventing or detecting subversive activity directed against Canada or in gathering necessary foreign intelligence for Canadian security. It read very similar to what the RCMP had proposed in its National Security Act drafts. The exception was that section 16 contained definitions of what "subversive activity" entailed. Subversive activity included espionage or sabotage, foreign intelligence activities aimed at collecting intelligence on Canada, foreign power activities that sought to launch an attack or other hostile act against Canada, and any activity of a terrorist group that was directing an attack in or against Canada, as well as any activities relating to establishing governmental change in Canada or elsewhere by force or violence, a definition that borrowed from the repealed section 98 of the Criminal Code. Surveillance for national security at the time contained another important difference when compared with other forms of surveillance. In an effort to place controls on police wiretapping, police were required to notify individuals of wiretaps ninety days after they were completed. But the Code exempted security operations from disclosure, for as Friedland points out, notifying a foreign embassy that they were being wiretapped by the government could lead to serious international incidents.[19]

The effort by the RCMP to put forward a National Security Act reveals how the Security Service wanted to ensure that its wiretapping activities were legal and above board. The RCMP Security Service and the commissioner regularly met with the justice minister and later the solicitor general, when the solicitor general became the minister overseeing the service, about its wiretapping orders. The government was always kept informed about these activities. With the creation of a National Security Act, the service demonstrated its support for the Mackenzie Commission findings and accepted that greater legal clarity was needed around the Official Secrets Act and wiretapping. But the federal government did not go as far as the RCMP wanted in amending the law. Rather than putting forward a clear and comprehensive National Security Act, the government instead created the Protection of Privacy Act. It devoted much of the new act to detailing how wiretapping by unauthorized means was a criminal offence and extolling the importance of privacy, while at the same time adding section 16 to the Official Secrets Act. This approach was reminiscent of strategies the Privy Council staff had recommended to the government in 1953 when they were contemplating how to amend the Official Secrets Act to allow for covert wiretapping. In that case, the Privy Council had recommended distracting other parliamentarians and the public by introducing many changes to the Official Secrets Act that would act as a "smoke screen" so that the amendment to allow for wiretapping could take place and hopefully go unnoticed.[20]

The service displayed a clear concern with making sure its actions were legal and approved by the government. In a letter from the Security Service's legal branch to an unknown recipient, Inspector D.K. Wilson stated how the service was preparing for the adoption of the Protection of Privacy Act in 1974. He wrote:

> I have been working with Services Section and the Security Service in anticipation of proclamation for the Protection of Privacy Act. With respect to Services Section work, all Divisions have been advised to commence working within the spirit of the legislation immediately for both political and practical purposes. That is to say, that working in this fashion will avoid unnecessary criticism and at the same time permit us to gear for the day when we will be recruited to work under the legislation.[21]

Wilson stated it was prudent to begin working as if the legislation had already received Royal Assent to ensure there was no interruption in the work the service was already engaged in. A service-wide memo for the Security Service indicated that the service had roughly three to six months until Royal Assent took place and the bill became law. All intercepts would be reviewed at HQ to ensure they conformed to the new legislation. Uniformity across all branches to ensure compliance under the new law was mandatory. Perhaps ironically, letters in these files about ensuring RCMP telephone intercepts were in compliance with the law contained stamps that stated, "WARNING ... YOUR TELEPHONE IS NOT SECURE. The content or any portion of this message irrespective of classification is not to be discussed over the telephone." The warning also served as a reminder that it was not only the RCMP involved in intercepting telephone communications.[22]

In 1974, after the passage of the Protection of Privacy Act, the RCMP's legal branch was concerned that the new section 16 of the OFA had no provision for getting a wiretap authorization in an emergency. They were advised by the government, including the assistant deputy attorney general, John Scollin, that until an amendment could be made, the RCMP could telephone the solicitor general and authorization could be given that way, although it was not ideal for security reasons.[23] With the new section in place, the RCMP took extra precautions when it came to wiretapping individuals, especially if they were Canadians, in order to be in compliance with what the government wanted. For example, on 9 November 1976 the director general of the Security Service and the solicitor general met to discuss the issue of wiretapping, and the minister requested that any warrants requiring his consideration involving Canadians be accompanied by an "aide-memoire," that is, a reasoning of why this order would be necessary. The RCMP made it clear to all staff in a memo that future warrants that did not arrive at the director general's office with the accompanying aides-memoire would not be considered and thus not presented to the minister. The purpose of the memo was to ensure that staff would be in compliance with government expectations and requirements and, as the RCMP put it, both the "spirit and intent of the legislation [the OSA]."[24]

The service also devoted much time and resources to standardizing and improving its filing systems as changes in legislation occurred. Some of the warrants issued in 1976 provide a window into the targets the RCMP was now looking at and how it was now more concerned with terrorist activities than communist subversion. Instead of listing specific individuals, the service developed a "blanket warrant" for targeting organizations. The reasoning for this appears in a memorandum written from "E" Division (British Columbia) inspector K.E. Hollas. In it he details the problems with targeting individuals with the Olympics who were scheduled to be in Montreal in 1976. These games were of great concern, likely because the previous games witnessed the 1972 massacre of Israeli athletes in Munich at the hands of the Black September Palestinian terrorist organization. In the memo Hollas states how it was not good enough to "react to a terrorist act, we must do everything in our power to prevent an occurrence, we must therefore proceed on the criterion of working on a preventative rather than a reactive basis, particularly, for the Olympics." The problem with the current system of obtaining warrants, he stated, was time and logistics. There was little time for setting up equipment for individual warrants, but he also pointed out how "it is hardly reasonable to expect that we will know the names and addresses of all individuals that we are targeting against in sufficient time to obtain warrants in the normal manner." He continued by stating that following the suggestion "to obtain warrants on organizations, rather than individuals" would help the service overcome its technical limitations. The change appears to have been suggested by someone other than Hollas: in the memo he is responding to another service member's suggestion to target organizations.[25]

Hollas also discussed the possibility that what he called "blanket warrants" could be abused. To combat the potential for service members to abuse such a broad power, he suggested limiting the period of use to no earlier than 15 April 1976 and no later than 31 August 1976 unless there was a good reason to extend the warrant. Details for the warrant would go to the solicitor general on a weekly basis to speed things up, and "blanket warrants" would be limited to extremist organizations and not used for counter-espionage operations. Orders had a standardized blurb detailing the reason for the warrant and the signature of the minister. A sample "blanket warrant" description appears below:

> Whereas I am satisfied by evidence under oath of Michael R. Dare [officer's name] a member of the Royal Mounted Police, that it is necessary for the prevention or detection of subversive activity directed against Canada or detrimental to the security of Canada or is necessary for the purpose of gathering foreign intelligence information essential to the security of Canada to intercept and/or seize any communication hereinafter described, namely, the telecommunications of unknown persons, present in Canada suspected to be members, adherents or supporters of organizations such as the Japanese Red Army, Bader Meinhoff Gang, Black September, Irish Republican Army, Front du Liberation du Quebec, American Indian Movement, Symbionese Liberation Army, Popular Front for the Liberation of Palestine, Jewish Defense League, Croatian Revolutionary Brotherhood, or other like organizations.[26]

The list of organizations reveals how the primary concern of the security services at this time was terrorist organizations, as Steve Hewitt demonstrates in his chapter in this book. What remains unknown is why the American Indian Movement found itself on this list or what intelligence (most likely from the United States) the service had received regarding it. The rest of the groups listed were known to support or engage in violence. Both far-left terrorist groups and fascist and far-right terrorist groups were also listed in this wiretapping order. In preparation for the Olympics, the service also noted that getting in touch with the minister on a weekly basis to approve wiretaps was going to be difficult, if not impossible, and an amendment to the OFA allowing for wiretapping warrants to be issued in an emergency would also not likely happen soon. The suggested solution from J.A. Nowlan was to serve these "class warrants" (the terminology evolved from "blanket warrants") dependent on two conditions: (1) that vital intelligence would be lost if not carried out, and (2) that a specific warrant would be applied at the first available moment the solicitor general could be met. Nowlan believed that this process was a "dangerous practice, although legal." It was dangerous because it could "lead us to the trap of putting [sic: lumping together] highly dangerous enemies along with the not so dangerous ones (relatively speaking)." The solution, he wrote, should be considered because it contained sound ethical checks and balances that could "withstand Parliamentary scrutiny at a later date, which would prove good faith and a desire not to abuse legislation seriously touching on human rights." The director general of the Security Services, Michael R. Dare, agreed with the plan and reiterated why speed was a concern. He provided a hypothetical example: a known Japanese Red Army member is set to arrive in Canada, and an opportunity may arise to bug the individual's car or perhaps a hotel room and the chance to act would be limited. A class warrant approving actions against organizations could resolve this problem. But Dare noted that the use of these warrants during the Olympics would always be contingent on the minister being satisfied that such a class warrant was truly necessary in the immediacy of the moment, and no other reasonable alternative could be found before an individual warrant could be issued by the minister. In sum, even if the service members agreed with this policy, the minister would always have the final say.[27] The service was granted official approval for class warrants from the deputy solicitor general on 16 March 1976 after discussing the issue with the Department of Justice.[28] With class warrants approved for use, Assistant Commissioner and Deputy Director of Operations Murray Sexsmith advised staff on 25 June 1976 that with respect to a particular class warrant (number 439) that "local [redacted] representative" begin preparation for "dedication of circuitry" in anticipation of authority for wiretapping to begin from HQ. He was presumably stating that the phone company should prepare for the wiretapping order as long as "recorders are not activated" prior to authority arriving from HQ. He also reminded staff that even though the new class warrants were in accordance with the law, the RCMP had broad powers at their disposal, so all guidelines had to be strictly followed, and "no interception of private communications" was to take place without approval and any accidental interceptions had to be destroyed.[29]

These records clearly detail the care and precaution the RCMP Security Service took with respect to its wiretapping operations and the power it had at its disposal. Ministerial authority was continuously required, and the service always sought to ensure that it was operating within the law and even drafted legislation for consideration in the form of the National Security Act. When extraordinary circumstances arose, like the Olympics, the service carefully scrutinized how to continue their work of looking for threats, in this case terrorist ones, while ensuring their actions were legal and had government approval. The evidence points to a service especially mindful of the power it had, not one operating as a "rogue" service. The documents show a service that did its best to ensure that the government signed off and approved of its work and continually suggested ways to follow the letter and spirit of the law even during exceptional moments where guaranteeing security was difficult. The government had clear and precise knowledge of what the RCMP was doing in regards to wiretapping and whom it was targeting and why, so much so in fact that the wiretapping applications and class warrants that were developed were drafted for them and approved by the Department of Justice. The RCMP received regular advice from the department on wiretapping and the law.[30] All of this indicates that it was extremely unlikely that the RCMP had gone "rogue" in the Cold War with respect to surveillance. Indeed, even in the 1970s and during the lead-up to the McDonald Commission, which noted that the RCMP's Security Service had engaged in illegal and "dirty tricks," the preliminary evidence suggests quite the opposite. It does not appear, and seems increasingly unlikely, that the government was ever kept in the dark about RCMP operations, even the service's actions against separatists in Quebec in the 1970s.

Conclusion: A Law unto Themselves?

The frequent and constant approvals sought by the Security Service for its wiretapping activities well into the 1970s are at odds with the scandal that precipitated the formation in 1977 of the Royal Commission into Certain Activities of the RCMP, or the McDonald Commission, named after its chair, David McDonald. Indeed, even as the commission was underway in 1978, RCMP regional staff were writing to HQ in Ottawa asking about wiretapping legalities concerning house guests staying with someone under surveillance. In the Montreal office, for instance, on 20 October 1978, regional staff asked Ottawa whether they were "legally allowed to listen to and report the information gathered while the visitor uses the target's phone." They knew they had to monitor all calls, but "do we report those who are not close family? Are we to report information from such visitors only if it pertains to subject's activities i.e. mentioned on warrant request?" The answer was that all communication had to be monitored and anything of value noted, but Ottawa noted that this issue had been raised before, though specifics were not mentioned in the memo. For instance, HQ had claimed that it was never clear whether some calls should not be monitored, such as between "target and lawyer, target and spouse, target and doctor etc." HQ had asked the government, and the McDonald Commission after it began, for guidance but their responses do not appear in the file.[31]

The McDonald Commission's final report recommended the creation of a civilian intelligence service and the end of the RCMP's involvement in domestic intelligence. This led to the formation of the Canadian Security and Intelligence Service (CSIS). But the commission had come about by way of scandal, and thus the origins of CSIS are wrapped up in that scandal and have underpinned its identity ever since, linking it to the actions of its predecessor. The commission found that the RCMP Security Service had engaged in illegal activities in their attempts to monitor separatists in Quebec. Such activities included burning down a barn to prevent a separatist meeting, stealing a membership list of the Parti Québécois, sending out fake Front de Libération du Québec (FLQ) communiqués, and having postal workers engaging in unauthorized mail openings. The scandal came to light when former RCMP members who were discharged and facing criminal charges began leaking information to authorities, which ended up being reported by the media. The solicitor general announced the creation of the commission in July 1977. But as this chapter makes clear, it was the government that set the agenda for the RCMP. The RCMP was tasked with collecting and even "disrupting" separatist activities in 1975, and in 1969, one year before the infamous 1970 October Crisis (which saw the FLQ terrorist group kidnap and murder Quebec politician Pierre Laporte and kidnap British trade commissioner James Cross), Prime Minister Trudeau stated in the Cabinet's Committee on Security and Intelligence how national unity was the most crucial issue of the time and serious defence was needed to protect it. The RCMP Security Service mandate on monitoring separatists was overly ambiguous and contained in a Cabinet directive but not in a law.[32] Pierre Trudeau in his memoirs recalled that the service was not encouraged to investigate a legitimate political party like the PQ or to engage in illegal methods, even though, Trudeau stated, the FLQ was trying to infiltrate the PQ and that had to be stopped by every means "the law put at our disposal."[33] Sources also reveal the RCMP regularly updated the government on its activities in Quebec in the 1970s.[34] During the McDonald Commission Solicitor General Warren Allmand stated that when he started his posting as solicitor general in 1973, he was told that the authority for wiretapping was contained in section 11 of the Official Secrets Act. He never elaborated on why he thought this section justified the legality of wiretapping or why he believed other forms of electronic surveillance were legal. The commission concluded that Allmand and other ministers believed that the RCMP's actions were legal. But absent from the public reports are the many times the RCMP Security Service consulted with ministers and the Department of Justice on the legality of their activities, as this chapter has revealed.[35] It was the government that always determined the legality of the RCMP's actions. In other words, ministers believed the actions of the RCMP were legal because they and their departments said their actions were legal without testing those opinions in court. It is reasonable to assume similar consultations may have occurred in regards to monitoring separatists, though more sources are needed.

What is clear is that throughout the 1960s and 1970s the RCMP Security Service took their wiretapping powers seriously and handled the practice with great care, seeking approvals for their actions from government and even drafting and suggesting new laws for greater legal clarity. Their actions were continually approved by multiple governments dating back to the 1950s. It is also clear that successive federal governments wanted to keep their wiretapping authority a secret or were not concerned enough about the legalities to act until 1973, and even then, little was added in terms of legal clarity to the OFA. The government's Cabinet directive stipulating that the RCMP engage in disruption of separatist activities bears some similarity to its attempt to keep wiretapping a secret with the OFA and section 11. Even Trudeau believed that whatever the law put at the government's disposal should be used to combat its enemies. It is the sovereign power or the government of the day that determines the law of the land and is responsible for creating it – not the security services. It is not unreasonable to assume that given that the government was willing to suspend the law with the War Measures Act in 1970, its security services believed that they were being ordered to do whatever was required and had the legal cover to do it. More study and more sources are needed to establish what the government knew and approved of in terms of RCMP activities during the Cold War. They may reveal that in regards to certain activities of the RCMP, there may be far more blame and scandal to uncover than previously believed.

NOTES

1 For example, the "historical context" section in the Library of Parliament's publication "Civilian Oversight of the RCMP's National Security Functions," which is a publication meant to inform MPs on the topic, notes how CSIS was created after the RCMP had been found to be engaging in illegal activities. See Canada, Library of Parliament, Tim Riordan, "Civilian Oversight of the RCMP's National Security Functions," Catalogue No. PRB-04-09E, Ottawa, Library of Parliament, 2004

2 Jeff Sallot, *Nobody Said No: The Real Story of How the RCMP Always Got Their Man* (Toronto: James Lorimer, 1979).

3 Dennis Molinaro, "'In the Field of Espionage, There's No Such Thing as Peacetime': The Official Secrets Act and the PICNIC Wiretapping Program," *Canadian Historical Review* 98, no. 3 (September 2017).

4 Molinaro, "In the Field of Espionage"; "Emergency Powers Act: Order in Council," Privy Council – Law and Practice – Emergency Powers Legislation, 1953–1956 (pc-lpepl), RG2, vol. 61, file P-50–2(b), Library and Archives Canada (LAC).

5 See Reg Whitaker, Gregory S. Kealey, and Andrew Parnaby, *Secret Service: Political Policing in Canada from the Fenians to Fortress America* (Toronto: University of Toronto Press, 2012), part 3; Gary Kinsman, *The Canadian War on Queers: National Security as Sexual Regulation* (Vancouver: University of British Columbia Press, 2010).

6 Olivia B. Waxman, "Q&A: The CIA Officer behind the New Spy Drama *The Americans*," *Time*, 30 January 2013, http://entertainment.time.com/2013/01/30/qa-the-cia-officer-behind-the-new-spy-drama-the-americans/?iid=ent-main-lead; Jonna Hiestand Mendez, "I Was Chief of Disguise at CIA. *The Americans* Got a Lot Right," *Washington Post*, 16 May 2018, https://www.washingtonpost.com/news/posteverything/wp/2018/05/17/i-was-chief-of-disguise-at-cia-the-americans-got-a-lot-right/?utm_term=.eee2178d442c.

7 Donald Mahar, *Shattered Illusions: KGB Cold War Espionage in Canada* (Rowman & Littlefield, 2016), 60–3.

8 Canada, RCMP, RCMP Report – Soviet Illegal Activity Involving Canada – 1930–1960, "Soviet Intelligence Service Illegal Activity against Canada: 1950s and 1960s," 1 June 1972, RG146, vol. 5986, file HIST B1-404, LAC.

9 T.M. Guernsey, "Guernsey to 'E' Division," 22 June 1954, Canada, RCMP, "Policy: Orders and Revocations," file 1P-12-3-6.

10 C.J. Sweeny, "Sweeny to the Officer i/c S.I.B 'E,'" 30 October 1961, Canada, RCMP, "Policy: Orders and Revocations," file 1P-12-3-6.

11 W.L. Higgitt, "Higgitt to the C.O. 'C' Division and the Officer i/c S.I.B 'O' Division," Canada, RCMP, "Policy: Orders and Revocations," file 1P-12-3-6.

12 W.H. Kelly, "Kelly to the C.O. 'C' Westmount the Officer i/c S.I.B 'E' and 'O,'" Canada, RCMP, "Policy: Orders and Revocations," file 1P-12-3-6.

13 D.S.I. Memorandum, "Re: Policy – Orders and Revocations," 13 April 1970, Canada, RCMP, "Policy: Orders and Revocations," file 1P-12-3-6.

14 "Ott to Tor," message number SI (E) 295/15, 26 August 1970, Canada, RCMP, "Policy: Orders and Revocations," file 1P-12-3-6.

15 [To and from illegible], "Re: Minister's Correspondence," [no date provided but document indicates a discussion about the contents that took place in October 1970], Canada, RCMP, "Policy: Orders and Revocations," file 1P-12-3-6.

16 Canada, *Report of the Royal Commission on Security* (Ottawa: Supply and Services Canada, 1969), 74–6; John Starnes, "Starnes to Cote, Deputy Solicitor General," 21 September 1971, Canada, RCMP, "Policy: Orders and Revocations," file IA-10-4-74.

17 M.L. Friedland, *National Security: The Legal Dimensions* (Hull, QC: Supply and Services Canada, 1980), 78–79.

18 National Security Act [draft], 21 September 1971, 9–12, Canada, RCMP, "Policy: Orders and Revocations," file IA-10-4-74.

19 Friedland, *National Security*, 79; Official Secrets Act, R.S.C. 1970, c.O-3.

20 Molinaro, "In the Field of Espionage," 468.

21 D.K. Wilson, "Wilson to [redacted]," 29 July 1974, Canada, RCMP, "Policy: Orders and Revocations," file 1P-12-3-6.

22 "[redacted] to 'E' Ops," 17 February 1978, Canada, RCMP, "Policy: Orders and Revocations," file 1P- 12-3-6.

23 E.P. Craig, "Craig to Legal Branch," 29 April 1974, Canada, RCMP, "Policy: Orders and Revocations," file 1P-12-3-6.

24 "HQ1 S.S. Communication Center to X6006," 10 November 1976, Canada, RCMP, "Policy: Orders and Revocations," file 1P-12-3-6.

25 K.E. Hollas, "Memorandum," [date illegible], Canada, RCMP, "Policy: Orders and Revocations," file 1P-12-3-6.

26 "Official Secrets Act Warrant to Intercept and/or Seize, Sample Only," n.d., Canada, RCMP, "Policy: Orders and Revocations," file 1P-12-3-6.

27 J.W. Nolan, "Nolan to Dare," 13 February 1975 and 25 November 1975, Canada, RCMP, "Policy: Orders and Revocations," file 1P-12-3-6; Michael Dare, "Dare to Deputy Minister Robin Bourne," 9 December 1975, Canada, RCMP, "Policy: Orders and Revocations," file 1P-12-3-6.

28 Roger Tassé, "Tassé to Allmand," 16 March 1976, Canada, RCMP, "Policy: Orders and Revocations," file 1P-12-3-6.

29 Murray Sexsmith, "Sexsmith to Commanding Officer 'A,' 'C' Westmount, 'O' Toronto Divisions and at Quebec Sub-Division Quebec City," 25 June 1976, Canada, RCMP, "Policy: Orders and Revocations," file 1P-12-3-6.

30 E.W. Willis, "Willis to 'A, B, C, D, E, F, G, H, J, K, L, O,'" re: Protection of Privacy Act, 5 June 1974, Canada, RCMP, "Policy: Orders and Revocations," file 1P-12-3-6.

31 J. Jodin, "Jodin to I/C 'E' Services HQ Ottawa," 20 October 1978, Canada, RCMP, "Policy: Orders and Revocations," file 1P-12-3-6; F. Forycan, "Forycan to Jodin," 23 October 1979, Canada, RCMP, "Policy: Orders and Revocations," file 1P-12-3-6.

32 Canada, *Commission of Inquiry Regarding Certain Actions of the Royal Canadian Mounted Police* [McDonald Commission] *Second Report*, vol. 1 (Ottawa: Minister of Supply Services Canada, August 1981), 75–84; D.W. Wall, "Record of a Meeting of the Cabinet Committee on Security and Intelligence, 19 December 1969," 5 January 1970; Whitaker, Kealey, and Parnaby, *Secret Service*, 298–303, 319–20.

33 Pierre Elliot Trudeau, *Memoirs* (Toronto: McClelland and Stewart, 1993), 131–3; Whitaker, Kealey, and Parnaby, *Secret Service*, 301; Cabinet Committee on Security and Intelligence, 1963–72, file 1-18-28.

34 See RG26, vol. 153, file 1-18-28, part 1, LAC.

35 McDonald Commission *Third Report* (Ottawa: Minister of Supply Services Canada, August 1981), 104.

8 Ford and the CIA: Spies and Détente

JOHN BREEN

A Republican presidential candidate from New York City is focused on bringing back "law and order" to American streets and connecting with "lower and middle class" white voters – "forgotten Americans." He knocks established Republican candidates out of the primary; his campaign manager ends up on the wrong side of the law; he is insecure and angry with the "liberal media"; he colludes with a foreign power during his election campaign; FBI wiretaps provide evidence of this subterfuge; and the sitting president, a Democrat, keeps this collusion secret and fails to inform the public. Though elected, the Republican candidate gets less than 50 percent of the popular vote.

This was Nixon in 1968.

That year kicked off with the Tet Offensive in Vietnam in January and February, shaking US resolve. By March, President Lyndon Johnson announced he would not seek re-election. On 4 April, Martin Luther King Jr. was assassinated; two months later Robert Kennedy was assassinated. By August, Richard M. Nixon was the Republican nominee for president, eventually defeating the Democratic candidate, Vice-President Hubert Humphrey. Less than six years later, Nixon would leave the presidency in a shambles; Vice-President Gerald Ford was left to pick up the pieces.

Al Capone was a murderous thug, and Eliot Ness took him down for tax evasion. So too was Nixon, responsible for significantly more carnage than Capone, brought down by a lesser, but in this case consequential, crime: that of the Watergate break-in. But it was his collusion with a foreign power to interfere with the presidential election of 1968 that may have led inexorably to his subsequent crimes, Watergate among them, and his downfall.

The Watergate break-in, which is most recognizably associated with Nixon, was really a downstream event, seemingly the result of lingering guilt and fear of discovery of his inceptive crime – as a candidate for president in 1968, he had ordered those around him to collude with the government of South Vietnam to resist ongoing peace talks, at the time being pursued by President Johnson, with support from the Russians. The "Chennault affair" involved Nixon's campaign advisers, under his direction, taking active measures to subvert US foreign policy to benefit Nixon's bid to be president. While the collusion had been suspected, from previously sequestered primary source materials in the Nixon library, John A. Farrell was able to demonstrate that, despite his many assertions of innocence – to interviewer David Frost, among others – "(H.R.) Haldeman's notes from the fall of 1968 show that Nixon was lying."[1]

President Johnson had called off bombing in Vietnam and hoped for peace talks to end a conflict that had slipped from a seemingly necessary fight against communism to an attrition-based, endless war. Knowing it to be hopeless, Nixon as a candidate made the political calculation to keep that knowledge from the American public: "I've come to the conclusion there's no way to win the war … we can't say that of course – in fact, we have to seem to say the opposite, just to keep some degree of bargaining leverage."[2]

The Soviets – in this instance at least – shared common interest with the United States, all parties apparently looking for a way out of Vietnam. The Soviets pressed their patrons in North Vietnam to be flexible, while suggesting to Johnson that a halt to the bombing would be met with a viable peace negotiation. Nixon saw this effort, timed for October – right before the election – as a clear threat to his candidacy. Should peace break out, it might elevate the chances of his Democratic opponent. Others, like Johnson's national security adviser, Walt Rostow, simply saw the negotiations as an opportunity to end a brutal conflict: "None of us would know how to justify delay."[3]

Seeming to place his quest for power above all else, Nixon nevertheless deployed Anna Chennault, a Republican fundraiser with the right connections in the region, to communicate with the South Vietnamese leadership that if they resisted Johnson's peace effort, they would get a better deal once Nixon won the election. Farrell says it this way: "Nixon personally directed the skullduggery – conducting backstage negotiations with a foreign country in violation of U.S. law."[4] Johnson's administration had established wiretaps and physical surveillance to confirm the collusion. Chennault, on Nixon's orders, had told the South Vietnamese ambassador that Nixon would win and that he should tell his boss to hold on. Why did Johnson not tell the voting public? He did not have a smoking gun, and Nixon denied it directly to the president in a pre-election phone call. While hints of Nixon's collusion were suspected immediately, the documents that truly proved the crime were sealed in the Johnson presidential library, and Nixon's lawyers kept Haldeman's notes secret for decades.[5]

Nixon won the election. The Vietnam War, now his war, dragged on for years and cost thousands of additional lives, American and Vietnamese. The Watergate break-in and its links to the executive were detailed in the press, Nixon's complicity revealed. The damage done was extensive – to the integrity of US-styled democracy and the nation's standing in the world, not to mention the presidency itself. When Nixon's helicopter took off for that final, iconic time on 9 August 1974, at least he waved two fingers. A photo taken shortly thereafter of newly sworn-in President Ford sitting in the Oval Office, empty bookshelves in the background, with Nixon's belongings removed and Ford's not yet delivered, is symbolic of the disarray Ford faced as he took on the challenge of rehabilitating the presidency.[6]

Nixon's relationship with his CIA had been tenuous and his interest in intelligence dubious. His national security adviser – Henry Kissinger – acted as gatekeeper, keeping CIA directors away from the president to ensure it was the National Security Council that took the lead in delivering daily intelligence briefings to the president. His director of central intelligence (DCI), Richard M. Helms, would later recall that he was not "sure how often Nixon ever glanced at the PDB [President's Daily Brief]," though the document was produced by the CIA.[7]

Helms clashed with President Nixon, who had asked for his help in ending an FBI investigation into the Watergate break-in. In apparent retribution, Nixon fired Helms and sent him to Iran as ambassador.[8] His replacement, James R. Schlesinger, arrived in 1973 to an agency in disarray, matching the country it served. He did little to right the ship in his few months at the helm. By the time he had been replaced by President Ford with William E. Colby – one of the original "disciples" of Office of Strategic Services (OSS) director "Wild Bill" Donovan – Schlesinger had fired more than five hundred analysts from the Directorate of Intelligence and over one thousand officers of the Directorate of Operations, and had sent out a directive to the workforce to provide him with information on "any activities now going on, or that have gone on in the past, which might be construed to be outside the legislative charter of the Agency."[9] There were apparently many such activities and plenty of officers willing to provide details.

Colby was a member of the original "Jedburgh" OSS paramilitary officer cadre parachuted into France after the D-Day invasion, and he had conducted direct action behind enemy lines in Norway. Unlike other directors, Colby could perhaps appreciate the ugly realities of presidential covert action, his role in the Phoenix Program in Vietnam exposing him to some of those harsh realities. As more of an operator than a bureaucrat, he was perhaps ill equipped to survive the oncoming political maelstrom.[10] That said, as events unfolded, and as will be discussed further in the conclusion to this chapter, Colby was not an innocent bystander and took a disturbingly active role in attempting to protect his president, the CIA, and perhaps himself.

Leaks and Commissions

An enterprising journalist, Seymour Hersh, published the first of his stories about the CIA's so-called "Family Jewels" in December 1974. These "Jewels" were a compilation of documents on, at best, questionable covert activities conducted largely by the CIA at the direction of successive Democratic and Republican presidential administrations, their unauthorized release in the press the unintended consequence of Schlesinger's directive – these were activities "outside the legislative charter" that had found their way to the press, as such activities tend to do. While Colby was meeting with Hersh in a vain attempt to dissuade him from publishing, Ford was skiing in Vail, Colorado, with his chief of staff, Donald Rumsfeld, whose deputy – Dick Cheney – was still in Washington and had taken an active role in addressing the evolving controversy. As detailed in numerous books and articles, and as revealed by Hersh in his groundbreaking article, the CIA over decades had opened US mail, infiltrated US student groups, and conducted illegal domestic break-ins, among other deplorable activities. Some of these activities took place as early as the Eisenhower administration, and certainly continued through Nixon's time in office.[11]

From the slopes of Colorado, Ford ordered Colby to provide him with a written report within forty-eight hours; Cheney took that information and produced his own memo, guidance for the president, focused on the political ramifications and the potential threat to the power of the presidency of these "Jewels."[12] Kissinger too provided his input:

> Colby has indicated that there are other activities in the history of the Agency, which though unconnected with the New York Times article, are also open to question. I have discussed these activities with him, and must tell you that some few of them were illegal, while others – not technically illegal – raise profound moral questions. A number, while neither illegal nor morally unsound, demonstrated very poor judgment. We should discuss this in detail upon your return.[13]

Following Cheney's protective guidance, Ford established the Rockefeller Commission with the namesake vice-president as its chair. The commission was thinly disguised as an effort to thwart overwrought legislative investigation; no one was fooled. Congress, its ranks filled with the "Watergate Babies" – ten new senators and seventy-five new congressmen and women, all looking to "reestablish Congress as an equal branch of government" – established the Church Committee in the Senate and the Pike Committee in the House.[14] Both investigative bodies would eventually learn much about highly questionable CIA activities, but it was Ford himself and his own "leak" of shockingly damaging information to the press that would cause the agency and the administration the greatest damage, calling into question executive power and the effectiveness of legislative oversight.

On 16 January 1975, Ford met with editors from the *New York Times* for what Rumsfeld writes in his 2018 memoir of Ford's presidency was an off-the-record chat. Ford unfortunately and inexplicably insinuated that there were CIA operations being investigated by the Rockefeller Commission that would "make your hair curl." In response to the obvious follow-up question, "Like what?," Ford blurted out, "Like assassinations."[15]

The details of covert action programs and clandestine operations are never meant to be disclosed to the public, and their US government provenance is never intended to be acknowledged. Revelations in the press inevitably lead to the unauthorized disclosure of sensitive information about clandestine sources and methods; they damage relationships with cooperative liaison intelligence services; and they have negative unintended consequences that impact on future operations. Learning organizations such as the Russian Federal Security Service or ISIS are able to exploit this leaked information to counter US law enforcement and intelligence capabilities. Friendly liaison services and their governments that are normally willing to support covert action are reluctant to do so when details of their cooperation could be revealed to the press or the subject of legislative investigations. The already low-probability effort to convince a prospective agent that a CIA case officer can keep them safe while the agent steals closely guarded information from their host country is made even more challenging when the agent is confronted with a front-page article on CIA espionage.

Richard Bissell, the CIA's former deputy director of plans – in charge of covert action during much of the Cold War – wrote about unanticipated consequences resulting from ill-conceived (and also well-conceived) covert operations, often called "blowback."[16] He suggested that revelations in the press were the main cause of such consequences. It was Bissell who infamously told President Eisenhower that the chances of a U-2 pilot surviving a shoot-down over Soviet sovereign territory was one in a million. The subsequent cover story, after pilot Francis Gary Powers beat the odds and survived, wrecked the Four Powers Paris Summit Conference of May 1960, and as Stephen

Ambrose described, "made [President Eisenhower] look indecisive, foolish, and not in control of his own government."[17] Bissell argued that CIA covert-action programs should adequately address this potential for blowback. While this tactical and operational planning takes place inside the CIA, the overarching strategy is formulated within the national security apparatus, originating from the president and the National Security Council, the NSC.

Ford utilized the NSC uniquely. Created in 1947, through the same legislation that established the CIA that same year, the NSC was instituted to debate and formulate national security policy in formal sessions via coordination among senior policymakers; it met thirty-nine times during the Ford administration.[18] Attendees varied but generally included President Ford; the vice-president; the secretaries of state and defence; the chairman of the joint chiefs of staff, acting as the primary military adviser; the director of the Central Intelligence Agency, acting as the primary intelligence adviser; and the director of the Arms Control and Disarmament Agency. National Security Advisor Dr. Henry Kissinger (until November 1975 – then succeeded by General Brent Scowcroft) planned NSC meetings and ensured preparation of briefing materials. The foci of NSC meetings during the Ford administration included the Middle East peace negotiations, aid to Israel, the Strategic Arms Limitation Talks (SALT), the Vietnam War, the Panama Canal treaty negotiations, the Helsinki Agreements, Angola, American–Soviet relations, military readiness, Southern Africa, and legislative intelligence investigations emanating from the "Jewels."[19]

While Ford would have perhaps appreciated the opportunity to focus NSC discussions on broader national security strategy, just a couple of months into his presidency, his attention was drawn to the damage caused by leaks of classified information.[20] In a 7 October 1974 NSC meeting, a few months before his ski trip to Vail and the emergence of the "Jewels" revelations, and before moving on to the not insubstantial issue of the day – nuclear negotiations with the Soviets – Ford took some time to complain about the recent leak of a classified working paper he had used with Israeli leader Yitzhak Rabin that included a US assessment of Israeli military capability. The New York Times – soon to play its role again as Ford's nemesis via Hersh – had obtained a copy of the paper: "I've been told that the New York Times has so much classified material, they don't know where to store it. This is unforgivable."[21]

Apparently he and his chief of staff, Rumsfeld, had discussed several options for how to deal with the leaks and had decided to give the Department of Defense, the State Department, and other agencies and departments forty-eight hours to provide the president a report on the situation, and potential solutions that might stop the leaks. Ford believed these unauthorized disclosures were a management problem, or at least that is how he communicated the challenge to his national security team. He also appeared to recognize that the FBI might be limited in its ability to stop the leaks: "The FBI has troubles in this area, and I don't know if they can ever be successful in stopping this. Thus, I see it mainly as a management problem in the Departments. A good manager stops it."[22] This was naive, and those in the room knew it.

Secretary of Defense James Schlesinger, the former CIA director whose order provided fodder for Hersh's article on the "Jewels," responded first. He pointed out that managers would likely need "an official secrets act or its equivalent" or the use of internal investigators and polygraphs to directly address the problem.[23] He was also the first to point out the obvious, that the negative effects of the Nixon presidency had reverberated into Ford's term: "The present climate is bad for this sort of thing. Internal morale is such that effective discipline is hard to achieve."[24] While Schlesinger had made a key observation (and he had some salient experience with creating poor morale), rather than address the morale issue, Ford continued to seek administrative fixes and proposed that they simply limit the number and distribution of classified documents.

Of note, early in the discussion at the NSC meeting, Ford said, "I have told my staff to contact the Attorney General to see what he and the FBI can do."[25] This, after he mentioned he had met with Chief of Staff Rumsfeld. Thus, it appears the president specifically asked Rumsfeld to go to the FBI to handle the leaks. But later in the NSC conversation, Ford is recorded as saying that he himself had talked with Attorney General Edward Hirsch Levi and "could have ordered an FBI investigation on this, but Don and I thought it would be better to see what you could do first."[26] Ford seems to have ultimately recognized that ordering his FBI to investigate would remind the American public (including Congress) a bit too much of the Nixon approach to handling such issues.

After the December 1974 publication of the "Family Jewels" by Hersh, in a 28 March 1975 NSC meeting, "leaks" again derailed the conversation. Discussing Israel, Kissinger complained about inaccurate maps leaked to the *New York Times*. Even when the leaks were not US-based, their importance was appreciated – CIA director Colby noted at one point in the meeting that Nguyen Van Thieu, then president of South Vietnam, had "tried to extract his troops from the highlands in time but his ploy failed. He was so afraid of leaks to the Communists that he told no one in advance, not even his own commanders who were caught by surprise."[27]

By May 1975, as Ford struggled to deal with the seizure of the US vessel *Mayaguez* by Cambodian forces in the aftermath of the fall of Vietnam, his NSC found itself dealing with numerous unauthorized disclosures. In a 14 May NSC meeting, Secretary of Defense Schlesinger noted the paradoxical value of leaks with regard to the administration's handling of the incident: "The leak regarding the B-52s is not too bad. It shows that the President will use them if necessary."[28] But in another NSC meeting the next day, dealing now with US policy vis-à-vis the Panama Canal, Rumsfeld noted,

> I've been doing some talking up on the Hill and I find there is a great deal of distrust and concern and leaking of documents to the Hill by the people in the Zone. I would caution against any new treaty concession being made to the Panamanians. The conservatives would join with the liberals on this.[29]

Later that summer, on 25 July 1975, in the written agenda for another NSC meeting, Kissinger made readers aware that leaks could impact negatively on SALT negotiations: "There is also the problem of the negative political impact, as well as the impact on mobile development funding, which would result if we rejected the proposal and the Soviet proposal were leaked to Congress."[30] Kissinger's talking points on the issue for Ford in July and in August again pointed out the danger of leaks: "Once the Russians leak to the Congress that they proposed a land mobile ban which we rejected, we will not only have a major political problem, but may also lose our land mobile development funds more readily than we would have under a deployment ban."[31]

In September, Kissinger again pointed out the potential damage, this time in talking points for Ford that touched on his (unclear whether he was thinking of Ford's or his own) legacy and the need to have a win in the national security arena with regard to nuclear negotiations with the USSR:

> We simply cannot afford bureaucratic infighting or leaks about who was tough and who was soft, who won and who lost ... We have a tough year ahead of us. I want us to go into it with a SALT agreement behind us, an agreement which represents a solid achievement and which has the unanimous support of the Executive Branch.[32]

In a January 1976 NSC talking points memo drafted by then national security adviser Brent Scowcroft regarding the US position on SALT prior to Secretary Kissinger's trip to Moscow, he noted, "The important thing at this point is that we present a unified front. I have already seen leaks in the press about various elements of our position and various attitudes around town. We can't afford that, and I want total support as we move forward in this vital enterprise."[33] By the time of a February 1976 NSC meeting, Ford's frustration with leaks was evident:

> If nothing out of this NSC meeting shows up in the newspaper, it will be an all time record for my time in office. It will be of major significance if nothing is leaked out. If it does, I'll throw up my hands and say that's it. The first god-damned newspaper story on this, I will say it ends the prospects for a SALT agreement.[34]

And in the last NSC meeting of the Ford presidency, a 13 January 1977 Semiannual Review of the Intelligence Community, attended by Ford, Vice-President Rockefeller, Secretary of State Kissinger, Secretary of Defense Donald Rumsfeld, Director of Central Intelligence George Bush, Chief of Naval Operations James L. Holloway, Assistant to the President for National Security Affairs Brent Scowcroft, and Dick Cheney, assistant to the president, among others, the topic du jour was again unauthorized disclosure.[35] They had important issues to discuss, such as Ford's executive response to the Senate and House intelligence community investigations, and the quality of national intelligence estimates. But the way the meeting rolled out exemplifies the impact of leaks on the effective functioning of an intelligence and national security apparatus.

Bush noted as the meeting began that Ford's Executive Order 11905 put the intelligence community in the proper "constitutional framework."[36] There was some subsequent joking about lack of funding for a private airplane for the CIA director, which all seems to be friendly colleagues teasing one another as a prelude to more serious discussion. But Bush also mentioned that counter-intelligence problems persisted, perhaps spurring Ford to ask how the "Moore case" was going. Both Ford and Bush were referring to the case of Edwin Gibbons Moore II, who just weeks earlier had attempted, in the most hapless way, to sell secrets to the Russians.

As night fell on 21 December 1976, Moore, a CIA employee with a troubled work history, tossed a package containing classified materials over the gate surrounding the Soviet embassy in Washington, DC. A Soviet embassy guard, thinking the package was a bomb, alerted the Americans. Inside the package, US security officials found a classified CIA telephone directory and instructions from Moore on how he should be paid. Moore was not a trained operator, and the payment instructions unfortunately (for him) led US law enforcement right to him. The FBI arrested Moore the next day at his home, in which they found hundreds of other classified documents Moore was apparently ready to also sell. Notably, during the subsequent trial it was revealed that Moore had written an anonymous letter in 1975 to then CIA director Colby, in the wake of the public "Family Jewels" revelations in December 1974, threatening to defect unless his paranoid grievances were addressed. His prosecutors linked the 1975 letter and his attempted espionage in 1976.[37] Moore, who likely was at best unbalanced and whose motivations were numerous, was at some level influenced by or triggered by Hersh's revelations in the *New York Times*.

Most in this NSC meeting either did not appreciate this linkage between espionage and the negative impacts of unauthorized revelations and revealed secrets, or they were uncomfortable expressing this understanding in front of the president. Instead the discussion progressed quickly to complaints about the justice department and, specifically, the attorney general – Edward Levi. According to Bush, the department sought release of classified information in order to prosecute Moore, information that Bush suggested was too sensitive to release, and that therefore Moore might go free.[38]

His concerns were not completely off base. There have been several examples in recent history of espionage cases derailed by the government's inability or unwillingness to release sensitive or classified information for use in prosecution. From the very beginning of the CIA, and its Second World War predecessor organization, the Office of Strategic Services, foreign spies sought access to US secrets, with some notable success. Duncan Lee was one such Soviet who penetrated the OSS (he was an aide to OSS director Bill Donovan) and later, the CIA. As Mark Bradley notes in his telling of the story, the FBI knew Lee was a Soviet spy based on extremely sensitive intercepts of Soviet communications; in order to prosecute, the government would need to use that information in an open court of law, essentially declaring that intercept capability to the Soviets, and risking the loss of other vital streams of intelligence. In the end, Lee was never prosecuted, and despite recriminations and some punitive measures enacted by the government, he ended his days in relative peace in Canada. In 1995, the NSA declassified its intercepts of Soviet communications and confirmed not only that Lee had been a spy, but that scores of other Americans had aided the Soviets.[39]

In the 1977 NSC meeting, Kissinger, referring to the Moore prosecution and reinforcing Bush's concerns, went so far as to suggest that the justice department and attorney general's guidelines, captured in EO

11905, represented a "threat to national security."[40] And while President Ford seemingly tried to move on by asking Bush to provide him with a report on the problem that he could give to the incoming Carter administration, Rumsfeld and Kissinger remained focused on the issue. Their concerns, reinforced by Vice-President Rockefeller, were specifically directed towards Attorney General Levi. Bush, who minutes earlier had given lip service to constitutional frameworks, now called Levi "an adversary."[41] Some of this was likely residual bitterness that Levi had previously supported legal limitations to presidential authority, or at least that is how the administration seems to have interpreted his past judgments.

In late October 1975, Levi had argued that the administration could not prevent the Church Committee from releasing its findings regarding CIA assassination plots.[42] And in a January 1976 memo to Ford, Levi offered his recommendation that several troubling aspects of CIA activity, including the assassination of foreign officials, be addressed with legal remedies. His solution was to have the administration support the pointed Church Committee prohibition against assassination, a solution that allowed for some significant wiggle room:

> There is currently no Federal law prohibiting an American citizen or, indeed, a government employee from assassinating a public official of a foreign country outside the United States. You have publicly expressed your concern over the possible existence of such a practice. We propose that you give enthusiastic administration support to the legislation proposed by the Senate Intelligence Committee to meet this problem … the legislative history of the bill contained in the Senate committee report … leaves open the possibility of a special Presidential power, even to ignore the narrow restrictions of the bill where the national security overwhelmingly dictates.[43]

Even this level of flexibility was not sufficient for Ford and his advisers. His EO 11905 reforming the intelligence community was published the next month, and in contrast to the Church Committee's definitional approach to restricting political assassination, the EO is vague and appears to purposely avoid limiting the power of Ford or future presidents.[44] This appears to have been Ford's approach generally: give the appearance of reform, but preserve power.

At least in the final NSC meeting, Ford seems to have recognized the impact of these unauthorized disclosures to the press: "What counts for this situation at this time? Is it the law, the mood in the country?"[45] But those around him – Rockefeller, Deputy Secretary of Defense Clements, and Kissinger – continued to point at the attorney general. Bush offered the slightest of defences and attempted to blame the entire judicial branch as an institution. As the discussion heated up, Rockefeller and then Kissinger made the suggestion that the president should take action immediately to, seemingly, tamp down the judiciary's ability to gain access to classified material for counter-espionage prosecutions. Rockefeller proposed an NSC resolution that the attorney general's EO 11905 guidelines be modified.[46]

As at other times when Ford seemed not to have control of a situation, he may have just been waiting to hear viewpoints before setting down a more reasonable course of action – he made it clear that he would continue to defer to his attorney general and suggested more study needed to be done. While Ford was made fun of on *Saturday Night Live* and in other outlets for, admittedly, his humorous gaffes, behind the scenes, he seems to have been a more thoughtful decision maker than the character portrayed by Chevy Chase. As noted by Trenta in his review of the Ford administration's response to the "Family Jewels," in the aftermath of the Nixon presidency and Senate and House committee hearings, and with the fall of Vietnam under his watch, Ford was able to masterfully preserve and perhaps even extend presidential power.[47]

Conclusion

Leaks of classified information have plagued the administrations of most every modern president. Nixon was obsessed with leaks. Indeed, Watergate burglars E. Howard Hunt and James McCord, both formerly employees of the CIA, and G. Gordon Liddy used documents provided by the CIA in other break-ins targeting the Democrats, including a September 1971 White House–directed burglary of the psychiatrist treating Daniel Ellsberg, who earlier that year had leaked the Pentagon Papers to the *New York Times*.[48] Nixon let leaks get the better of him; Ford sought not to make the same mistake. Unfortunately, even as he attempted to focus his NSC on crucial matters of the day and move beyond the impact of leaks, Ford's administration, including Kissinger and CIA director Colby, among others, sought to use the tactical release of classified information offensively.

In a February 1975 meeting to discuss investigations of CIA domestic activities by the Church Committee, just a few months after the December 1974 publication of the "Family Jewels," Kissinger complained that members of the committee staff were "professional leakers."[49] Acknowledging that they were motivated by their political beliefs, he appeared resigned to the idea that the Church Committee had been likely to weigh the political cost–benefit of the morally repugnant activities detailed in the Family Jewels document: "Then we are in trouble."[50]

During the February meeting CIA director Colby at first appeared to be looking again for bureaucratic solutions, suggesting that non-disclosure agreements might keep officials from revealing information to the press. But even he eventually seemed to realize that the system was inexorably porous. Disturbingly, it's Colby who appears to have been the catalyst for the nefarious suggestion that the leaks themselves could be used to disrupt the work of the Church Committee. He suggested that he testify in executive session; with a small number of individuals in the room, any leaks would be easier to trace back to their source and presumably could be used to go after the leakers and thereby weaken the effectiveness of the commission.[51] Laurence Silberman, deputy to Attorney General Levi, linked those hoped-for revelations to Ford's ability to exert executive privilege and limit further the scope of the investigation: "Our position on executive privilege would be better if we had a leak first … we must first give them less sensitive information, so if it leaks we aren't hurt so much."[52]

This is a stunning proposal. The deputy attorney general was essentially suggesting a covert-action operation directed against the US Congress, using Colby's testimony as a vehicle to provide leak-worthy, but less-than-damaging information to the committee. Providing "feed information" to foreign intelligence services via a double agent is a tried-and-true technique to sow doubt within and about an opposing organization. In this case, the director of the CIA would be the double agent, ostensibly testifying in support of a congressional investigation, but actually there to provide organized feed material that could be traced back to a suspected leaker. That the number two law enforcement officer in the nation was suggesting such an operation against the legislative branch of the US government is certainly shocking. He goes on to propose leaks of additional information – about FBI activities during Lyndon Johnson's administration. And elements within the FBI may have been complicit in this proposed activity: "The Bureau would like to dribble it out. This will divert attention and show relative cooperation with the committee. This relates only to illegal activities."[53]

The "flash-back" tactic – a deliberate technique of the Ford administration in its strategic attempt to deal with the Church Commission – was meant to divert attention from Republican malfeasance by demonstrating (in this case with leaks) that questionable activities took place earlier in Democratic administrations.[54] While logically fallacious, this technique can at least be an effective, overt technique of political misdirection. Employing it via internally focused covert action is simply wrong.

As detailed in this chapter, the Ford administration was obsessed with the unauthorized disclosure of classified information in many of the same ways the Nixon administration had been. Indeed, several of Ford's closest advisers – Kissinger and Schlesinger among them – were holdovers from Nixon's administration and had dealt with a president obsessed with leaks. In multiple NCS meetings, and certainly in other deliberations, leaks became a topic of some deliberation and distraction. Ford and his advisers worried about them and speculated on their impact, but ultimately appeared to have recognized that they were inevitable, and perhaps even useful, their utility recognized by the operator in the room (Colby) and proposed as a deception operation against Congress. There is no evidence that this proposal was acted upon. The difference between Ford and Nixon thus appears to be only that Ford chose not to act on his darkest impulses, even though such impulses were as ever present with his advisers as with Nixon's.

Lastly, Nixon's collusion with a foreign power, and his obsession with its discovery and with leaks (which would reveal his incipient crime), reverberate in the consciousness, if not the conscience, of today's body politic. Watergate, the ensuing investigation, threatened impeachment, and Nixon's resignation played out in the press, mesmerizing and disgusting the US public. Ford and his colleagues then dealt with the aftermath, with regard not only to a hostile Congress and a disaffected public, but also to dissent from within. It's not clear that Ford's administration was leakier than any other, yet the leaks perhaps seemed more impactful in Nixon's shadow.

Individuals leak information to the press for a multitude of reasons. In many ways, their motivations mirror those of spies recruited to provide secrets to a foreign power. Some may feel that they otherwise have little power to effect change. They may believe that their only option is to thwart an immoral or otherwise dangerous policy by revealing its elements to the public through the media. A journalist might make the argument to a wavering source that an individual can uniquely effect positive change; a foreign recruiter of spies might say the same. In both cases, the work of the journalist or the recruiter of spies is made easier when they can point to the poor behaviour of the host government.

So, as Nixon's crimes played out in the press, with leaks to the press and intrepid reporters following leads to ground, the fourth estate wielded significant social influence. Ford appears to have realized this, but sought administrative (and legal) means to curb its influence, though with relatively little success and to his great frustration.

As modern politics becomes more and more tribal, with recriminations and counter-accusations, how does an administration deal with the inevitability of leaks? Nixon presents one alternative; Ford, another. Nixon broke the law, broke into doctors' offices and political opposition headquarters, fired those attempting to investigate, and took active measures with government resources at his disposal to attack his enemies; Ford wrung his hands but largely ignored the leaks. He complained about them in closed-door meetings with his closest advisers and fretted about their impact, but he generally went about the business of running the country despite them. Indeed, Ford may have himself been the most impactful leaker of his own administration when he famously blurted to reporters about CIA assassinations.

Luca Trenta speculates that Ford's revelation at that January 1975 lunch with journalists was strategic – an example of the "flash-back" tactic. By revealing this information to the press, Ford had intentionally shone a light on past administrations. Eisenhower, Kennedy, and Johnson all had their own incriminations. The "flash-back" is a tried-and-true technique – if everyone is to blame, no one is to blame. Thus, Ford and those around him had a strategic approach to dealing with leaks and their impact. Bureaucratic obfuscation and strategic ambiguity allowed Ford the flexibility to deal with a hostile Congress and a wary public while still running the country and preserving the reputation of the presidency. Will future administrations choose Nixon's management style or Ford's nuanced approach?[55]

NOTES

1 John A. Farrell, *Richard Nixon: The Life* (New York: Doubleday, 2017), 638.
2 Ibid., 321.
3 Ibid., 341.
4 Ibid., 342.
5 Ibid., 343–4.
6 CBS News, "Nixon Departure from White House," 9 August 1974, video, 4:03, https://www.c- span.org/video/?8671-1/president-nixons-departure -white-house, and CBS News, "Photographer Recalls Moments That Encapsulated Nixon Resignation," 7 August 2014, https://www.cbsnews.com/news /photographer-recalls-moments-that-encapsulated-nixon-resignation/.
7 Central Intelligence Agency, *The President's Daily Brief: Delivering Intelligence to Nixon and Ford*, August 2016, https://www.cia.gov/library /publications/intelligence-history/presidents-daily-brief-nixon-ford /PDB_Nixon_Ford_August_2016.pdf

8   Christopher Marquis, "Richard Helms, Ex-C.I.A. Chief, Dies at 89," *New York Times*, 22 October 2002, https://www.nytimes.com/2002/10/24/us/richard-helms-ex-cia-chief-dies-at-89.html.

9   Tim Weiner, *Legacy of Ashes: The History of the CIA* (New York: Doubleday, 2007), 325, and John Prados, *The Family Jewels: The CIA, Secrecy, and Presidential Power* (Austin: University of Texas Press, 2014), 17.

10   John B. Green, "Review Essay: *Disciples: The World War II Missions of the CIA Directors Who Fought for Wild Bill Donovan*," *Military Review* (May–June 2016): 126–8, https://www.armyupress.army.mil/Portals/7/military-review/Archives/English/MilitaryReview_20160630_art020.pdf.

11   Jefferson Morley, *The Ghost: The Secret Life of CIA Spymaster James Jesus Angleton* (St. Martin's), 240.

12   Box 5, folder: "Intelligence–Colby Report," Richard B. Cheney Files, Gerald R. Ford Presidential Library, https://www.fordlibrarymuseum.gov/library/document/0005/1561477.pdf.

13   Kissinger's memo to the president, 5, box 5, folder: "Intelligence–Colby Report," Richard B. Cheney Files, Gerald R. Ford Presidential Library, https://www.fordlibrarymuseum.gov/library/document/0005/1561477.pdf.

14   Morley, *The Ghost*, 243.

15   Donald Rumsfeld *When the Center Held: Gerald Ford and the Rescue of the American Presidency* (New York: Free Press, 2018), 117.

16   Richard Bissell, *Reflections of a Cold Warrior: From Yalta to the Bay of Pigs* (New Haven, CT: Yale University Press, 1996).

17   Stephen Ambrose, *Ike's Spies: Eisenhower and the Espionage Establishment* (New York: Anchor Books, 2012), 280.

18   https://www.fordlibrarymuseum.gov/library/guides/findingaid/nscmeetings.asp.

19   Ibid.

20   Box 1, folder: "NSC Meeting, 10/7/1974," National Security Adviser's NSC Meeting File, Gerald R. Ford Presidential Library, https://www.fordlibrarymuseum.gov/library/document/0312/1552376.pdf.

21   Box 1, folder: "NSC Meeting, 10/7/1974," 2, https://www.fordlibrarymuseum.gov/library/document/0312/1552376.pdf.

22   Box 1, folder: "NSC Meeting, 10/7/1974," 2, https://www.fordlibrarymuseum.gov/library/document/0312/1552376.pdf.

23   Box 1, folder: "NSC Meeting, 10/7/1974," 2, https://www.fordlibrarymuseum.gov/library/document/0312/1552376.pdf.

24   Box 1, folder: "NSC Meeting, 10/7/1974," 2, https://www.fordlibrarymuseum.gov/library/document/0312/1552376.pdf.

25   Box 1, folder: "NSC Meeting, 10/7/1974," 2, https://www.fordlibrarymuseum.gov/library/document/0312/1552376.pdf.

26 Box 1, folder: "NSC Meeting, 10/7/1974," 3, https://www.fordlibrarymuseum
    .gov/library/document/0312/1552376.pdf.
27 Box 1, folder: "NSC Meeting, 10/7/1974," 16, https://www.fordlibrarymuseum
    .gov/library/document/0312/1552382.pdf.
28 Box 1, folder: "NSC Meeting, 10/7/1974," 17, https://www.fordlibrarymuseum
    .gov/library/document/0312/1552389.pdf.
29 Box 1, folder: "NSC Meeting, 10/7/1974," 17, https://www.fordlibrarymuseum
    .gov/library/document/0312/1552390.pdf.
30 Box 1, folder: "NSC Meeting, 10/7/1974," 3, https://www.fordlibrarymuseum
    .gov/library/document/0312/1552393.pdf.
31 Box 1, folder: "NSC Meeting, 10/7/1974," 1, 8 (talking points), https://
    www.fordlibrarymuseum.gov/library/document/0312/1552393.pdf. Box 1,
    folder: "NSC Meeting, 10/7/1974," 5, https://www.fordlibrarymuseum
    .gov/library/document/0312/1552394.pdf.
32 Box 1, folder: "NSC Meeting, 10/7/1974," 3, https://www.fordlibrarymuseum
    .gov/library/document/0312/1552395.pdf.
33 Box 1, folder: "NSC Meeting, 10/7/1974," 3, https://www.fordlibrarymuseum
    .gov/library/document/0312/1552399.pdf.
34 Box 1, folder: "NSC Meeting, 10/7/1974," 21, https://www.fordlibrarymuseum
    .gov/library/document/0312/1552401.pdf.
35 M. Todd Bennett and Alexander Wieland, eds., *Foreign Relations of the
    United States (FRUS), 1969–1976*, vol. 38, part 2, *Organization and Man-
    agement of Foreign Policy; Public Diplomacy, 1973–1976* (Washington, DC:
    United States Government Printing Office, 2014), 83; minutes of a National
    Security Council meeting, 13 January 1977, 1030–1130.
36 Bennett and Wieland, *Foreign Relations of the United States (FRUS), 1969–
    1976*, vol. 38, part 2, 83; minutes of a National Security Council meeting,
    13 January 1977, 1030–1130.
37 Robert Meyers, "Moore Guilty of Trying to Sell CIA Files," *Washington
    Post*, 6 May 1977.
38 Bennett and Wieland, eds., *Foreign Relations of the United States (FRUS)*,
    1969–1976, vol. 38, part 2, 83; minutes of a National Security Council meet-
    ing, 13 January 1977, 1030–1130.
39 Mark A. Bradley, *A Very Principled Boy: The Life of Duncan Lee, Red Spy and
    Cold Warrior* (New York: Basic Books, 2014), 261–2.
40 Bennett and Wieland, eds., *Foreign Relations of the United States (FRUS)*,
    1969–1976, vol. 38, part 2, 83; minutes of a National Security Council meet-
    ing, 13 January 1977, 1030–1130.
41 Ibid.
42 Luca Trenta, "An Act of Insanity and National Humiliation: The Ford
    Administration, Congressional Inquiries and the Ban on Assassination,"
    Journal of Intelligence History 17, no. 2 (2018): 135.

43 Ibid.
44 Bennett and Wieland, eds., *Foreign Relations of the United States (FRUS), 1969–1976*, vol. 38, part 2, 66; memorandum from Attorney General Levi to President Ford.
45 Trenta, "An Act of Insanity," 137.
46 Bennett and Wieland, eds., *Foreign Relations of the United States (FRUS), 1969–1976*, vol. 38, part 2, 83; minutes of a National Security Council meeting, 13 January 1977, 1030–1130.
47 Bennett and Wieland, eds., *Foreign Relations of the United States (FRUS), 1969–1976*, vol. 38, part 2, 83; minutes of a National Security Council meeting, 13 January 1977, 1030–1130.
48 Trenta, "An Act of Insanity," 137–9.
49 Bennett and Wieland, eds., *Foreign Relations of the United States (FRUS), 1969–1976*, vol. 38, part 2, document 6, "Memorandum from Director of Central Intelligence Schlesinger to All Central Intelligence Agency Employees," https://history.state.gov/historicaldocuments /frus1969-76v38p2/d6.
50 "Memorandum of Conversation in Secretary Kissinger's Office, Investigations of Allegations of CIA Domestic Activities," 20 February 1975, http:// cryptome.org/nara/wh/wh-75-0220.pdf.
51 Ibid.
52 Ibid.
53 Ibid.
54 Ibid.
55 Trenta, "An Act of Insanity," 131.

9 Maintaining Innocence: The Curious Case of Wartime Intelligence History

TIMOTHY ANDREWS SAYLE

Canada's communications intelligence and communications security agency, the Communications Security Establishment, has stepped out of the shadows and embraced a new approach to public relations. CSE's website details the history of the organization, including a list of partnerships with the United States, the United Kingdom, Australia, and New Zealand – partnerships that were once considered of the utmost secrecy.[1] The CSE Twitter account (@cse_cst) provides historical information and data privacy tips and cracks jokes with the Twitter account of the Canadian Security Intelligence Service (CSIS) (@csiscanada).[2] In 2018, in partnership with the Canadian Science and Technology Museum, CSE presented a travelling exhibit related to cryptology and cybersecurity.[3] Earlier that same year, CSE distributed a number of rubber duckies, wearing sunglasses and stamped with CSE's name, at recruiting and other public events.[4]

This is a new and dramatic departure for the CSE, an agency whose forebears were kept hidden from public view. In 1955, the much larger American communications intelligence agency, the United States National Security Agency (NSA), issued classification guidelines noting that the "association of NSA with cryptology, COMINT [Communications Intelligence], COMSEC, [Communications Security] or the service cryptologic agencies" was deemed "UNCLASSIFIED."[5] This contrasted sharply with the CSE's precursor, the Communications Branch, National Research Council (CBNRC): the very existence of CBNRC, let alone its roles, was secret. In fact, in the 1950s, when the Canadians learned that the NSA was proposing to downgrade the security classification of US–Canadian cooperation on communications intelligence issues, CBNRC insisted that the existence of the agreement by which the NSA and CBNRC cooperated be treated by the Americans as "TOP SECRET code-word material," the highest level of classification in the

NSA's hierarchy.[6] Only a few years later, in 1960, defectors from the NSA publicly revealed the existence of CBNRC, and in the 1970s a CBC news program exposed more about the secretive Canadian communication intelligence agency. The exposure led to CBNRC's rechristening as the Communications Security Establishment (CSE) and its transfer to the Minister of National Defence's portfolio.[7] CSE was not publicly "avowed" by the government of Canada until September 1983 during the Special Senate Committee on the Canadian Security Intelligence Service, and for the rest of the 1980s and into the 1990s, public information about CSE was limited.[8] This chapter considers the challenges to writing intelligence history, including the challenges faced by official historians. It also seeks to break down the notion of a single "government line" on the secret past, and reveal the various lenses by which different groups within government view the dangers and benefits of releasing historical records related to intelligence issues. New sources – not necessarily the original records themselves, but records detailing debates over the release of historical records and the drafting of official history help intelligence historians understand the limitations of their research but also the possible benefits to governments of a more open approach to intelligence records.

The Canadian communication intelligence capability that became CBNRC and later CSE was born in the Second World War. In the late 1970s and early 1980s, historians in the Department of External Affairs (DEA) researched and wrote a draft history of the DEA's wartime experience that included a chapter on Canadian intelligence. The chapter set off a series of consultations within the government of Canada and with American and British allies. It was decided, ultimately, that the story of Canada's wartime intelligence history could not yet be told. Throughout the 1980s, with the public avowal of CSE and the implementation of the Access to Information Act, greater light was shone on Canada's wartime efforts. In 1993, John Bryden published *Best-Kept Secret: Canadian Secret Intelligence in the Second World War*, a comprehensive account of the subject, although one – as explained below – that Bryden thought remained limited in some ways by government secrecy. The history of the government of Canada's efforts to keep secret what officials referred to as "our World War II heritage" reveals the challenge for a smaller intelligence partner faced with demands by larger allies. The allies do not bear all of the blame, however, for it is clear that Canadian secrecy on wartime intelligence matters was upheld by Ottawa not as a matter of security or as a counter-intelligence effort, but as an attempt to meet allied demands and avoid roiling the waters of domestic politics at home. Ultimately, the debate over whether or not to publish the DEA history, and how to respond to Bryden's research efforts, reveals a debate – even confusion – within government about the potential value in publicizing Canada's intelligence history. While Canada's allies encourage study of their national intelligence history, the government of Canada is only beginning to move towards a more open acknowledgment of its historical experience. Only time will tell how much further Canada's intelligence organizations and the Privy Council Office are willing to move beyond rubber duckies.

The Missing Chapter

In 1978, historians in the Department of External Affairs began work on a history of the department. The final volumes were not published until the 1990s, owing to a series of delays. The volumes are sound histories, filled with important detail regarding the conduct of Canadian foreign policy and the men who made it. By the end of the writing of the first draft, however, there was a "missing dimension" to the volume that covers the Second World War. There was no chapter on intelligence. This is not because the Department of External Affairs played no role in intelligence gathering and analysis during the war, nor is it because of some oversight on the part of the departmental historians tasked with writing this history. A full history of Canada's "entry into the intelligence and security world" during the Second World War had been drafted and redrafted for publication. In 1980, higher-ups at the DEA had "given a yellow light" to the inclusion of the history of Canadian foreign intelligence; by 1982 that yellow light "was switched to red."[9] The draft chapter was reviewed by the Communications Security Establishment and intelligence organs in both the United States and the United Kingdom, who insisted that several parts of the story must be kept secret. Had the chapter gone to print after the revisions and deletions required by the CSE, the United States National Security Agency, and the United Kingdom's Joint Intelligence Committee (JIC), the history would have been incomplete and misleading, and so it was excluded.[10]

Early in February 1981, Don Page, a historian and the deputy director of the Historical Section of the Department of External Affairs, sent his draft to the Security and Intelligence Division of the DEA for review. The chapter devoted significant attention to three elements of Canada's wartime intelligence role: the development of the Examination Unit (XU), Canada's cryptanalysis unit; the department's Special Intelligence Section, which would analyze and report on the raw intelligence; and Canada's close cooperation with and support of British Security Coordination (BSC), London's North American intelligence outpost. While conducting his research, Page had found a few documents in the archival files of the department and a handful of important declassified records at the Public Archives (today Library and Archives Canada, or LAC). Because the documentary record was so sparse, Page had relied on interviews with veterans of the intelligence effort to tell the story.[11] That story, as E.P. Black, the deputy undersecretary, put it, was "fascinating" and "well-worth publishing." Black, who had served in intelligence liaison roles during the Cold War, was well aware that Canada remained an important part of the Allied peacetime intelligence system born in the Second World War. The story, he understood, was where it all began; it was "how we lost our innocence and illusions."[12]

Page reminded the DEA reviewers that while the DEA had "played a role in assisting ... the development" of the history, it was not to be an "official history" nor one that expressed the views of the department. Nonetheless, the departmental reviewers found "a few passages that bother[ed]" them and wanted to "shoot it to CSE" for review. Black agreed, wondering whether it should be "checked in London and Washington."[13]

On 1 June, CSE sent a request to its British counterpart, the Government Communications Headquarters (GCHQ), asking for approval of the part of the draft dealing with signals intelligence. The Canadian High Commission in London was then informed that "all such security/historical questions" and their answers needed to be coordinated by the Joint Intelligence Staff in the Cabinet Office.[14] Page then wrote to Ivan Callan, the intelligence liaison at the British High Commission in Ottawa, on 4 June, describing the project as "semi-official" and the work of historians and officers from the department. He asked that Callan might "give us a clearance of the sections of this text" dealing with BSC and the XU – and that it was "imperative" he get the "final okay" by 1 July 1981.[15] The material was also sent to the United States, seemingly by the CSE directly to the NSA.[16]

With remarkable speed for government bureaucracy, Callan had his answer for Page by 26 June. The answer was not a happy one. That day, Bulstrode of the British Joint Intelligence Committee sent Callan a cable labelled "Confidential UK Eyes Alpha Comint Channels." Bulstrode apologized to Callan for requiring him to take a "rather tough line with the Canadians," but said that it was required as Page's draft had "aroused considerable concern here in London." The cable – which Callan passed to the Canadians – included a list of requested deletions and alterations.[17]

By the early 1980s, many of the secrets of the Second World War were secret no longer. Much of the information in Page's draft that London had objected to was already in the public domain, having been published by historians or investigative journalists. And yet the Canadian draft contained information that while perhaps known was not officially acknowledged; there were details that had not been con-firmed by British authorities let alone made publicly available in British archives. London had worried that a history authored by Page, who, as mentioned, was deputy director of the Historical Section of the Ca-nadian Department of External Affairs, would be assumed by readers "to have been based upon official archives and be authoritative." As a result, the Canadian publication might seem to confirm events and practices the release of which was "contrary to the United Kingdom guidelines on release of intelligence and intelligence related records."[18]

The first specific concern for the British was reference to signals intel-ligence, and especially mention of Canadian efforts to intercept Vichy French and Japanese diplomatic traffic. It was United Kingdom pol-icy to avoid admitting "to any effort against diplomatic targets even in wartime," and so the UK "did not wish" to be "publicly associated with either the interception or exploitation of diplomatic communications by the Canadians."[19]

Even though the British official history referred, elliptically, to the reading of diplomatic material, the UK signals intelligence effort against Latin America, which Page described, was not authorized for release in the UK. London wanted it deleted from the Canadian draft. Page's discussion of the value of reading French diplomatic traffic to Moscow, and the breaking of Free French cyphers, was "particularly worrying." Revelation of these issues, Bulstrode wrote, might be "regarded as very offensive by the French" and damaging to both UK–France and Can-ada–France relations. Page's draft also alluded to British partnership in continued signals intelligence cooperation after the war. United King-dom policy did "not permit the admission of sigint activity in peace-time," and London again recommended deletion.[20]

Even the later section on BSC and Camp X, which the British accepted as already the stuff of "extensive" discussion in books, had never been acknowledged by the British authorities, and London would not pro-vide clearance for their inclusion in Page's text. Nonetheless, "in order to be as helpful as possible," London suggested a number of specific deletions and alterations that, if made, would allow the more general discussion of these entities to remain. A crucial requirement for the London JIC was that the book itself be introduced with an extended caveat: not only was the book not to represent the Department of Ex-ternal Affairs, but the reader should be warned not to assume that any discussion of "activities of foreign government" represented officials views of those governments, either.[21]

Upon review of the cable from London, it was clear to Page that Lon-don wished for "the removal of all reference … to British collaboration" except for some minor references to Camp X. This British response provided two major challenges for the Canadian historians. First, Page complained that the omission would result in a historical account that was not only "misleading but dishonest." If all references to British signals intelligence were to be removed, Page realized that the draft, as it stood, would suggest that the Canadians were conducting a signals intelligence effort on its own and without connection to the "total war effort." Yet "Canada could not do this on its own; it had to have assistance and the British were, of course, logical teachers."[22]

Second, primary records of the events the British wished to deny had already been released by the Public Archives in Ottawa. Canada, up until the introduction of the Access to Information Act in 1983, had operated on a "thirty-year rule" allowing the declassification of most government records after a thirty-year rolling embargo. Owing to this rule, there were already, at the Public Archives, copies of both Vichy and Japanese diplomatic traffic intercepted by the Examination Unit, and reports showing cooperation with both the US Joint Intelligence Committee and the British Intelligence Mission in Washington. Since 1972, there had also been available in the archives correspondence between the British High Commission and the Department of External Affairs acknowledging British assistance to Canadian signals intelligence activities. Denying this information, already publicly available in the archives, made little sense to Page.

Page hoped that if he introduced a specific caveat in the text of his chapter that the "author has had no access to any security or intelligence files," and noted the information had been made available from publicly available sources and interviews given in confidence, he could proceed with his current draft.[23] Callan sent on this counterproposal to London, and he told Page the idea caused Her Majesty's Government to take "a more relaxed view of the detail given."[24]

The British were willing to relax only so much. Callan met with Page and the DEA intelligence officials and provided a list of some specific points that continued to worry London. In one case, Page noted that "BSC collaborators had been known to have previously used their skills in illegal ventures." The British provided the non-accusatory suggestion that these individuals' skills "were only likely to be of use in peacetime in illegal ventures." Mention of a BSC agent who had posed as a reporter from the Southam newspaper chain also worried the British, who feared damage to the Southam chain – and also that such a story would fuel current accusations that intelligence agencies frequently use the press as cover. Page also explained how Tommy Stone of the Department of External Affairs had produced "materials for a forged letter that would persuade the president of Brazil to end the landing rights of an Italian airline being used by German agents entering Latin America." Even though Page had gleaned this information from published secondary sources, the British requested it be removed. The list went on and on. Page was not thrilled and, tongue in cheek, suggested that his proposed disclaimer note that the text had "been amended in certain places to meet the sensitivities of a foreign government." Nonetheless, he agreed to the amendments, and the British and Canadians had, by September, come to a tentative agreement that would allow the draft to go forward.[25]

There would be more and larger obstacles, however. When security and intelligence officers of DEA first saw the draft, they agreed among themselves but did not tell Page that "perhaps the time had come, as it would inevitably, for the public to be told when Canada got into the intelligence business." They passed the draft to CSE and pointed out, verbally but not in writing, that "most, if not all of the material in it came from sources already in the public domain."[26] On 1 December 1981, CSE responded, and did not think the time had come to be quite so open. Pat Spearey, the director general, policy, of CSE, wrote to the DEA on behalf of the chief of CSE, Peter R. Hunt, about Page's description "of our World War II heritage." CSE had concerns about the draft: they asked Page to delete any reference to Captain E.N. Drake's Discrimination Unit, the army's cousin of the XU. They also wanted no reference to any "continuing Canadian post-war intercept and exploitation organization," that is, the forerunner of CSE.

The major obstacle, however, came not in CSE's requests, but those passed on from the NSA. The American requests for alteration of the draft, Spearey warned, were "more demanding than those of the U.K. Authorities." In particular, Spearey wrote, and Page later learned, there was a "tri-centre desire to limit discussion" of the

> scope of wartime collaborative efforts in the interception and exploitation of foreign radio transmissions, the success of cryptographic efforts against communications such as the Vichy diplomatic codes, the deliberations of the 1942 Washington conference, the division of effort between the Allied Nations, and the secure communications facility linking the BSC and Ottawa.[27]

Page was surprised, given what he thought were agreements worked out between him and officers of the Intelligence Analysis Division (ZSI) after the meeting with Callan.[28]

In the intervening months, however, while the CSE had been reviewing the draft and receiving NSA's replies, Page had been hard at work improving the chapter. He sent his new draft chapter to the Department of National Defence (DND), where it came in for "most scathing" reviews. His colleagues at DND warned Page that, "in view of the extensively documented British official history of Intelligence," Page's almost completely undocumented account, "which tells only the External Affairs side of the story" and left out DND, would "make the Department look rediculous [*sic*]." Page and his team were invited to peruse the DND files at the Public Archives, some of which were publicly available and some of which remained closed. At the archives, he learned that Eric Brand's "History and Activities at Operational Intelligence Centre–NHQ, 1939–1945" had been declassified and available publicly since November 1970, open to "anyone who wishes to come in off the street to see it." The available records also made it obvious that there was no need to delete the fact that the allied intelligence organizations were collaborating. Some closed files from the chiefs of staff files and the Department of Transport also allowed him to correct and expand the chapter. When he had finished reworking the draft, he told DEA officials that DND had "subsequently read and approved for release all the additions to the text."[29]

Page's new draft was sent to CSE, where it was not well received. "From the perspective of CSE and that of our collaborating centres," Spearey wrote to the DEA, "the current manuscript is more revealing than its predecessor." CSE wanted Page to forget the new version and instead return to the previous draft CSE had seen; if all revisions as per CSE's December letter were made, CSE "would be prepared to see this chapter go to publication." If Page insisted on trying to move forward with the new version, CSE threatened a delay of "many months" and new approaches to London and Washington that would likely result in a "call for the deletion of most of Mr. Page's newest additions." CSE's January letter was instructive, however, in that it emphasized just where the resistance to Page's draft was originating – not so much in Ottawa, but in Washington. For it was "particularly in the view of our foreign collaborators" that postwar and even earlier wartime communications intelligence "organizations, effort and relationships" continued to "require the protection afforded by classification."[30]

In March of 1982, the axe finally fell on the draft chapter. The interdepartmental Intelligence Advisory Committee (IAC) decided that "details of our WWII intelligence operation should not be published at this time" in any form; the current manuscript "clearly had the approval of the Department and ... would, therefore, be logically understood by the reader to be an accurate and complete account." Despite all of the caveats, and the nature of the chapter being something different from an official history, it could not go forward.[31] The "primary objection of the Committee," according to Black, "remains one of policy, not security in the narrow sense." The subjects identified in the CSE letter, which really channelled NSA concerns, were "sensitive topics on which the IAC would not be prepared to sanction comment until Canada's allies are in a position to issue their own histories." Publication of the details in Page's draft would "draw unwelcome attention to sensitive activities of the intelligence community."[32] The historians continued to press the matter, pushing for inclusion of Page's revised draft, even after memoranda were sent by the IAC to the Historical Division, "effectively and explicitly cancelling what had legitimately been seen as implicit approval given by our response to the original and subsequent texts of the history."[33] In the end, the intelligence chapter was left out of what was to be the final manuscript.

The Story Gets Out

Page, however, still had his draft chapter, and a story worth telling. In late 1983, he made a formal request to security officials in the DEA for permission to publish an article, "Canada's Entry into the Allied Intelligence Community," in *Quester*, the newsletter of the Canadian Forces Supplementary Radio Systems.[34] DEA security and intelligence officials now believed that "with the public avowal of the activities of NSA, GCHQ and CSE, little real damage can be done by acknowledging that Canada was into the act from the early days." Page had put together his history using material that was available in the public domain, and DEA officials recognized that "had this text been the product of original private research into public material, and not identifiable as the work of someone in the pay of the Canadian Government, there could have been no possible objection."[35]

But there was objection, for again, the manuscript raised alarm bells at CSE. Page had given a lecture at the University of Manitoba that concerned the signals intelligence agency. Mona Browne, special assistant to the chief, CSE, wrote to the DEA and warned that for Page's work to be published at the "unclassified level," CSE would want to consult with its British and American partners. Browne acknowledged that the discussion over the book manuscript had taken place "in the pre-avowal era of Canada's SIGINT program," and so "some of CSE's previous concerns have fallen away," but she assumed the US and UK would have reservations. And even if CSE's concerns had lessened, they had not disappeared: reintroduction of CSIS legislation was bound to generate press attention, and CSE's concerns were directly related to the "recent public debate on Canadian intelligence and security programs." The less public debate, it seemed, the better for CSE. Thus Page's lecture and now this effort to publish the draft was "viewed with some discomfort."[36] Ultimately, and with permission of James Bartleman, the Director General of the DEA's Bureau of Intelligence Analysis and Security, Page published his piece in *Quester*, which due to restrictions was not an unclassified arena. But that was hardly the end of the story.

After publishing the piece, Page asked for permission to present the paper at an academic conference, the Consortium for the Study of Intelligence, to be held at York University in Toronto in June 1984.[37] There is no record of the DEA's response to Page, but the evidence suggests he did not receive permission. The paper was delivered, and indeed distributed, at the Consortium – but not by Page.

The archival record is partially sanitized, but sanitized poorly, and it is clear that Peter St. John, a professor at the University of Manitoba, gave the paper at the conference. The paper got the attention of the American and British authorities, especially as the text was distributed to participants in a form that contained information that even the DEA had asked Page to excise.[38] The NSA informed CSE that it maintained a "proactive capacity and dialogue" with academic publishers to ensure that information the NSA considered secret would not be published.[39] The chief, information policy, at NSA used this power "to get an understanding" from the coordinator of the Consortium for the Study of Intelligence that the paper would not be published in a mode that would link it to any government authority, that is, presumably Page and the DEA.

Just how the paper was delivered by St. John remains mysterious; perhaps his name was left off the program. The NSA official who wrote to Browne at CSE signed off by mentioning "a matter of curiosity" about "whatever was done about the case of the ghost speaker and the speech that was not supposed to be given!"[40] In turn, Browne wrote to the DEA to "stress once more our desire" that the "manuscript does not receive further dissemination in Canada."[41]

Page promised that he would never authorize publication of his draft, but warned that St. John might try to publish the paper and it was out of his hands. The saga, however, had an obviously chilling effect on the Historical Section at the DEA, for Page said "he would avoid the subject of intelligence in future while carrying out research."[42]

A version of the manuscript, however, would see the light of day: in February 1985, Peter St. John published "Canada's Accession to the Allied Intelligence Community" in *Conflict Quarterly*. Page read it and "found it strikingly similar to my own essay," even if St. John had not corrected some of the mistakes Page had identified in his own work. The text, however, did match closely one in which Page had deleted references that had been problematic to the allies: there were no references to Latin American traffic, the Free French, and other details.

In the mid-1980s, there was a further burst of scholarly activity on Canada's wartime intelligence. Wesley Wark, then an associate professor of history at the University of Calgary, published "Cryptographic Innocence: The Origins of Signals Intelligence in the Second World War" in the *Journal of Contemporary History*.[43] Wark had used the Access to Information Act to gain partial access to the official history of the Examination Unit. The act, which was proclaimed on 1 July 1983, would be put to use by other researchers studying the RCMP Security Service, the precursor to the new Canadian Security Intelligence Service.[44] The legislation allowed for a boom in the literature, but as one scholar put it, it did not mark a period of "new openness." CSIS, for instance, had entered the "new age of access to information and mandatory archival control kicking, screaming, and resisting every step of the way."[45] When the government refused to release some documents, as per the act, researchers sued for release; a Mr. X won a release of records related to wartime cryptography that would be important to further studies.[46] Despite the frustrations caused by the act, academic and independent scholars, if they had information, could not be barred from publishing it as Page had been. The contrast between Page's experience and the next major effort at a history of Canada's wartime intelligence reveals the importance of outside researchers given the limits on institutional historians.

Best-Kept Secret

In January 1990, a little more than five years after the publication of the St. John article, the Access to Information and Privacy coordinator at the Department of External Affairs received a letter from an author researching a book on the "history of Canada's intelligence gathering activity during the Second World War." John Bryden had previously published *Deadly Allies: Canada's Secret War, 1937–1947*, on chemical and biological weapons, and had now turned his sights on this subject. In his initial research, Bryden had determined that External Affairs had played an important role in intelligence during the war, but that "this appears to be a story that is almost completely unknown."[47] The fruits of Bryden's efforts would ultimately be published as *Best-Kept Secret: Canadian Secret Intelligence in the Second World War* – an excellent and detailed account of the topic. The path to publication, however, is instructive. Bryden took two lines of approach to conducting his research: seeking release of information from the government of Canada and interviewing veterans of the wartime intelligence effort. Both turned out to have frustrations and limitations.

Initially, Bryden had hoped to avoid filing a formal request under the Access to Information Act because the process can be so lengthy. Ultimately, however, he was persuaded to file requests. In response, he received 1,966 total pages of documents from CSE, but 700 of them were "totally blank" and others were variously severed.[48] Some information, like minutes of the Joint Intelligence Committee, had been totally denied him under other requests. As for the JIC records, he told DEA officials that the British and Americans were releasing such information and was curious why the Canadians were not. E.R. Johnston, the Access to Information and Privacy coordinator at the DEA, told Bryden that "unless we were given chapter and verse, we have no knowledge of release of such information," and so would not release it. This situation was what Johnston himself described as something out of *Catch-22*.[49]

Documents released in American and British archives allowed Bryden to piece together some of the story. At the National Archives of the United States, he was able to freely peruse a "numbered collection of intercepts" of Vichy traffic that had readily identifiable Canadian input. Yet Ottawa would not release similar records.[50] Even in Ottawa itself, at the Public Archives, were documents recording DEA diplomat Herbert Norman discussing Ultra signals intelligence, yet no information relating to Ultra was released in response to Bryden's access request, suggesting it was an area that the government of Canada felt compelled to keep secret.[51]

Page, of course, had had a similar experience in finding some material that had already been released in the Canadian archives that contained information CSE would insist should remain secret. CSE officials had worried that someone at the Department of National Defence had "picked up some dust-covered boxes, and without reviewing the contents, sent them to Archives." At the time, the Canadian archives seemed not to have an ability to handle sensitive material. Just what records remained, and who held them, was something of a mystery; for instance, CSE could find no documents related to the formal transfer of the Examination Unit to CBNRC and asked if the DEA happened to have any.[52] The DND seems to have been responsible for declassifying records without the "necessary consultation" with CSE, and once that material was in the public domain, "it cannot be recalled and we must live with the consequences." The consequences provided both opportunity and frustration for historians, and for government were "a hazard of the ATI game!"[53] Bryden's requests for declassification seem to have sparked an effort to better understand and ultimately release Department of External Affairs records related to intelligence in the Second World War, but the process was "somewhat hampered by limited resources."[54]

Research by interview also proved challenging. Bryden identified a number of veterans of the Examination Unit he wished to interview, but as they had previously sworn a secrecy oath, they were wary of speaking candidly and preferred to discuss only specific issues Bryden could raise from his research in open material.[55] Bryden went so far as to write to Ward Elcock, the deputy clerk for security and intelligence, and counsel at the Privy Council Office, to ask about these oaths of secrecy, now more than forty-five years old. Elcock explained that there was "no statute of limitations for an oath of secrecy: if the subject is still sensitive, then the oath still applies." It would be up to the responsible department, in this case CSE, to determine on a case-by-case basis whether or not an issue remained sensitive. Bryden advised CSE that he was seeking these interviews and provided a list of subjects so that CSE could send a cautionary letter to the potential interviewees. The letter, from Ronald J. Browne in CSE's Information and Records Section, was sent to four or five former Examination Unit employees. The letter explained the limits imposed on CSE by the Access to Information Act, but also noted that they had passed Bryden "hundreds of documents known to be in the public domain," including a list of things that presumably they might discuss: wartime activities of the Examination Unit, and the administration and creation of the Joint Discrimination Unit at the end of the war. At the same time, Browne warned that CSE had retained "details of our relationships with wartime allies, methodologies of analytic discrimination and cryptanalysis" and the names of certain individuals. These subjects, then, were off-limits.[56]

The interview process was not as fruitful, it seems, as Bryden had hoped. In his correspondence with CSE and the DEA, he warned that the cycles of publishing meant that the subject would not be explored by a major author again until decades after the publication of his books; by that time, the former employees would be deceased.[57] Now was the time to write their history. Intriguingly, at the same time that Bryden was seeking out interviewees, the Foreign Intelligence Bureau of the Department of External Affairs began conducting its own interviews "of the original employees of the Examination Unit (who have retired some time ago), to ensure that the historical record and the atmosphere of the early days of the Establishment's predecessor organization are not lost."[58] These records seem to be still closed to researchers.

In letters to both CSE and the DEA, Bryden made clear that he was frustrated that there were still parts of Canadian history that he did not know and that he could not explain to his readers. From his research abroad, he knew that "Canadian roles are consistently downplayed by our allies, and that we tend to downplay them out of deference to the British and the USA." Officers of the Department of External Affairs who read his letters were privately sympathetic.[59] Bryden effectively made the case that the history of Second World War signals intelligence was being written anyway – the problem was that it was being written incorrectly, without Canada, and to Canada's disadvantage. Canada's role in "Y" intelligence, and the importance of Canadian stations to identifying U-boats – even providing the "vital cross-bearings" during the chase of the *Bismarck* – was almost entirely absent from the secondary literature. Bryden noted, too, that F.H. Hinsley's voluminous histories *British Intelligence in the Second World War* pay Canada short shrift and that several other works attribute the breaking of Abwehr spy ring codes to MI6 and not the Examination Unit.[60]

By piecing together documents that were previously, and perhaps incorrectly, declassified in Canada, and the records in the American archives – and even, in the French archives, the original copies of Free French telegrams that the Canadians intercepted and deciphered – Bryden was able to tell an important story. Still, as he wrote, he had been unable to look inside the Examination Unit itself to understand the equipment it used and the cyphers it worked on. He could recreate some of this by reading what Bletchley Park veterans had been allowed to write about their experience, which was clearly similar to that of the Canadians – but he could not fill in these gaps with reference to Canadian records or Canadian interviews.[61]

Future, Dark or Light

There is some evidence that Bryden's appeals, and the simultaneous appreciation in DEA that Canada was being written out of wartime intelligence history, had some effect. In 1991, in response to an Access to Information request regarding BSC, the DEA's Access to Information coordinator recommended release and stated that there was "a benefit to be had from releasing records that show what Canada contributed to the war effort, rather than continuing to protect certain information that diverts credit to others."[62] Still, there was no noticeable relaxation of secrecy regarding Canada's intelligence agencies' archival records. Part of the explanation for this lies in the fact that Canadian intelligence exists as part of a multilateral intelligence network. Legal efforts to challenge some aspects of intelligence secrecy have been rebuffed not because of a direct threat to Canadian security, but because Canada is a "net importer" of intelligence and may lose access to secrets shared by its allies.[63]

All of Canada's intelligence partners have faced the same concerns over their intelligence networks and the need to protect secrets. But Canada's partners have made much more effective efforts to publicize, even utilize, their intelligence "heritage." In 2017, the United States Central Intelligence Agency made more than twelve million pages of historical records available on its website.[64] The NSA also hosts electronic copies of key archival releases. To be sure, much of the availability of American intelligence records is due to concerted lobbying and legal challenges by scholars and public organizations. This is not the only route to more open intelligence archives, however. The United Kingdom and Australia have commissioned or authorized several histories of their respective countries' intelligence agencies, including MI5, MI6, the UK Joint Intelligence Committee, and the Australian Security Intelligence Organization (ASIO).[65] A Canadian historian is currently writing the official history of GCHQ.[66] Clearly London and Canberra see benefits to these efforts to publicize their intelligence history. While there exist internal histories of some parts of Canada's intelligence agencies and organizations, none have been purposefully released; what is available is available only because of ATI requests. Dennis Molinaro's chapter in this volume, for instance, is the product of diligent efforts to pry records loose via ATI. Sadly, however, requests for archival records on intelligence matters have, until recently, been regularly ignored to the point of refusal by the Privy Council Office. Only since roughly 2017 has more archival information been released under ATI due to the sustained efforts of the Canadian Foreign Intelligence History Project, a group of scholars and concerned citizens seeking the release of historical intelligence records for use in scholarship. Their efforts have been greatly enhanced by the hard work and determined efforts of the Access to Information and Privacy Branch at Library and Archives Canada, who seem to face an uphill battle in convincing line departments that information dating back to the first half of the twentieth century can be safely released.[67]

There is a real cost in refusing to share Canada's intelligence history, and the cost is not to counter-intelligence efforts or to security. The historiography of intelligence studies sometimes compares a British "never-never land" and an American "wonderland."[68] "Wonderland" has a different meaning for students of Canadian intelligence and security. In 2008, the former director of the Canadian Security Intelligence

Service, Jim Judd, told an American diplomat that Canadians held an "Alice in Wonderland" view on security issues. Judd, speaking in the midst of the post-9/11 war on terror, complained about court decisions and Canadian public opinion towards security matters, claiming that "government security agencies" were on the "defensive and losing public support for their effort to protect Canada and its allies."[69] Whose fault is it that Canadians know so little about the intelligence and security history of Canada? The government security agencies have done so very little to build up public support and in fact have actively resisted those interested in engaging with them. One easy way to build up support for these agencies is to encourage the study of their past – surely this desire for support accounts for some of the British and Australian efforts to publicize their own intelligence history.

Bryden, for his part, wondered if there was some connection between the "alienation" in both Quebec and the western provinces that he saw around the time of his writing:

As Canadians, we seem to have little in our immediate past to be proud of. Maybe part of the reason for that is that our governments, or their bureaucracies, have been so self-effacing that they have preferred to bury the accomplishments of Canadians rather than risk even the aroma of censure, either from the Canadian public or our allies.[70]

CSE's public campaigns, and Library and Archives Canada's willingness to open archival records, might mark the beginning of a trend towards more openness in Canada, but it is too soon to tell. Page, whose historical work on wartime intelligence was, in effect, censored, should have the last word: "Canadian institutions have on the whole been slow to realize that hiding their past will only darken their future."[71]

NOTES

The author wishes to extend special thanks to Mr. Alan Barnes, whose ATI requests made this research possible. All of the archival materials used in this chapter, while available at Library and Archives Canada, are also available digitally via the Canadian Foreign Intelligence History Project.

1 Communications Security Establishment, "Partnerships," 31 October 2011, https://cse-cst.gc.ca/en/about-apropos/peers-homologues.
2 In July 2016, CSE wrote to CSIS, "@csiscanada Welcome to Twitter! Allow us to offer some neighbourly advice: 'password' is never a good password!" with an accompanying image of a white spy and a black spy.

Tweet by @cse_est, 13 July 2016, https://twitter.com/cse_cst/status/753246566903910400.

3 Communications Security Establishment, "Cipher | Decipher Travelling Exhibition," 16 July 2018, /en/cipher-decipher.

4 Tweet by @cse_est, 12 January 2018, https://twitter.com/cse_cst/status/951877269231894534.

5 Appendix to NSA Regulation Number 121-7, "Guide Lines for Security Classification," 8 April 1955, NSA FOIA Reading Room.

6 Memorandum for the Members of USCIB, "Downgrading of References to U.S.-Canadian Collaboration to SECRET," 1 April 1954, NSA FOIA Reading Room.

7 Graham Templeton, "When Canada Learned It Had Spies," *Vice Motherboard*, 5 August 2015, https://motherboard.vice.com/en_us/article/bmjq3a/when-canada-learned-it-had-spies.

8 Philip Rosen, "The Communications Security Establishment: Canada's Most Secret Intelligence Agency" (Library of Parliament, September 1993), http://publications.gc.ca/Collection-R/LoPBdP/BP/bp343-e.htm. For a good overview of CSE and its predecessors before the events of 11 September 2001, see Martin Rudner, "Canada's Communications Security Establishment from Cold War to Globalization," *Intelligence and National Security* 16, no. 1 (March 2001): 97–128, https://doi.org/10.1080/714002836.

9 ZSPA/CFW (Hooper) to ZSP (Bartleman), 22 June 1984, Record Group 25 BAN 2016-0036 (RG25), box 32, file 7-5-2, part 3, Library and Archives Canada (LAC).

10 Ultimately, the final manuscript was not all that final – due to other delays, the DEA history was not published until 1990, with only slim mention of intelligence matters. John Hilliker and Donald Barry, *Canada's Department of External Affairs: The Early Years, 1909–1946* (Montreal: McGill-Queen's University Press, 1990).

11 The interviewees were George Glazebrook, Professor Gilbert Robinson, Arthur Menzies, Gordon Hilborn, Marcel Roussian, Sir William Stephenson, Earle Hope, and Mrs. Mary Oliver.

12 "Permission to Publish Attached Section on Special Wartime Activities in the Forthcoming DEA History," FAH (Page) to ZSP (Hooper), 11 February 1981, RG25, box 32, file 7-5-2, part 1, LAC.

13 Calkin to Black, undated, RG25, box 32, file 7-5-2, part 1, LAC; EPB (Black) to SZP, undated, RG25, box 32, file 7-5-2, part 1, LAC.

14 HICLON to EXTOT HC-249, 1 June 1981, RG25, box 32, file 7-5-2, part 1, LAC.

15 Page to Callan, 4 June 1981, RG25, box 32, file 7-5-2, part 1, LAC.

16 "Mr. Page's enquiry," Mary D. to Mr. Hooper and Mr. Dornan, 2 June 1981, RG25, box 32, file 7-5-2, part 1, LAC.

17 JICTEL 539 from Bulstrode to Callan, 26 June 1981, RG25, box 32, file 7-5-2, part 1, LAC.
18 Ibid.
19 Ibid.
20 Ibid.
21 Ibid.
22 "DEA History Project – Chapter III Special DEA Wartime Activities," FAH (Page) to ZSI (Calkin), 2 July 1981, RG25, box 32, file 7-5-2, part 1, LAC.
23 Ibid.
24 Callan to Calkan, 14 August 1981, RG25, box 32, file 7-5-2, part 1, LAC.
25 "Callan's comments regarding special DEA wartime assignments," FAH (Page) to ZDI (Calkin), 14 September 1981, RG25, box 32, file 7-5-2, part 1, LAC.
26 ZSPA/CFW (Hooper) to ZSP (Bartleman), 22 June 1984.
27 Spearey for Hunt to Hooper, 17 March 1982, RG25, box 32, file 7-5-2, part 1, LAC.
28 "Chapter III – The Arcana of Diplomacy," FAH (Page) to ZSP (Hooper), 29 January 1982, RG25, box 32, file: 7-5-2, part 1, LAC.
29 Ibid.
30 Spearey for Hunt to Hooper, 17 March 1982.
31 CIH (Carter) to PFZ (Black), 16 March 1982, RG25, box 32, file 7-5-2, part 1, LAC.
32 Black (PFZ) to Carter (CIH), 14 April 1982, RG25, box 32, file 7-5-2, part 1, LAC.
33 ZSPA/CFW (Hooper) to ZSP (Bartleman), 22 June 1984, RG25, box 32, file 7-5-2, part 3, LAC.
34 "Your memorandum to SZP dated September 19, 1983," ZSS (Cleark) to SCH, 30 September 1983, RG25, box 32, file 7-5-2, part 3, LAC.
35 ZSPA/CFW (Hooper) to ZSP (Bartleman), 22 June 1984.
36 Mona Browne for Chief, CSE, to R.W. Clark, Director, Security Division, DEA, 5 December 1983, RG25, box 32, file 7-5-2, part 3, LAC.
37 SCH (Page) to ZSI (Lavertu), 16 February 1984, RG25, box 32, file 7-5-2, part 3, LAC.
38 ZSPA/CFW (Hooper) to ZSP (Bartleman), 22 June 1984.
39 Mona Browne to Michael Shenstone, ADM Political and International Security Affairs, 4 December 1984, RG25, box 32, file 7-5-2, part 3, LAC.
40 M.J. Levin, Chief, Information Policy, NSA, to Mona Browne, Special Assistant to the Chief, CSE, 5 November 1984, RG25, box 32, file 7-5-2, part 3, LAC.
41 Mona Browne to Michael Shenstone, 4 December 1984.
42 Shenstone to Peter R. Hunt, Chief, CSE, 20 December 1984, RG25, box 32, file 7-5-2, part 3, LAC.

43 Wesley K. Wark, "Cryptographic Innocence: The Origins of Signals Intelligence in Canada in the Second World War," *Journal of Contemporary History* 22, no. 4 (1987): 639–65.

44 Gregory S. Kealey, "The Royal Canadian Mounted Police, the Canadian Security Intelligence Service, the Public Archives of Canada, and Access to Information: A Curious Tale," *Labour/Le Travail* 21 (Spring 1988): 199–226.

45 Gregory S. Kealey, "In the Canadian Archives on Security and Intelligence," *Dalhousie Review* 75, no. 1 (1995): 26–38.

46 Wark, "Cryptographic Innocence," 641.

47 [Writer's name sanitized as per privacy legislation] [Bryden] to E.R. Johnston, Access coordinator, DEA, 10 January 1990, RG25, box 32, file 7-5-2, part 6, LAC.

48 [Name sanitized] [Bryden] to Browne, forwarded to Johnston, 7 December 1990, RG25, box 32, file 7-5-2, part 6, LAC.

49 (CCBI) Johnston to file, 16 May 1990, RG25, box 32, file 7-5-2, part 6, LAC.

50 [Name sanitized] [Bryden] to Browne and Johnston, 4 June 1990, RG25, box 32, file 7-5-2, part 6, LAC.

51 [Name sanitized] [Bryden] to Browne, forwarded to Johnston, 7 December 1990.

52 (CCBI) Johnston to file, 16 May 1990.

53 Browne to [name sanitized] [Bryden], 2 August 1990, RG25, box 32, file 7-5-2, part 6, LAC.

54 "Releasing to Public Access of Wartime Intelligence Files," INS (John C. Legg) to JIX, 5 October 1990, RG25, box 32, file 7-5-2, part 6, LAC; (CCBI) Johnston to file, 16 May 1990.

55 (CCBI) Johnston to file, 16 May 1990.

56 Unaddressed form letter from Ronald J. Browne, undated but marked 10 July 1990, RG25, box 32, file 7- 5-2, part 6, LAC.

57 [Name sanitized] [Bryden] to Johnston, 7 December 1990, RG25, box 32, file 7-5-2, part 6, LAC.

58 John M. Fraser, Director, Foreign Intelligence Bureau, to A.S. Woolner, Chief, Communications Security Establishment, 5 July 1990, RG25, box 32, file 7-5-2, part 6, LAC.

59 (CCBI) Johnston to file, 16 May 1990; "Researcher [sanitized]," JIX to INS, 17 December 1990, RG25, box 32, file 7-5-2, part 6, LAC.

60 [Name sanitized] [Bryden] to Browne, forwarded to Johnston, 7 December 1990.

61 Ibid.

62 "Archives Consultation re Cooperation with Foreign Agencies," JIX to INS, 21 January 1991, RG25, box 32, file 7-5-2, part 7, LAC.

63 Ruby v. Canada (Solicitor General), [2002] 4 S.C.R. 3, 2002 SCC 75, https://scc-csc.lexum.com/scc-csc/scc-csc/en/item/2017/index.do.

64 Daniel Victor and Erin McCann, "Kissinger's Files and Invisible Ink Recipes: C.I.A. Trove Has It All," *New York Times*, 22 December 2017, https://www.nytimes.com/2017/01/18/us/cia-released-documents.html.

65 David Horner, *The Spy Catchers: The Official History of ASIO, 1949–1963*, reprint edition (Crows Nest, AUS: Allen & Unwin, 2016); Christopher M. Andrew, *The Defence of the Realm: The Authorized History of MI5* (Allen Lane, 2009); Keith Jeffery, *The Secret History of MI6: 1909–1949* (Penguin, 2010); Michael S. Goodman, *The Official History of the Joint Intelligence Committee*, vol. 1: *From the Approach of the Second World War to the Suez Crisis* (Abingdon, UK: Routledge, 2015).

66 Chris Nelson, "It's No Enigma: Calgary Professor John Ferris Chosen to Write U.K. Spy Agency History," *Calgary Herald*, 30 April 2018, https://calgaryherald.com/news/local-news/its-no-enigma-calgary-professor -chosen-to-write-history-of-u-k-spy-agency.

67 Centre for Security, Intelligence and Defence Studies,"Canadian Foreign Intelligence History Project (CFIHP)," https://carleton.ca/csids/canadian -foreign-intelligence-history-project/ (accessed 30 October 2018). For a notable access success and scholarly publication in the security realm, see Dennis Molinaro, "'In the Field of Espionage, There's No Such Thing as Peacetime': The Official Secrets Act and the PICNIC Wiretapping Program," *Canadian Historical Review* 98, no. 3 (September 2017): 457–81.

68 Wark, "Cryptographic Innocence"; Richard J. Aldrich, "Never-Never Land and Wonderland? British and American Policy on Intelligence Archives," *Contemporary Record* 8, no. 1 (June 1994): 133–52; Gill Bennett, "Declassification and Release Policies of the UK's Intelligence Agencies," *Intelligence and National Security* 17, no. 1 (2002): 21–32; Len Scott, "Sources and Methods in the Study of Intelligence: A British View," *Intelligence and National Security* 22, no. 2 (2007): 185–205.

69 "CSIS Ex-Chief Slams Courts, Canadians: WikiLeaks," CBC, 29 November 2010, https://www.cbc.ca/news/canada/csis-ex-chief-slams-courts -canadians-wikileaks-1.889732.

70 [Name sanitized] [Bryden] to Browne, forwarded to Johnston, 7 December 1990.

71 Don Page, "Whose Handmaiden? The Archivist and the Institutional Historian," *Archivaria* 17 (Winter 1983–4): 172.

Postscript

REID MORDEN

The divide between the investigative powers necessary for law enforcement and those necessary to protect national security is not an obvious one. However, while both of these spheres of official activity are carried out under the umbrella of the rule of law, they are quite distinct from one another and their needs and requirements differ substantially.

— Stanley A. Cohen, Senior General Counsel,
Department of Justice, Canada[1]

At its core, this Inquiry involves the appropriate response of our democracy in Canada to the pernicious phenomenon of terrorism, and ensuring that, in protecting the security of our country, we respect the human rights and freedoms that so many have fought to achieve.

— Commission of Inquiry Report, Prefacing Statement
by the Commissioner, the Hon. Frank Iacobucci,
Former Justice, Supreme Court of Canada[2]

Those who fail to learn from history are doomed to repeat it.

— Winston S. Churchill, after George Santayana

In his introduction, Dennis Molinaro outlines the current threats or perceptions of threats that preoccupy intelligence services today. He rightly points out that in a post-9/11 world their focus has shifted efforts to counterterrorism (CT). His conclusion that this has been to the detriment of devotion to countering hostile intelligence gathering and various kinds of subversion or espionage is, perhaps, more moot. He perceptively notes that the cooperation and degree of openness among the intelligence services of the "Five Eyes" (FVEY) is unprecedented, although different perceptions and priorities remain.

The preceding chapters are essentially set in the early years of the Cold War and, not so coincidentally, the opening chapters of Five Eyes cooperation. Otherwise, in a series of well-researched pieces these chapters address the main preoccupations and circumstances of intelligence services at that time in hopes that actions or reactions will then provide lessons for the present. It is a reasonable premise as many, if not most, of the concerns of intelligence services in that period are alive and well in their thinking today.

As a brief recap of the main themes, the chapters deal with legal frameworks within which intelligence services work, the knotty problem of intelligence overreach and intrusion, the need for independence of intelligence services in reaching conclusions and consequent action, the treatment of socially distinct groups, such as the LGBTQ community, the protection of sources or agents, leaks, and the communications problems attendant in a world where much takes place in the shadows.

The postscript traces the development of the security intelligence effort in Canada, set, in large measure, against the backdrop of the issues examined in previous chapters. It also looks at responses to current intelligence challenges. In both cases this chapter leans heavily on perceptions and experience from the writer's tenure as Director of the Canadian Security Intelligence Service (CSIS) as it matured from its establishment in 1984, when it inherited the mantle of its predecessor, the Security Service of the Royal Canadian Mounted Police (RCMP).

In looking at today's security challenges, it is well to keep in mind the words of Niccolò Machiavelli from 1517: "Whoever wishes to foresee the future must consult the past; for human events ever resemble those of preceding times. This arises from the fact that they are produced by men who have been, and ever will be, animated by the same passions. The result is that the same problems always exist in every era."[3]

To illustrate briefly, humanity's capacity to inflict unspeakable cruelties on their fellow humans is woven through known history, often tinged with religious zealotry. Take the vicious power struggle covered with a veil of religious conflict that constituted the Thirty Years War of the seventeenth century. Take the burnings at the stake over religion as with Joan of Arc, or non-Catholics of Bloody Mary's England, or those same burnings through superstition in the Salem witch trials on this side of the Atlantic. And remember the prisoners of war executed out of hand by both sides during the Spanish Civil War and the Second World War, as well as incidents like the massacre of innocent people in the village of Mỹ Lai during the conflict in Vietnam. The list can go on and on.

For context, a little history of Canada's engagement in the world of shadows may be in order. Within Canada, intelligence is usually taken to mean security intelligence that is designed to be preventive. Countering espionage, subversion, or terrorism dictates the structures, equipment, and activities of intelligence organizations involved. And, like all living organisms, intelligence structures and methods evolve over time as threats change and technology advances.

In this defensive sense, Canada is no stranger to intelligence activities. In fact, it has a long history in the security intelligence business in response to a succession of threats, real and perceived, which the territory now called Canada faced even before the country's creation in 1867.

For the 120 years prior to the creation of CSIS in 1984, there was an interlocking of Canada's security intelligence service with the federal police force. It began with Premier Sir John A. Macdonald's creation of the Western Frontier Constabulary in 1864. This was to be a "detective and preventive police force, for the purpose of watching and patrolling the whole frontier from Toronto to Sarnia." The Constabulary operated along the Upper Canada borders and rail lines, reporting on activities related first to the American Civil War, then to the Fenian movement, whose goal was to overthrow English rule in Ireland. The Montreal Water Police, an agency like the Constabulary, had similar responsibilities in Lower Canada.

In 1868 the federal government set up a twelve-member Dominion Police force in charge of guarding public buildings and carrying out the previous responsibilities of the Western Frontier Constabulary. In 1920, the Dominion Police, then numbering 140, was amalgamated with the 2,500 members of the Royal North West Mounted Police to form the RCMP.

Between the two world wars in the twentieth century, the security intelligence function, now within the body of the RCMP, remained small and inconspicuous. It grew as a result of the espionage activity related to the Second World War. However, the defection of cipher clerk Igor Gouzenko from the Soviet Embassy in Ottawa in September 1945 and the information he brought with him, removed any thoughts the government might have had about reducing the security intelligence function to pre-war levels.

Gouzenko's revelations of a number of elaborate Soviet espionage networks operating in Canada ushered in the modern era of Canadian security intelligence. His information showed that the Soviets of the day were interested in more than cultivating disaffected workers; they were intent on acquiring military, scientific, and technological information by whatever means available to them. Thus, as the postwar period gave way to the Cold War, Canadian security intelligence operations grew in response to this new threat. And, as the fear of the pervasive "red menace" took hold, particularly in the United States and especially in the period of Senator Joseph McCarthy's ascendance, the shock of the extent of Soviet activities in Canada sowed the seeds of security service overreach.

Espionage, however, soon became only one aspect of the complex world facing those involved in Canadian intelligence work. The 1960s provided challenges to Canada of an entirely unprecedented order. Members of the Front de libération du Québec (FLQ) used assassination, kidnapping, bombing, and other acts of terrorism in order to achieve their political goal of making Quebec an independent country.

Some of the overzealous activities of the RCMP Security Service during this period led the governments of the day to establish two Royal Commissions of Inquiry.[4] Frances Reilly and Marcella Bencivenni's chapters highlight these very points by showing us how in both the United States and Canada fighting the "red menace" could be mixed with political rivalry as well as by revealing the pitfalls that can occur when law enforcement is mixed with intelligence.

Behind these immediate concerns also lay the belated recognition of balancing the need to identify potential threats while also scrupulously protecting the rights of Canadians to exercise legitimate political dissent. Both royal commissions, separated by a decade in the '60s and '70s, recommended that the security intelligence functions be separated from the RCMP and that a civilian service be formed to carry out those functions. Both commissions recognized that the problem of balancing the need for accurate and effective security intelligence with respect for democratic rights and freedoms could not be adequately resolved as long as security intelligence responsibilities remained part of the federal police force. The result, finally, was the creation of CSIS in June 1984.

Towards the end of that decade, the Cold War began to wind down and the issues related to international terrorism became increasingly prominent, although they had never been completely absent in Canada's security intelligence world. As Hewitt's chapter demonstrates, transitioning from the counter-intelligence (CI) world to the counter-terrorism world was unchartered territory, and in Canada the RCMP initially drew on its CI experience, which did not work well at first.

In the immediate post–Second World War era, people hijacked aircraft in order to go somewhere, for example, to Cuba or out of Eastern Europe. Later, in the 1970s people hijacked aircraft as a means of getting other terrorists out of jail. Even later, in the 1980s and 1990s, the tragedies of Air India and Pan Am 103 took place without any risk to life or limb of the hijackers; they remained on the ground. However, the assassinations of Indian prime ministers Indira and Rajiv Gandhi in 1984 and 1991 were harbingers of a new and darker ruthlessness.

Another such precursor was the 1993 truck bombing of the North Tower of the World Trade Center in which six people were killed and a thousand injured.

This ruthlessness, which eschewed personal safety considerations for the perpetrators, burst into full flower on 11 September 2001. The terrorists in the World Trade Center disaster effectively demonstrated that every country in the world is vulnerable to attack. Whatever protections North Americans believed they had, by virtue of their separation from offshore disputes, no longer offered comfort.

This postscript is not designed to explore the root causes of the various terrorist movements that have wrought so much carnage to so many people, especially the innocent. Suffice it to say that terrorism and the violence associated with it are not new to Canada. Armenian extremists have murdered a Turkish military attaché in Ottawa and a security guard at the Turkish Embassy there. Supporters of the Provisional Irish Republican Army (PIRA) smuggled detonators from Canadian mining operations for use in the indiscriminate bombings that wracked Northern Ireland for years. And, dramatically and tragically, there was the death of a baggage handler at Narita airport in Japan and of over three hundred passengers on Air India flight 182, both through the acts of Sikh extremists.

Canada cannot ignore the fact that its own policy leads us into areas of ideological and religious conflict where violence, official or otherwise, is often seen as the means of resolution. Canada is no longer simply a haven for those seeking escape from hatred and strife in their homelands. Nor does Canada any longer act as a simple parking place for those few who abuse its hospitality and bring those homeland problems to our door. Now Canada's own policies and actions motivate those who disagree with them to retaliate.[5] Current issues with China, Saudi Arabia, and Venezuela have economic and political repercussions, but it must also be remembered that Canada has been added to ISIS and Hezbollah "hit lists" for actions taken in the Middle East and Afghanistan.[6] As the pendulum in the present swings back to the world of counter-intelligence, one can imagine new challenges for the Five Eyes in trying to adapt and change. So much for a brief trip through Canada's intelligence history. What does the landscape look like now?

Legislative Framework

It is a commonplace that a country's institutions reflect its society and their values. One such value in Canada is respect for the rule of law. It is probably also fair to say that when wrong is detected, Canadian governments generally, either on their own initiative or in response to public pressure, have probed the difficulty and taken actions to remove it or otherwise ameliorate the problem. The creation of CSIS was the result of one such set of actions.

The civilianization of security intelligence was a watershed event in Canada. Perhaps even more important, CSIS came into existence based on an act of Parliament that outlined its mandate and, even more remarkably, found a balance between the security needs of the state and protection of the rights and freedoms of its citizens. In the post 9/11 era, that balance has shifted to give greater heft to the nation's security requirements through amendments to the CSIS Act itself, and through other anti-terrorist legislation. Whether the adjusted balance is proper for Canada in this more violence-prone world will continue to be an active debate and the subject of judicial review in specific instances.

What is key, in the context of this book, is that CSIS came out of the starting gate in 1984 with clear legislative guidance as to how it should conduct its activities. It could be persuasively argued that if guidance such as that contained in the CSIS Act had been the framework for the RCMP Security Service, many misdeeds would have been avoided and history might be quite different. As the antidote for the inclination of security organizations to overreach, the argument for legislative backdrop is overwhelming. A trail of successful individual complaints, coupled with review body criticisms and judicial pronouncements attest to the effectiveness of the strictures that bind today's CSIS operations.

However, simply settling the new CSIS into a legislative backdrop does not convey a full picture of Canada's intelligence activities. The Canadian intelligence community has grown and evolved as needed – not always tidily and not always without controversy. Before 9/11 the Canadian security and intelligence community could be roughly divided into four groups, not necessarily evenly weighted: foreign intelligence, security intelligence, military intelligence, and criminal intelligence. Of those four categories, security intelligence and criminal intelligence would be at the heavy end of any scale. Departments and agencies involved included the Communications Security Establishment (CSE), National Defence (DND), CSIS, Foreign Affairs and International Trade (now Global Affairs Canada), and the RCMP.

Post 9/11, the government scrambled to close significant gaps in its legislative and organizational framework (e.g., the creation of the Department of Public Safety) to respond to the threats posed in an increasingly dangerous and ruthless world. Additional players with roles to play in the intelligence makeup also emerged such as Emergency Measures Canada, Citizenship and Immigration Canada (CIC), the

Canadian Border Services Agency (CBSA), the Canadian Customs and Revenue Agency (CRA), Justice, and Transport Canada. Other government players with responsibilities in public safety include organizations such as Health Canada, the Canadian Food Inspection Agency, Fisheries and Oceans, the Canadian Nuclear Safety Commission, and the Financial Transaction Tracking and Assessment Centre (FINTRAC), which deals with money laundering.

Strides have been made in the past few years to render activities of major actors like the CSE, CBSA, and the RCMP accountable through review mechanisms more or less analogous to the review regime set out in the CSIS Act. While others mentioned above have not attracted specific review bodies, a new attempt to strengthen Canada's intelligence accountability regime has been made with the creation in November 2017 of a broadly representative Committee of Parliamentarians on National Security and Intelligence. In view of the committee's recent arrival on the scene, its impact and effectiveness remain to be conclusively demonstrated.

Ultimately, many of the misgivings lawyers and civil libertarians have about the balance between the security needs of the state and protection of the rights of citizens as set out in related legislation have been and will continue to be addressed by the courts under the Charter of Rights and Responsibilities, a part of the Canadian Constitution.[7] The courts have acted and will continue to act as an effective brake on any inherent excess contained in the laws as drafted or in too broad interpretations of their mandates by intelligence organizations.

Cooperation

If a major and continuing threat is terrorism, which transcends boundaries, then the ability of Canada's security and intelligence community to function effectively with its foreign partners has never been more important. The links with other countries have been forged over many years and are vitally needed now. They are necessary not just to ensure that the immediate tasks are carried out as effectively as possible but also to continue to demonstrate Canada's determination to counter terrorism and display the professional capabilities to do so. For better or worse, it becomes a factor in Canada's overall relationships abroad, at a time of political volatility in those very relationships.

In the post–Second World War period, the Five Eyes (Australia, Canada, New Zealand, the United Kingdom, and the United States) have traditionally been the core of Canada's international intelligence relationships. The association with Australia and New Zealand comes, in part, from traditional Commonwealth ties and represents Canada's view of itself as a Pacific nation. However, the major partners in intelligence exchanges have always been the UK and the United States.

At the same time, Canadian intelligence is an integral part of other information-exchange arrangements. For example, the broader Commonwealth interchange includes episodic meetings in one Commonwealth capital or another in which exchanges both formal and informal are made on issues of moment, either generally or with one party in particular. Moreover, the networking benefits of this global grouping should not be dismissed. Personal acquaintance can be and has been valuable, particularly in the trans-boundary world of terrorism.

NATO also has its intelligence dimension, which is valuable in large measure in the same context as the Commonwealth exchanges noted above. In both cases, sharing of information is circumscribed depending on the perceived reliability (and security reputation) of the intelligence services involved.

As far as exchanges between and among the Five Eyes are concerned, there remains a wariness that is embedded deep in the psyches of practitioners. Professionals in the business are instinctively cautious about sharing, whether they are Canadian, British, or American. There may be doubts about the security of information that is shared and there may be questions as to how the information may be used or misused. Canada has direct recent experience in the latter with the misuse of Canadian information provided to the United States about Maher Arar, who was seized at a New York airport and subsequently rendered abroad, where he was subjected to physical abuse by his custodians.

The past again provides interesting points of reference to the present. Kealey and Taylor's chapter on the secret Commonwealth meetings reveals how countries had their own agendas and needs but still tried to find some way of cooperating to deal with the new threats they faced. The new challenges the Five Eyes face in regards to China and Russia will again pit these same countries into deep debate and discussion on how to find a way forward in a new threat environment.

In addition, there are different perceptions and intelligence priorities among parties. Among the Five Eyes, these were generally fairly muted throughout the Cold War. They had a common enemy in the USSR and its Warsaw Pact allies and they acted to oppose and thwart their intelligence activities.

As the terrorist threat grew and broadened in the eighties, a driving priority for the British were the activities of the various groups active during the "Troubles" in Northern Ireland, particularly the Provisional Irish Republican Army (PIRA) and the Irish National Liberation Army

(INLA). While not insensitive to British concerns, Canada's main preoccupation at the time was clearly directed at those parts of the Sikh community seeking independence for the Punjab (Khalistan) through the use of violence. This represented not a dialogue of the deaf between Canada and the UK but not a synchronous merging of concerns either.

Without in any way diminishing the importance to Canada of exchanges and cooperation among the Five Eyes, in reality, as in so many other spheres, nothing is more important than the intelligence relationship with the United States. 9/11 and its aftermath stretching through to relations with the US administration in 2019, brought us face to face with some stark realities, above all the implications of the steadily accelerating integration of the North American economy. Most dramatic was the 9/11 shutdown of the border through which pass some 75 per cent of Canada's exports of goods alone, exports that fuel 20 per cent of Canada's GDP.[8]

A Canada that had become accustomed to an almost automatic exemption from punitive trade measures aimed at the rest of the world, found that this was no longer the case; a Canada that assumed a special relationship and a sympathetic ear from succeeding US administrations, found neither; and a Canada often free with gratuitous advice and criticism, has found it prudent to select more carefully the issues on which it wishes to be actively at odds with the United States.

Moreover, while intelligence work is undoubtedly best carried out in the shadows, an increasingly transparent world will make that tradition harder to sustain. Instant communication, wider dissemination of data, both secret and open, and the need to reach out to non-traditional partners define a new, and uncomfortable, working environment for intelligence and security practitioners.

Treason

If international cooperation is the positive face of interactions among intelligence and security services, the spectre that one country or another is harbouring a traitor or even a mole within a service remains the ultimate nightmare. MICE, or money, ideology, compromise, and ego, have traditionally been the main components fuelling treasonous behaviour. To which might be added "nationalism" making the acronym MINCE.

These drivers remain key in exploring this major element in any defensive or security service's mandate. About ten years ago, K.L. Herbig produced a major study for the US Department of Defense entitled "Changes in Espionage by Americans, 1947–2007."[9] Although this study sought to explore the motives that impelled Americans to commit treason or engage in treasonous acts, a similar situation can be said to apply to Canada. In this study Herbig breaks down the motives by time segments. From 1947 to the 1970s, she asserts that the main driver was ideology, reflecting a fascination for or approval of the USSR and its policies. By the '70s, disillusionment had set in among those who were tempted to spy for the Soviets, and money as a motivator came to the fore. However, since the 1990s, money has become less important and divided nationalist loyalties have superseded all other factors.

These categories do not mean that issues of compromise and ego are absent. As to ego, the prime example remains British traitor Kim Philby. Philby may well have been sufficiently disgusted with British and Western societies to throw his lot in with the Soviets, but it seems clear that a major motivator for his treasonous activities was the ego-driven resolve to demonstrate that he was, in fact, smarter than those around him.

With respect to compromise, the nature of vulnerability has changed. In an increasingly transparent world, sexual practices as the cause of vulnerability have given way to pressures on members of immigrant communities either by threats against family remaining in the country of origin or appeals to the immigrants' patriotism towards the old country. Pressures put on the Vietnamese community in Canada in the period following the war in that country perhaps exemplify the former approach to pressure while the appeals to patriotism have been clearly documented in cases involving members of the Chinese community in the United States. In short, they amount to an exhortation to the emigrant to play a role in restoring China to its rightful place as a great power. Hidden behind these blandishments, sometimes implicit, is the threat to the well-being of family who have remained in China. A third important example involves Tamil immigrants living in Canada. Canada is understood to have the second-largest Tamil diaspora in the world. It has grown quickly since 1983, with the Tamil insurrection in Sri Lanka and throughout the on-and-off conflict that ended only in 2009. The Tamil community in Canada has been subject to intense pressures from the Tamil insurgents, especially for financial resources. Threats to family remaining in Sri Lanka were direct and vicious.

Whatever the mix of motivations, treasonous activities remain a major concern for governments and their security services. Throughout the 1970s, the theft of technological knowledge was a prime objective of the Soviet intelligence services and their allies. Canada was a prime target, technically advanced, particularly in the field of communications, and with close proximity to the United States. Ironically, as the world of technology opened up, a good part of the Soviets' targets could probably have been sourced from a copy of *Popular Mechanics*. In careerist terms, however, there remains a certain cachet in material obtained by covert means.

Three Canadian examples serve to illustrate the sometimes mixed motives that lead individuals to betray their country. Josef Ratkai was born in Antigonish, Nova Scotia, but was brought up in Hungary. While completing his studies there Ratkai was targeted by Soviet intelligence to utilize his Canadian connection to act as a courier for them, largely working in the Maritime provinces and targeting strategic marine issues. There is little doubt that pressure was exerted with respect to his Hungarian family and the prospect of making some additional cash. Ratkai was caught in 1988 in a hotel in Newfoundland in a "sting" instigated by the US Naval investigative service and orchestrated by the RCMP, which carried out the actual arrest.

Royal Canadian Navy S/Lt. Jeffery Delisle was convicted in 2013 of passing classified information to Russia's military intelligence organization, the GRU. Delisle has asserted that he didn't do it for the money but out of resentment when he found out that his wife of the time was having an affair. His denial that money was a motivator is questionable given that he had earlier been forced to declare personal bankruptcy.

A security service's greatest nightmare is betrayal by one of its own. In this case, the culprit was a second-generation member of the RCMP Security Service. Gilles Brunet was the son of Josephat Brunet, first director general of the separate division that became the RCMP Security Service. An excessive drinker and extravagant spender, Brunet needed the extra income offered by the Soviet intelligence apparat. First fired by the RCMP for unrelated reasons, Brunet succumbed to a heart attack before his identity as the Security Service mole could be verified.

The Brunet case also revealed a weakness in the Security Service's recruiting methods at the time. Caught up in the paranoia of the "red menace" and always concerned that a potential traitor would slip through the recruitment vetting process, the Security Service made a conscious effort to recruit from within families already represented in the RCMP. Generally speaking, this approach worked well, but the Brunet case demonstrated that if the process went wrong, the results could be disastrous.

Agent Running and Source Handling

For an intelligence service to interact with people, its lifeblood lies with its agents and sources of information, or the collection of information from living beings, known in the trade as HUMINT. As one senior official in an allied service once told me, "we do three things, we recruit agents, we run them, we collect from them and, on the whole, we do it rather well." For any service to be effective, it must do those three things "rather well."

In many ways, the toolkit of the source or agent recruiter or case officer, is the mirror image of the MICE (or MINCE) described in the section above, because very often those same inducements, personality frailties, and pressures come into play once a potential source has been identified. However, whatever the stresses inherent in a recruitment, the long-term running of a source requires a multidimensional skill set from the case handler. He or she must be an intellectual and social companion, skilled debriefer, and a sensitive and adroit psychologist. The case officer must always have one eye on the possibility that this successful recruitment and source of information may be a plant, a dangerous double agent.

Deery's chapter outlined the Australian experience of running a source within an communist front organization. That narrative well describes the judgment calls required to direct the source towards areas where the information can be maximized. It also depicts the stresses and dangers to which the source had committed herself. What is important is that the main considerations for successful agent/source running outlined in that chapter remain as valid today as they did in Australia in the 1950s.

Pressure Points

To induce potential sources or agents to provide information or otherwise cooperate, recruiters have a variety of pressure points to deploy. The frailties encompassed in MICE or MINCE provide a rich hunting ground to achieve a source's cooperation, willing or otherwise. One such pressure point about which much has been written, including in this book, concerns the treatment and attitudes of intelligence services towards homosexuals. Taking its narrative from British experiences in the mid-twentieth century, Lomas and Murphy's chapter takes a different approach than other works on this subject by asserting that much of the concern, certainly from the British Foreign Office, stemmed from risk to its reputation rather than any dangers that homosexuals within the public service or the foreign service might pose in terms of disloyalty. Reputational or societal embarrassment is a powerful tool in the hands of manipulators intent on breaching security walls. Homosexuality may have been the pressure point until the late '60s or even into the '70s but in the contemporary era (as well as in the past) myriad other practices ranging from child exploitation, to drug use, to having recourse to sex workers represent the pressure points relevant today.

In Canada, in the depths of the Cold War, a security service made up overwhelmingly of male heterosexuals took the words of the MacKenzie Commission on Security to heart and went to ludicrous extremes to identify and root out homosexuality within the public service.

Out of the Shadows?

There is always pressure from the media and the academy for more openness in intelligence activities. These criticisms reveal a number of new elements that intelligence services need to weigh when looking at the degree of openness that may be desirable in the conduct of their operations.

Intelligence work is best carried out in the shadows, but an increasingly transparent world makes that tradition harder to sustain. Sayle's chapter highlights the difficult and not always straightforward path to getting documents released in Canada. But in the world of intelligence collection, instant communication, wider dissemination of data, both secret and open, and the need to reach out to non-traditional partners define a new, and uncomfortable, working environment for intelligence and security practitioners.

The explosion of information means that policy officials will be more reliant on information brokers. If collection is easier, selection is harder. This more open world is blurring the Cold War's distinction between collection and analysis.

In contrast to the days of the Cold War, intelligence today is in the information business, not just the secrets business. In the age of information, it is time for the intelligence community to split its resources between what Greg Tiverton of RAND Corporation has described as "puzzles and mysteries." Puzzles have particular solutions, but we need access to the necessary (usually secret) information. Puzzles were the intelligence community's stock in trade during the Cold War: How many missiles does the Soviet Union have? How accurate are they? What is East Germany's order of battle? The opposite of puzzles are "mysteries," questions that have no definitive answer. For example, will North Korea strike a new nuclear bargain? Will China's Communist Party cede domestic primacy? When and where will ISIS attack next? No one knows the answers to these questions. The mystery can only be illuminated; it cannot necessarily be "solved."

The unravelling of strategic mysteries is very different from puzzle solving. While analysts do need access to secrets, their crucial partnerships are those with colleagues outside intelligence and outside government, in the academy and think-tank world, in non-governmental organizations, and in the world of private business. In short, intelligence gathering is in the information business, not dealing in secrets.

In this age of information, collection of intelligence becomes easier as the world swims in massive amounts of data. Making sense of the data becomes the central problem for intelligence agencies now and into the foreseeable future. Without proper analysis, intelligence becomes lost if we can't make sense of it. This process is not without its effect on the individual citizen. Modern intelligence systems must be able to access in a timely, accurate, proportionate, and (hopefully) legal way information about individuals and their movements and activities that resides in databases subject to data protection or privacy legislation, or that may be held by other governments or global commercial organizations such as airlines or banks.

This definitely does not refer to traditional police inquiries into the records of an individual identified as a suspect. Effective pre-emptive intelligence may, for example, depend upon data-mining techniques applied to records in bulk form. Such techniques inevitably involve trawling through the records of the innocent as well as the suspect to identify patterns of interest for further investigation.

In short, much of the information needed to track terrorist groups, including their financing, resides in these databases within our own societies. This is clearly controversial as we have seen in the United States over data collection without warrant and here in Canada over CSIS' retention of the so-called "metadata" files.

The "mission management" of planning intelligence access to these pools of information in a complementary way becomes correspondingly more complex, especially when we take into account the domestic and legal considerations that come into play, particularly if the result is ever to be used as evidence in court. In this area we are a long way from traditional intelligence collection activity.

The goal in the end is not for analysts to make themselves smarter but to make policy better, improve military decisions, and enable improvement for law enforcement. In short, the key feature of twenty-first-century intelligence is going to be the pressure to use it for anticipatory purposes to protect the citizen.

Molinaro's chapter provides us with more insight into how the RCMP struggled to find its way in a world where technology was changing but legislation was failing to catch up. History here can show us the importance of having legislators and the intelligence community on the same page.

One thing the citizen need not worry about is whether in today's world they will have to change the way they conduct their lives. That is because others will change them for them. Since 9/11, think of how the lives of the travelling public have become more bothersome every time they enter an airport. Added security is only the part that the public sees and experiences. Virtually no one notices the cameras catching everyone's movements from one part of the airport to another. The public has little idea of the analysis applied to the personal information required for travel to a number of other countries, including Canada's closest neighbour. And the public doesn't generally notice the technology designed to identify and winnow out suspicious substances they may be carrying in their luggage.

In short, technology is a ubiquitous reality that will become even more intrusive. News media outlets constantly comment on the impact – personal, political, or military – of sophisticated technologies and the uses to which they are put. Persons or organizations that seek to cause harm are astute users of these technologies, and security intelligence services are all too often required to react after the fact. The evolving state of intrusive technologies, in fact, makes security intelligence outreach to the public a vital tool in the constant battle to protect the state and its citizens from harm.

A Sense of Danger

If 9/11 was supposed to be a wake-up call for Canadians it also signalled a return to an unwarranted sense of complacency. In Toronto, less than a month after 9/11, the writer spoke to the Canadian Council of Chief Executives – the CEOs of Canada's 150 largest companies – on how Canada could update and upgrade its security. As we walked back to our offices after the event, the CEO of one of our major banks said to me: "That was very interesting, Reid, but, of course, it won't happen here." As recent history shows, whether in the mosque killings in Quebec City or in the murder of army Cpl. Nathan Cirillo, a member of the ceremonial guard at Canada's National War Memorial, it *can* happen here.[10] In the latter incident the shooter proceeded to the Parliamentary buildings where legislators were present at caucus meetings. He was shot by Parliamentary security staff before he could wound or kill anyone else.

The number one task of intelligence and early-warning providers is to persuade the consumer of a real threat of danger. In doing so the provider must display credibility, which hinges on several essential elements. The purposes and the organizational processes must be clear, the product should meet the real needs of the clients, concepts and messages should be straightforward, and strong analytical backup must be available. Armed with these prerequisites, the warning provider is equipped to engage the client, thereby acquiring the consumer's total commitment. The success of this task depends on how accustomed the consumer or policymaker is to utilizing intelligence in making major decisions. In Canada, this task is harder because policymakers, whether senior bureaucrats or politicians, are not aggressive users of intelligence in their day-to-day decision making.

The task is further complicated by the need to temper the sense of danger with a solid dose of pragmatism. The crystal ball will not often yield much beyond a hazy picture of possibilities and probabilities. Quality of analysis is key as is, above all, the avoidance of overstating – a flaw found in all governments and notably in the military and the security establishments.

The locus of the central warning apparatus also has some importance. Most countries have emergency measure organizations whose mandates may include natural and man-made mishaps, such as major train wrecks, fires, or floods, but not counterterrorism. Their roles are to ensure that first responders (e.g., fire and police departments, hospitals) are acting to contain the problem and to coordinate the involvement of national resources if they are needed to augment local resources. Their roles are essentially the same whether they operate in a unitary or federal setting, although dealing with several levels of government on urgent matters has its own set of challenges.

For the most part, these emergency measure organizations do a competent job in coping with disasters. They are less well equipped to deal with terrorism, particularly if the information they are receiving is imprecise, which it will often be, or looks at a longer-term horizon. In these circumstances, information or intelligence providers need a credible responsibility centre to provide a comfort level, especially if actions on their part involve expenditures and engage local budgets.

When an event occurs, the government department responsible for public safety or the senior unit that serves the head of government in security and intelligence (S&I) matters will intervene. If an event is imminent, it is probably the latter that becomes engaged. The world of S&I yields little good news, especially post 9/11, and heads of government, like all politicians, are anxious to be as insulated as possible from bad news. However, once an event unfolds, those same heads of government want to be assured that the best and the brightest in the government – by definition those immediately advising him or her – are in control of the situation.

As regards the problem of persuading policymakers and decision makers to take warnings seriously, the first challenge for intelligence providers is to get their products out of the hands of the security professionals in the entity they are targeting and into the hands of those senior enough to be able to act on the information provided. While people talk blithely about sharing, this runs counter to every tenet in the S&I ethos. A brief example. At a point in my tenure, CSIS launched an analytic series of papers on security issues that was distributed to departments of government through their departmental security officers (DSOs). After some months without any feedback, positive or negative, a survey was conducted among recipient departments. Almost without exception, word came back from the DSOs that they had found the reports to be very good. In fact, they were seen as "so hot" that again almost without exception the DSOs had locked them securely away in their safes. The upshot was that no one who might have put this material to good use had access to it.

This example also shows that security professionals do not like to share. They worry about being loose-lipped with the occupant of the neighbouring office, never mind the uninitiated within their own government or, horror of horrors, with foreigners. These barriers are real and breaking them down is vital. For example, the cop on the beat must have enough background that he or she can play a role in a bottom-up flow of practical information. Nor should local leaders become mesmerized by information from the national government. It is too easy to conclude that such information must be good. But this is not necessarily the case because the agencies that purvey intelligence to the national government also tend to believe that what they are producing is gold-plated and are consequently resistant to bottom-up input. Other challenges exist too, as Breen's chapter points out, such as when consumers seek to politicize intelligence or hide it for their own gain or even consider leaking it as part of a wider strategy.

Assuming providers have hit on a strategy to overcome this problem, packaging becomes important. The old legal axiom, *res ipsa loquitur* – the thing speaks for itself – definitely does not apply here. All of the barriers to understanding – short time horizons, competing demands on time, lack of understanding of the issues – can apply. Therefore providers of intelligence must think more carefully about what message they wish to convey and what understanding of it they hope to achieve – for example, plant a seed, educate, spur to action.

They cannot rely on whatever bare-bones facts they have at hand, nor the professional shorthand they would use in talking to their S&I counterparts. They should particularly avoid the kind of overstatement to which they are prone: a misguided view that the darker the picture the more attention it will get. Often, this approach does nothing but reduce the credibility of the intelligence provider. It is not my experience that policymakers will shy away from difficult or expensive decisions, but they will almost universally need material that persuades not only them but their peers and superiors as well.

Everybody has "skunk works," a usually small unit expected to think outside the box and provide innovative solutions. Within the bureaucracy this usually means a policy analysis or environment scanning unit dedicated to identifying trends or predicting events. The trouble is, far too often, these are trophy units that are tolerated but exist outside the decision-making mainstream. The urgent, or the immediate, will unfortunately almost always outpace the important.

Assuming that the intelligence providers, using short or long-term analysis, have established their credibility with their particular set of consumers, how do they maintain that credibility and further convince the policymaker that the threat is real? This can be accomplished by using what might be called "aggressive prudence." This begins by careful calibration of the level and urgency of the threat. Given the overabundance of data available, this immediately takes us back to the quality of the analysts and their output. Threats can be assumed or manufactured out of this welter of data to fit most purposes, and intelligence executives must therefore exercise considerable discretion and judgment. The easy way out is simply to forward all disturbing data to the policy-/decision makers and recommend a steady stream of alerts. That way, no one gets blamed if an event occurs because no one can say they were not warned.

Canada has experienced the tragic consequences of going down this route in one of the most serious terrorist attacks before 9/11 and PanAm 103 – the bombing of the Air India 182 flight from Canada to London and India. The intelligence providers conveyed a stream of warnings to the national law enforcement body, which in turn passed on the information to the federal transport authorities. Without an absolutely specific threat confronting them, the latter did not authorize the additional screening and inspection resources that, in hindsight, would have seemed the appropriate response to the information they were receiving. In explaining their inaction, they were clearly sceptical of the repeated but inconclusive warnings – a tragic case of the boy who cried wolf. Would the response have been different post 9/11? Probably, but the trap of warning fatigue remains.

If not the blanket approach, then what could be used to capture and maintain the trust and interest of the decision makers? Intelligence providers need to step outside their own closed world and accommodate the broader landscape. They have the unenviable task of knitting the various strands of society together and maintaining that elusive balance between security and individual rights. They can then move from the general to the particular. Essentially, the starting point for any set of security arrangements is a review of the threat, the risk, and the vulnerabilities of a given site, facility, or operation. This applies as much to municipalities and communities as it does to corporations. This leads to a more detailed threat, risk, and impact assessment (TRIA) and from there to a crisis management plan. This involves:

1 identification of all assets at risk, including personnel, physical assets, and intellectual property;
2 identification of probable threats. Threats will likely include premeditated direct attack or infiltration by individuals seeking opportunities for theft or destruction of people or assets, including intellectual property;
3 determination of the risk, or probability of occurrence, for each threat category;
4 delineation of the impacts associated with each threat should they occur individually or in concert with other threats.

Intelligence and Law Enforcement

The protection of the state and its citizens cannot be effective unless there is a close, respectful, and mutually confident partnership between intelligence professionals and their law enforcement counterparts. Law enforcement is both a contributor to and a customer of intelligence. This raises the issue of the degree to which there should be closer institutional links between intelligence and law enforcement. In Canada this starts with the RCMP and CSIS. Relations between these two organizations have not always been cordial, a fact that has been clearly documented in both legal proceedings relating to the bombing of Air India 182 and the subsequent Commission of Inquiry (the Major Commission) on the same subject.[11] Neither Canadian governments nor citizens will tolerate any continuation of these turf wars and apparent lack of trust and cooperation.

The essence of the problem rests with the different objectives of intelligence, especially security intelligence, and law enforcement. Broadly put, security intelligence equals prevention and law enforcement equals prosecution. The most proximate link, however, is the operations of organized crime, which essentially cut across both criminal and terrorist activity. Organized crime is often defined as activities driven by the desire for financial gain while terrorism is driven by political or social goals. However, organized crime and terrorism have become increasingly close.

Many would argue that there is little to distinguish between terrorists and organized crime. Certainly the groups often overlap and intersect in terms of their aims and objectives and lines of business (e.g., money laundering, drug running). Given these interactions, there should be a concern about the presence of organized crime in Canada's ports and, increasingly, at our airports. If nothing else, this situation adds urgency to the need for seamless cooperation and intelligence exchanges among such agencies as CSIS, the RCMP, CRA, CBSA, Immigration, airport and port authorities, and their supporting local police forces.

Relevant here is the question of CSIS officials or CSIS material appearing in court, which has been an ongoing concern. For example, CSIS evidence was used in a US District court in North Carolina in a case involving the illegal sale of missile parts to third parties associated with a well-documented terrorist organization. There have been other benchmarks over the last thirty years that relied on the Canadian Charter of Rights and Responsibilities and contributed to what might be called the judicialization of national security. These cases involved such principles as:

1 establishing an accused's right to disclosure of all information relevant to their case that is in the Crown's possession regardless of whether it is inculpatory or exculpatory, or whether the Crown intends to introduce it into evidence or not;[12]
2 establishing that these cases should be heard in open court;[13]
3 setting the stage for Special Advocates created by subsequent legislation to ensure fairness on security certificate hearings leading to deportation;[14]
4 imposing extraordinary obligations on CSIS officers to retain operational notes when conducting investigations that are not of a general nature – i.e., whenever an investigation targets a particular individual or group and it may have to pass the information on to external authorities or to a court.[15]
5 establishing the obligation for security officials to testify at judicial or quasi-judicial proceedings.[16]

Some observers believe these developments will hinder the effectiveness of Canada's security officials. In fact, the evidence so far indicates otherwise. The Toronto 18 case (a conspiracy to create a terrorist incident that resulted in charges against eighteen of the conspirators) illustrates what can be done by CSIS and the RCMP working together, within the structures imposed by the courts. CSIS shared information gleaned from their own investigation of the accused with the RCMP through a number of disclosure and advisory letters (including CSIS wiretaps), participated in Joint Management Teams, and frequently discussed the dual investigations. CSIS also worked to ensure that the RCMP got into the right investigative path without providing more information than was necessary to ensure that public safety was protected. In addition, CSIS developed two informants whom they later passed on to the RCMP to become police agents; their evidence in court eventually assisted in the Crown securing eleven convictions under anti-terrorism legislation.

Despite all this cooperation, Justice Dawson (ON SC 2009) decided that CSIS and the RCMP had created enough of a "firewall" between their parallel investigations that CSIS's contribution would not subject them to broader disclosure obligations. However he did uphold the principle that if the CSIS and RCMP investigations had become intertwined enough as to effectively be one investigation, then broader disclosure would apply. A similar case in the BC Supreme Court reached a similar conclusion. These two decisions demonstrate a willingness on the part of the judiciary to allow for greater integration of CSIS and RCMP operations to meet the threat of terrorism, yet to preserve sensitive CSIS information from being disclosed.

As a sidebar, it should be noted that Canadian judges would be less than human if they didn't at least reflect on what has become a distressing trend on the US federal bench. In essence, judges there, when faced with security or terrorist issues, have often said, in effect, "that's above my pay grade and anyway, surely the federal government is in the best position to judge." A typical example occurred when a US federal judge dismissed Maher Arar's civil suit, ruling that the issues of national security and foreign policy it raised were special factors beyond the competence of that particular court. These types of issues will increasingly come before the courts and will bring with them unfamiliar issues and contexts as intelligence, criminal behaviour, and terrorism come together.

It is vital that judges meet this new set of challenges directly. One important reason to do so lies with the court's role in protecting the rights of individuals. This is a role both prophylactic and remedial. It is also one that cannot be left solely to the discretion of the executive or legislative arms of government. This becomes a matter of some importance as the state begins most security cases with a substantial advantage, claiming the need for secrecy because of possible damage to the country's foreign policy interests and the dangers if intelligence methods are disclosed. A minefield perhaps, but one which must be traversed if the balance is to be struck between the interests of the state and the rights of the individual.

Craig Forcese's book on security law (one of the first in the area with a Canadian perspective) comments that the Federal Court has indicated that, in finding that balance between rights and security, government claims of national security already have a finger on the scale.[17] This is followed by a citation of one of the Johannesburg Principles on National Security, Freedom of Expression and Access to Information,[18] that national security claims to restrict disclosure are not legitimate if the underlying purpose of the claim is to shield government from embarrassment or exposure of wrongdoing.[19]

Delving behind the government's cloak of secrecy may in fact be one of the most complex tasks judges will face. Nevertheless, our intelligence organizations (CSIS, CSEC, RCMP) are bound by our laws, which are quite transparent, and those charged will often be brought to court under provisions of the Criminal Code, territory generally familiar to the judiciary. Even here, however, security issues may bring dimensions to criminal cases that go beyond the familiar, and beyond precedent, at least in Canada.

Moving through the Twenty-First Century – How Well Equipped Are We?

With the end of the Cold War, the intelligence communities in many allied/industrialized countries began looking for new mandates or targets. Through the 1990s many of these services began to delve into such issues as organized crime, drugs, and economic and corporate intelligence. Success, or gaining a successful "market niche," was elusive, at least as far as the latter two sectors were concerned. However, investigations into organized crime and drugs were more fruitful, and although they overlapped with law enforcement, they easily meshed with the concentration on countering the growing terrorist threat. The latter phenomenon, culminating in 9/11, has brought about a reassertion of the original focus of most intelligence services.

If the preponderance of the resources in CSIS had traditionally been devoted to counter-intelligence or counter-espionage activities, things began to change with the winding-down of the Cold War and the increasing seriousness of terrorist activity. The result was that, by 9/11, CSIS counterterrorism activities dominated its concerns. More recently, the balance of resources has been readjusted to take into account the return of levels of espionage not seen since the Cold War. In light of Russian and Chinese aggression, counter-intelligence activities have reasserted their importance for security and intelligence organizations.

Unlike countries with which Canada traditionally most closely associated (e.g., the United States, the UK, and Australia), Canada has no offensive or foreign intelligence service. In this more fractured and dangerous world, the question arises again as to whether Canada should develop its own foreign intelligence service like the CIA or the BSIS (MI6). In this writer's view, the answer is no. Moreover, an attempt to create one will prove to be a very expensive mistake. In the first place, Canada is already in the foreign intelligence collection business, primarily through the information-gathering activities of Global Affairs Canada and the Department of National Defence, which of course includes Canada's eye in the sky, the Communications Security Establishment. Second, those departments, plus CSIS and the RCMP, have extensive partnerships and contact points throughout the globe into which essential data flow. Third, the CSIS Act has great flexibility in permitting foreign collection and activities. Moreover, the combination of Canada's own resources plus its networks with allies and other international partners seem adequate to respond to terrorist threats to Canada.

Society and Security

In the minds of many, Canada is a solution looking for a problem. But, of course, it does have problems. In the world of terrorism, particularly disturbing is the rise of domestic, home-grown terrorism among young people, fuelled in part by persistent economic disadvantage. In a report by the Institute for Research on Public Policy (IRPP), *Belonging? Diversity, Recognition and Shared Citizenship in Canada*,[20] suggests that Canadians have done a reasonable job to date in managing diversity. However, the same study warns that we have unfinished business in recognizing and respecting difference and in strengthening social integration.

Luc Portelance and Ray Boisvert (both former senior executives at CSIS and Portelance later heading the CBSA) have written a paper on the state of Canada's security today and they say:

> Canada must improve the effectiveness of its counter-radicalization strategy. The European situation and our own experience point to a problem that is both foreign-influenced and homegrown. Prevention must begin at home working closely with our communities and all levels of government. Moreover, the development and delivery of a counter-narrative must not be seen as the exclusive domain of the police, intelligence or military

services of government. Neither should it be viewed as a technology problem …This is a strategic, long-term battle of ideas that will only be won through effective message targeting and content management strategies.[21]

In the same context, a study by the Canadian Labour Market Report posits the following:

The rising number of new immigrants who are living in poverty in Canada is a "tinderbox" that could explode into an "inferno" of social discontent. The Report goes on that more than 36 percent of immigrants who have been in the country for less than five years live in poverty. That compares to 25 percent in the 1980s.

The study goes on to say that poor immigrants could grow increasingly disenchanted because many were attracted to Canada by policies that give points "for skills and education, but such credentials are often not recognized … A continued failure of new immigrants to assimilate economically could turn into an inferno, if it were also accompanied by negative reactions on the part of domestic-born Canadians."[22] Reinforcing this point, a study in the Senate, tabled by Art Eggleton, is described by him in the *Globe and Mail*: "We learned that despite the challenges many communities face, and thanks to our multicultural and integration policies, we have a broad sense of inclusion in Canada. The rising numbers of immigrants who own homes, who take out citizenship and who intermarry point to inclusion."[23]

But everything is not perfect. We have fault lines. We have far too many people living on the margins. This has been made more challenging by rising income inequality in Canada, where 4 per cent of Canadian households control 67 per cent of total wealth, and where middle and low incomes have stagnated or decreased.[24]

Conclusion

Some themes have resonated throughout this book. Perhaps first and foremost, today's dangerous and complex world demands better analysts from more diverse disciplines. Second, biases and feelings constantly intrude. Third, the struggle for the attention of the front office, in either the public or private sectors, is constant. Fourth, governments will always be driven by the urgent rather than the important. Fifth, a major task for the intelligence producers is to avoid consumer "warning fatigue," equally important at the heights of policymaking or in the trenches of the first responders.

NOTES

1 Stanley A. Cohen, *Privacy, Crime and Terror, Legal Rights in a Time of Peril* (Markham, ON: LexisNexis Canada, 2005), 52

2 Report of the Internal Inquiry into the Actions of Canadian Officials in relation to Abdullah Almalki, Ahmad Abou-Elmaati, and Muayyad Nureddin by Commissioner, the Hon. Frank Iacobucci, Commissioner's prefacing Statement. Privy Council of Canada, Monograph, http://publications.gc.ca/pub-?1d+9-651236&sl=0.

3 Niccolò Machiavelli, *Discourses on the First Ten Books of Titus Livius, Third Book, Chapter XLIII: Natives of the Same Country Preserve for All Time the Same Characteristics,* 1517.

4 Royal Commission of Inquiry on Security (MacKenzie Commission), estd 1966, Printing and Publishing, Supply and Services Canada, reprinted 1977, Cat. 21-1966-5; Royal Commission of Inquiry into Certain Activities of the RCMP (McDonald Commission) estd 1977, publicsafety.gc.ca/cnt/rsrcs/lbrr/ctlg/dtls-en.aspx?d=PS&i=98363807.

5 Reid Morden, Comment, *Globe and Mail,* 30 July 2005.

6 Reid Morden, Comment, *Globe and Mail,* 2 November 2006.

7 The Constitution Act, 1982, Part l, https://laws-lois.justice.gc.ca.

8 https://www.export.gov/article.id=Canada-MarketOverview (14 December 2018).

9 Katherine L. Herbig, *Change in Espionage by Americans, 1947–2007,* Technical Report 08-05 (Monterey, CA: Defense Personnel Research Centre, Diane Publishing, March 2008).

10 "Attentat terroriste dans une mosque," *TVA Nouvelles,* 29 January 2017; "Ottawa Shooting: Cpl. Nathan Cirillo Dies of Wounds, Gunman Also Shot Dead," *CBC News,* 22 October 2014.

11 Commission of Inquiry into the Investigation of the Bombing of Air Indian Flight 182, 2010 https://www.publicsafety.gc.ca/cnt/rsrcs/pblctns/rspns-cmmssn/rspns-cmmssn-eng.pdf.

12 *R v Stinchcombe,* 1991 3 SCR 326.

13 *Vancouver Sun v Attorney-General of Canada, Attorney-General of BC,* 2004 SCC 43.

14 *Charkaoui v Canada (Minister of Citizenship and Immigration),* 2007 SCC 9.

15 *Charkaoui v Canada,* 2008 SCC 38.

16 Commission of Inquiry into the Investigation of the Bombing of Air India Flight 182 2010.

17 Craig Forcese, *National Security Law, Canadian Practice in International Perspective* (Toronto: Irwin Law, 2008), 408.

18 "The Johannesburg Principles on National Security, Freedom of Expression and Access to Information," UN Doc. E/CN.4/1996/39 (1996).

19 Ibid., 383–4

20 Keith Banting, Thomas J. Courchene, and F. Leslie Seidle, eds., *Belonging? Diversity, Recognition and Shared Citizenship in Canada* (Montreal: Institute for Research on Public Policy, 2007).

21 Luc Portelance and Ray Boisvert, "Is It Time for a National Security Reset in Canada?," 11 February 2016, text provided by authors, and as adapted for newspaper publication in the Comment section of the *National Post* on the same date.

22 Peter Dungan, Morley Gunderson, and Tony Fang, *Macroeconomic Impacts of Canadian Immigration*, Working Paper 2165434 (Toronto: Rotman School of Management, 22 October 2012).

23 *Reducing Barriers to Social Inclusion and Social Cohesion*, Report of the Standing Senate Committee on Social Affairs, Science and Technology, June 2013, www.senate-senat.ca/social.asp.

24 Ibid.

Contributors

Marcella Bencivenni is Associate Professor of History at Hostos Community College of The City University of New York. She is the author of *Italian Immigrant Radical Culture: The Idealism of the* Sovversivi *in the United States, 1890–1940* (New York University Press, 2011, repr. 2014), and co-editor of *Radical Perspectives on Immigration*, a special issue of the journal *Socialism and Democracy* (Routledge, 2008). She is currently serving as the editor of the *Italian American Review*. Her new research projects include a biography of Carl Marzani, the first political victim of McCarthyism, and a study of the Triangle fire of 1911 in Italian immigration history and memory.

John Breen is Former Chair for National Intelligence Studies at the US Army's Command and General Staff College (2014–2017). He had assignments in Europe, the Middle East, and South Asia. Dr. Breen has extensive substantive operational knowledge of numerous foreign environments as well as the disciplines of counterproliferation, cybersecurity, and counterterrorism. He received his PhD from the University of Rochester, Rochester, NY.

Phillip Deery is Emeritus Professor of History at Victoria University, Melbourne. He has published over one hundred articles and book chapters in the fields of communism, labour history, espionage, and the Cold War. One of his more recent publications is "American Communism" in the *Cambridge History of Communism*, vol. 2: *The Socialist Camp and World Power 1941–1968* (2017). His books examining the Cold War are *Red Apple: Communism and McCarthyism in Cold War New York* (New York: Fordham University Press, 2014, 2016); *The Age of McCarthyism: A Brief History with Documents, Third Edition* (Boston: Bedford/St. Martin's,

2016) with Ellen Schrecker; and *Espionage and Betrayal: Behind the Scenes of the Cold War* (Milan: Feltrinelli Press, 2011) with Mario Del Pero.

Steve Hewitt is Senior Lecturer in the Department of History and the American and Canadian Studies Research Centre at the University of Birmingham.

Gregory S. Kealey is the founding editor of *Labour/le Travail*, which he edited from 1976 to 1997 and remains on its editorial board. His books include two prize-winning titles: *Toronto Workers Respond to Industrial Capitalism* (1980, 2nd ed. 1991); and *Dreaming of What Might Be: The Knights of Labor in Ontario* (1982; winner of the Corey Prize of the AHA and CHA). He has also published *Workers In Canadian History* (1995). He has edited some forty volumes including eight volumes of RCMP Security Bulletins (with Reg Whitaker) and the five-volume *Readings in Canadian Social History* (with Michael Cross). A collection of essays that he has edited with Lara Campbell and Dominique Clement, *Debating Dissent: Canada and the 1960s*, was published with the University of Toronto Press in 2011. In 2010 he published, along with Reg Whitaker and Andy Parnaby, a history of the Canadian secret service entitled *Secret Service: Political Policing in Canada from the Fenians to Fortress America*, with the University of Toronto Press. In 2017 the University of Toronto Press published his collection of essays, *Spying on Canadians*, and he was awarded the Order of Canada.

Daniel W.B. Lomas is Lecturer in International History at the University of Salford. His research looks at the postwar interface between intelligence and policy in Britain. His book *Intelligence, Security and the Attlee Government, 1945–1951* is available from Manchester University Press.

Dennis G. Molinaro holds a PhD in history from the University of Toronto. He is the author of *An Exceptional Law: Section 98 and the Emergency State 1919–1936*. He has published work in leading journals on the Gouzenko affair and the history of wiretapping, which was featured on national media. He has taught on the subject of modern espionage at the University of Toronto and Ontario Tech.

Reid Morden was the director of the Canadian Security Intelligence Service from 1988 to 1992. Morden served as Deputy Minister of Foreign Affairs from 1991 to 1994. Morden was named director of CSIS in 1988, and served in that capacity for four years. He has served as President of Atomic Energy of Canada Limited (1994–8), and worked in the private sector with Kroll and KPMG Forensic Inc. In 2000 Morden received the Order of Canada, and in 2005 he was appointed to assist the commission of inquiry dealing with the case of Maher Arar. Morden presently runs the security analysis firm Reid Morden & Associates, while acting as Executive Director of the Volcker Inquiry into the United Nations' Oil-for-Food Programme. He is also a Director of the HSLA industry trade group. Morden has sat on the Board of Governors for Trent University, was an adviser to the Schulich School of Business' MBA program and is a Grand Officer of the Order of the Southern Cross.

Christopher J. Murphy has been a Lecturer in Intelligence Studies at the University of Salford since 2006. He researches the history of the British intelligence community, from the origins of the Security Service (MI5) and Secret Intelligence Service (SIS, or MI6) from 1909 to the present day. He has specific research interests in the work of the Special Operations Executive (SOE) during the Second World War and the historiography of intelligence studies.

Frances Reilly received her PhD in History from the University of Saskatchewan in 2016. Her dissertation, "Controlling Contagion: Policing and Prescribing Sexual and Political Normalcy in Cold War Canada," focused on how homosexuality and communism were defined as contaminating threats. Frances is currently working on a monograph about RCMP Cold War surveillance and Operation Profunc.

Timothy Andrews Sayle is an Assistant Professor at the University of Toronto. His most recent book is *Enduring Alliance: A History of NATO and the Postwar Global Order*. He is also a principal co-investigator and editor of an oral history project examining President George W. Bush's decision to "surge" troops to Iraq in 2007. Dr. Sayle is a Senior Fellow of the Bill Graham Centre for Contemporary International History and an associate of the Center for Presidential History at Southern Methodist University. He teaches the history of international relations with attention to the various factors that determine strategy and statecraft in the state system.

Kerry Taylor is Head of the School of Humanities at Massey University, New Zealand. He has published widely on the history of the New Zealand communist movement and labour movement. His books include *Culture and the Labour Movement and on the Left: Essays on Socialism in New Zealand*. He is associate editor of the *New Zealand Journal of History* and on the editorial board of *Labour History*.